।। छान्दोग्योपनिषद् ।।

THE CHĀNDOGYA-UPANIṢAD

॥ छान्दोग्योपनिषद् ॥

THE CHĀNDOGYA-UPANIṢAD

Text in Sanskrit; and Translation with Notes in English from the Commentaries of Śaṅkarācārya and the Gloss of Ānandagiri and the Commentary of Śaṅkarānand.

by

Raja Rajendralal Mitra

BKP

Bharatiya Kala Prakashan

DELHI (INDIA)

First Published 2001

Published by : C.P. Gautam
BHARATIYA KALA PRAKASHAN
3421-A, IInd Floor, Narang Colony, Tri Nagar,
Delhi-110035, Ph : 7153083

ISBN : 81-86050-80-9

Laser Type Setting
Pranav Graphics
58, Vir Nagar, Jain Colony,
Near Rana Partab Bagh,
Delhi-110007
Ph.: 7252384, 7422128

Printed by
SANTOSH OFFSET
Delhi

PREFACE

The chronology of the Old Testament has influenced almost all the speculations of Oriental scholars in regard to the possible date of the *Vedas* and the *Upaniṣads.* It is very difficult to say anything with positive confidence on this subject, but this much is certain, that the Upaniṣads, at least the ten principal ones, are not in any way posterior to the *Vedas.* The argument that a philosophy like that embodied in the Upaniṣads cannot exist side by side with the nature-worship of the *Vedas,* loses its force when the *Sūktas* of the *Veda* are regarded as symbolic only of those esoteric truths which were taught through the *Upaniṣads* to the select few. Symbology helps the solution of many a riddle over which philology has either sat in despair or which it has understood only to misunderstand. The history of all the great religions of the world shows, that there is nothing inconsistent in the possible existence of a sublime philosophy with the empty formalities of popular religion. And this circumstance in itself is an indirect argument against the later origin of the *Vedas* and the *Upaniṣads.*

Veda means knowledge, and *Upaniṣad* means both the exoteric philosophy of *Brahman,* the *Advaita,* and sittings for the discussion of that philosophy. The *Upaniṣads* are aptly called the *Vedānta,* the end of the *Veda,* that which is reserved for those who have freed themselves from the useless bonds of formal religion. The *Veda* consists of three parts : *Mantra, Brāhmaṇa* and *Upaniṣad,* including the *Āraṇyakas.* The *Mntra* portion contains hymns addressed to various powers, all symbolic of important truths intended, on the one hand, to teach the religion of faith and forms to the ignorant, and the philosophy of sublime unity to the initiated, on the other. The one is the *Karma-mārga,* the religion of *forms,* and the other is the *Jñāna-mārga,* the religion of philosophy or knowledge. There is a way between the two, leading from *Karma* to *Jñāna,* called *Upāsanā,* or the invoking of any particular power of nature. This is different from the general *Karma-mārga,* inasmuch as *Karma* does not mean anything performed with a special aim and for a special purpose. *Karma-mārga* is only the general religion of faith which leads to *Upāsanā* and *Jñāna.* The word *Karma* should in this place not be confounded with that philosophical law of necessity which is called by that name.

The *Upaniṣadas* teach the philosophy of absolute unity. By unity is meant the oneness of the subject, all experience of objective existence being regarded as in and of it. Experience implies consciousness, and consciousness, apperception or "pure reason" is the only reliable, self-illumined, absolute factor of our knowledge. All else is but mere representation in and through the mode of this consciousness. The world of being is nothing, considered apart from consciousness which, in its turn, is entirely independent of experience. It cannot in any manner be negatived, for the very negation implies its existence. This is the realm of the absolute, ever-existent, *Brahman,* an abstraction appropriately expressing this ides of unity in duality, being a term expressive of the whole of that which can be none other than a compound of Thought and Being.

This Absolute is not the Unknowable of Agnosticism, nor the inexplicable atom of Materialism. Materialism is in fact out of question, inasmuch as the Absolute of the Upaniṣad is not a result of organisation nor a property of matter. It is something always independent of everything, and self-illumined, self-subsistent. It is everywhere; but for it the world of experience is nowhere. But the Agnostic who stands half-way between Materialism and Transcendentalism identifies the Absolute with the Unknowable and makes it the source of all that translates itself into experience. This doctrine is entirely untenable, for that which is Unknowable is not the Absolute, but that which produces the various modifications and representations of it through experience.

That something which IS and is not known *per se* by the very law of consciousness not permitting such knowledge, is the Unknowable *par excellence.* But to describe the fountain of knowledge, absolute consciousness, which is seen in daily individual experience, as the Unknowable or even the unknown would, at least, be a strange perversion of metaphysical language.

The effect of this philosophy on practical ethics is immense. Any system of ethics not based on some clearly demonstrated world-idea falls short of practical use, and is *pro tanto* a deviation from the path of adequately fulfilling the object of existence. The variety of experience is not real, nay even experience itself is nowhere from the point of the Absolute. To lead that life wherein the variety of experience does not affect either for weal or woe is the highest practical rule of conduct in accordance with the proper aim of existence. This does not imply entire inertia as some would understand it. The variety of experience *creates* distinction, and sets up false limits where there exist none. Pain and pleasure, good and evil, virtue and vice, merit and sin, are all conventions based on this variety of experience, and admitted for the sake of that experience. But in the Absolute no such distinctions are possible, and the highest bliss which cannot be described in words other than those implying negation of everything positive known to us, consists in forgetting the source of separateness and realising that unity which is the very being and nature of the cosmos. And more than this philosophy holds that the individual is a copy of the great cosmos and that through the unity of the two in the Absolute there is always possible and easy way from the one to the other. When the sense of separateness is killed out, the Absolute in the individual, and the microcosm is at once understood as the macrocosm. Pain and pleasure, evil and good, are all merged in the unity of the Absolute where all is that indescribable something which is neither pleasure nor pain, but something supremely sublime and happy, so to speak. This process of killing out this idea of separateness is no inertia, so far as ordinary language is understood; and though it may not be that blind submission to the will of an authropomorphic deity, it is certainly the highest possible activity and energy on a superior plane. It is not neglect of duty nor renunciation of the world either; it is mere forgetting of self and its environments. This is *mokṣa. Mokṣa* in the popular sense is a something to be achieved, in the *Upaniṣad* it is already achieved, every being is one with the Absolute, is, in fact the Absolute; what is to be achieved is destruction of the sense of separateness, which being accomplished, *mokṣa* is easily realised. The disregard of this vital difference between the two ideas has led many Orientalists to regard the *mokṣa* of the *Vedānta,* and the *nirvāṇa* of the Buddhists, as something bordering on pure inertia or entire annihilation.

The illusion-theory is another puzzle in the way of many. Some try to set it down to later interpolation. That this is not so, will be evident from the text of the *Upaniṣads;* but a suggestion by the way may be usefully given. Experience is endless, and this endless variety creates distinctions which lead to the sense of separateness. All that is illusion in the phenomenal, is only these distinctions or limitations and the sense of separateness created by them. The basis or substratum of the illusion cannot be said to be nothing nor something. It is as indescribable as the Absolute and is known to BE, though never apart from or outside of the Absolute.

Many students of Indian philosophy enamoured of the idea of *mokṣa* taught by it seek to achieve it by various processes, physical or mental, generally, known as *Yoga.* Those who do so without being fully saturated with the spirit and substance of the *Upaniṣads* merely take a leap in the dark and court certain death, spiritual as well as physical. The first requisite is proper familiarity with the first principles of *Advaita* philosophy *(Śravaṇa)*; and entire love with them *(Manana).* Then follows that sublime state wherein the sense of separateness is being slowly forgotten. But even here nothing but strict practice of the noble virtues and perfect altruism will be necessarily required of the student.

M.N. DVIVEDI

CONTENTS

॥ छान्दोग्योपनिषद् ॥
THE CHĀNDOGYA-UPANIṢAD

SAṄKARA'S INTRODUCTION

The Chāndogya-Upaniṣad[1] comprises eight chapters, and commences with the words : "Om, this letter, etc.' Of this work a brief commentary according to the order of the text is compendiously given for the benefit of enquirers.[2]

Its connection.[3] [The performance of] the ceremonies prescribed [in the Vedas] when conjoined with a knowledge of the gods,[4] fire, life and the rest, becomes the cause of transition to the Brahmaloka,[5] by a luminous path, *(arcirādi mārga)*; without such knowledge it leads to the Candraloka (region of the moon) by a darksome path *(dhūmādi mārga).* Those who follow the impulses of their passions,[6] losing both these paths, are doomed to inextricable degradation. But as by neither of these two paths can absolute beatitude be obtained, and as a knowledge of the non-dual soul independent of ceremonies is necessary to destroy the cause of the threefold mundane transition, this Upaniṣad is revealed.

By a knowledge of the non-dual soul, and by no other means, is absolute beatitude obtainable; for it is said : "Those who believe otherwise (*i.e.,* in duality) are not masters of their own selves, and inherit transient fruition;[7] while he who acknowledges the reverse becomes his own king." Moreover a believer in the deception of duality suffers *pain* and bondage (transmigration), as the guilty suffer from the touch of the heated ball;[8] while a believer in the truthful soul without duality, like the not guilty escaping unscathed from the touch of the said ball, absolves himself from all liability to pain and bondage; hence a knowledge of the non-dual cannot be co-existent with works.[9]

When a belief in such texts as, "The being one without a second" : "All this is the divine soul," once grows in the mind to annihilate all distinctions about action, actors and fruitions, nothing can withstand that belief.[10] If it be said, that a belief in ritual ordinances will prove prejudicial to it—this is denied : Since rites are enjoined to one who is conscious of the nature of actor and recipient and is subject to the defects of envy, anger and the rest, he alone is entitled to their fruits. From the injunction of ceremonies to him who knows the Vedas, may it not be inferred that the conscient of the non-dual is also enjoined to (perform) ceremonies?— No; because the natural distinctive knowledge of actor, recipient and the rest which is included in ceremony, is destroyed by [a proper understanding of] the Śrutis : "The being one without a second" : "All is the Divine soul, " etc. Therefore actions are enjoined to him only who is ignorant, and not to the conscient of the non-dual. Accordingly it has been said : "All those (who are attached to ceremony) migrate to virtuous regions; he, who reposes in Brahman, attains immortality."

In this discourse on the knowledge of the soul without duality the object and exercise of the mind in both cases being the same, are also related certain auspicious forms of adoration *(upāsanā)*, [1st such] the recompense of which closely approximate to salvation, [2nd such] the subject of which founded on the Śrutis : "Om is mind," "Om is corporeal," is Brahman differing but slightly from the non-dual, [and 3rd such as] are connected with ceremony, although their recompense is transcendent.

The knowledge of the non-dual is an operation of the mind, and inasmuch as these forms of adoration are modifications of mental action, they are all similar; and if so, wherein lies the difference between the knowledge of the non-dual and these forms of adoration ? The knowledge of the non-dual is the removing of all distinctive ideas of actor, agent, action, recompense and the rest engrafted by ignorance on the inactive soul, as a knowledge of the identity of a rope removes the erroneous notion of a snake under which it may be [at first] preceived; while *upāsanā* (adoration) is to rest the mind scripturally upon some support, and to identify the same with the thinking mind;—(a process) not much removed from this transcendent knowledge. Herein lies the difference.

Since these forms of adoration rectify (the quality of) goodness (*satva*), display the true nature of the soul, contribute to the knowledge of the non-dual, and are easy of accomplishment from having supports, they are therefore primarily propounded; and first of all, that form of adoration which is allied to ceremony, inasmuch as mankind being habituated to ceremony, adoration apart from it is, to them, difficult of performance.

Foot Notes

1. "The knowledge of Brahman is called Upaniṣad, because it completely annihilates the world, together with its cause (ignorance) with regard to such as possess this knowledge, for this is the meaning of the word sat ('to destroy,' 'to go') preceded by *Upani (upa,* 'near,' *ni* 'certainty'). A work which treats of the same knowledge is also called Upaniṣad."

2. The *Chāndogya Brāhmaṇa* of the Sāma Veda, whereof this Upaniṣad forms a part, contains ten chapters (prapāṭhakas); of these the first two are called the *Chāndogya Mantra Brāhmaṇa,* the rest constitute the *Chāndogya-Upaniṣad.* ŚAṄKARA, having commented upon the *mantra* portion, now begins with the Upaniṣad, which will account for the abruptness and brevity of this Introduction.

3. That is the relation subsisting between the Upaniṣad any the rituals of the Vedas, or, in other words, the scope and tendency of the work.

4. The word *deva* (god) is used in the Vedas to signify and thing great, glorified or much attended to; and accordingly we find the vital functions called devas. In the Ṛg-Veda pestles and mortars—and even the leather strainers used in the preparation of the moon-plant juice—when they form the subject of a hymn—are honoured with the same epithet. In the Bible the English equivalent of this word is often used in much the same sense; thus : "Whose end is destruction, whose god is their belly." Philippians, chap. iii, v. 19.

5. "The Vedāntic disclosure of a future state, considering the souls of men as ascending or descending according to their respective actions, treats of several worlds or stages of existence, the highest of which is Brahma-loka. The being of

untainted piety and virtue obtains *mukti* or liberation from all changes of existence, becomes immortal, obtains God, revels in the enjoyment of Him, and, as says the Śvetāsvatara Upaniṣad, 'has the Universe for his estate.'—Tatvabodhinī Patrikā.

6. This part of the sentence may be rendered, "Those who follow nature *(svabhāva),*" etc., as an allusion to the Svābhāvika Buddhas, who deny the existence of immateriality : and assert "that matter is the sole substance, which in its varied forms of concretion, and abstraction, causes the existence and destruction of nature or palpable forms." Ānandagiri, however, does not allude to the Svābhāvikas.

7. The passage may be rendered : "They are dependent, and become of regions perishable, etc." The version above given is after Ānandagiri.

8. An allusion to the ordeal by fire. For the manner in which men underwent this ordeal, see Macnaghten's Hindu Law, vol. i, p. 311.

9. That is, ceremony and knowledge are opposed to each other as light and darkness, and therefore cannot co-exist in the same recipient—Ānandagiri.

10. That is, when a knowledge of the true nature of soul shows the futility of ceremonies and their fruits, that impression cannot be undone by other causes.

FIRST CHAPTER

Section I

ॐ आप्यायन्तु ममाङ्गानि वाक्प्राणश्चक्षुः श्रोत्रमथो
बलमिन्द्रियाणि च सर्वाणि सर्वं ब्रह्मोपनिषदं माहं ब्रह्म
निराकुर्यां मा मा ब्रह्म
निराकरोदनिराकरणमस्त्वनिराकरणं मेऽस्तु तदात्मनि
निरते य उपनिषत्सु धर्मास्ते मयि सन्तु ते मयि सन्तु।।
।। ॐ शान्तिः शान्तिः शान्तिः ।।

---

1. ओमित्येतदक्षरमुद्गीथमुपासीत ओमिति ह्युद्गायति तस्योपव्याख्यानम्।।

Om ![1] this letter, the Udgītha, should be adored. Om is chanted its description.

Om ! this letter should be adored. The letter[2] Om is the most appropriate *(lit.*, nearest) name of the Deity *(paramātma* or supreme spirit). By its application, He becomes propitiated, as men by the use of favourite names. From its perfect applicability and definitive and comprehensive character, the sound Om exclusively is here pointed out by the particle इति "the", "this". It is, further, emblematic[3] of the divine soul, as images are of material objects. Being thus a designation and a representative of the Supreme Spirit, it is known in all the Vedāntas as the best means towards the accomplishment of His adoration. Its repeated use at the commencement and close of all prayers, and Vedic recitations, establishes its pre-eminence : and for these reasons this eternal letter, denoted by the term Udgītha from its constituting a part of the Udgītha,[4] should be adored; to this Om, as the substance[5] of all actions and the representative of the Supreme, firm and undeviating attention should be directed.

The Śruti itself has assigned a reason why the word Udgītha is expressive of Om; "this is chanted (Udgāyate)." As the chanters of the Udgītha hymns begin with Om, by Udgītha Om is implied. By "its description" is implied the narration of the mode of its adoration, of its attributes and fruition : प्रवर्त्तते "commenceth," (understood) should be the concluding verb of the sentence.

2. एषां भूतानां पृथिवी रसः पृथिव्या आपो रसोऽपामोषधयो रस ओषधीनां पुरुषो रसः पुरुषस्य वाग्रसो वाच ऋग्रस ऋचः साम रसः साम्न उद्गीथो रसः॥

The earth *constitutes* the essence of all substances; water is the essence of the earth, and annual herbs of water; man *forms* the essence of annual herbs, and speech is the essence of man; Ṛk, is the essence of speech, Sāma of the Ṛk, and of the Sāma, the Udgītha is the essence.

"Of all substances," moveable and immoveable, the earth is the "essence" (रस)] *i.e.*, source, (गति) place of dependence, (परायण) asylum (अवष्टम्भ) "Water is the essence of the earth"; water being (as it were) the warp and weft[1] of the earth, is called its essence. "Annual herbs," being matured and elaborated by "water," form the essence of that element. Of annuals "man is the essence," being matured by aliment.[2] Of that "man, speech is the essence"; speech being his pre-eminent attribute is styled his essence. Of all speeches the Ṛk hymns are the essences, being pre-eminent; of all the Ṛk hymns, the Sāma Veda is the essence, being more pre-eminent, "and of the Sāma" Om, the Udgītha, the subject of this discourse, "is the essence," being sublimer still.

3. स एष रसानाꣳ रसतमः परमः परार्ध्योऽष्टमो यदुद्गीथः॥

The Udgītha is the quintessence of all these essences; it is the Supreme, the most adorable, the eighth.

Thus this Om named Udgītha, being the last of all successive essences, is (called) the quintessence (रसतम) ; being an emblem of the Deity, it is the most adorable—परार्ध्य, from *ardha* "place" and *para* "pre-eminent"—worthy of the abode of the Supreme; that is, worthy of being adored as the Deity. "The eight" :—calcutating from the essence of the earth, the Udgītha is the eighth.

4. कतमा कतमर्क्तमत्कतमत्साम कतमः कतम उद्गीथ इति विमृष्टं भवति॥

What ? What is the Ṛk ? What ? What the Sāma ? What ? What the Udgītha ? These are questioned.

It has been said that Ṛk is the essence of speech ; *it is now asked,* what is that Ṛk ? What that Sāma and what the Udgītha ? The repetition of the word "what" [कतमः—क with the affix डतमच् in the text] is expressive of the earnestness *of the enquirer.* The affix डतमच् is used in asking questions regarding different classes,[8] there is no plurality of the class Ṛk, how is then such an affix used here? The word जातिपरिप्रश्न being a compound of जातौ and परिप्रश्न (questions into a class) applying to the individual hymns of the class Ṛk, and not of जातः and परिप्रश्न (questions regarding classes) it is not objectionable. It might be said, that the instances कतमःकठः] "which Kaṭha" ?[9] and the like, can be explained by taking this word to be a compound of जातेः and परिप्रश्न] and not of जातौ and परिप्रश्न; but that cannot be, the enquiry being into the individual hymns of the class Kaṭha. Were this compound composed of जातेः and परिप्रश्न some additional rule would be necessary for the elucidation of the passage in the text. "These are questioned," *i.e.,* these interrogations are made. Questions being put, their replies follow :

5. वागेवर्क् प्राणः सामीमित्येतदक्षरमुद्गीथस्तद्वा एतन्मिथुनं यद्वाक् च प्राणश्चर्क् च साम च॥

Ṛk is speech, Sāma is life, and Om, this letter, is the Udgītha. Verily this and that, speech and breath *(prāṇa)*—Ṛk and Sāma,—make a *mithuna* (couple).

"Ṛk is speech," etc. The identity of speech and Ṛk *established in the text,* is not prejudicial to the Udgītha being the eighth (verse 3), the topic being different—that of proving the all-gratifying attribute of Om. Speech and breath *(prāṇa)* are the sources of Ṛk and Sāma, hence speech is said to be Ṛk, and breath *(prāṇa)* Sāma. By the use, in due order, of [the words] speech and breath, the sources of Ṛk and Sāma, the whole of the Ṛk and Sāma hymns are included; by the Ṛk and Sāma being thus taken in all the ceremonies capable of performance through them are *necessarily* included; and by them all motives, *which impel to ceremonial works,* are also included. And thereby all doubts regarding the all-comprehensiveness of "Om, this letter the Udgītha," are removed.

"Verily this and that " indicate the Mithuna couple; and what that Mithuna is, is thus related. "Speech and breath" (prāṇa) the sources of all the Ṛk and Sāma hymns, from the *(couple)* Mithuna. "Ṛk and Sāma" *in the text* signify the sources of Ṛk and Sāma, and not a distinct couple of Ṛk and Sāma; otherwise there would be two couples one of speech and breath, and the other of Ṛk and Sāma, and the use of the singular ("this and that make a couple") would become inadmissible; hence it follows that speech and breath the *sources* of Ṛk and Sāma constitute the couple.

6. तदेतन्मिथुनमोमित्येतस्मिन्नक्षरे सꣳसृज्यते यदा वै मिथुनौ समागच्छत आपयतो वै तावन्योन्यस्य कामम्।।

The Mithuna unites with the letter Om, as couples uniting together gratify each others desires.

"The couple" defined above "unites with the letter Om". Thus this couple which has the attribute of gratifying all desires being " united," incorporated with the letter Om, the all-gratifying power of the letter is likewise established. The exclusively phonetic nature of the letter Om, its being utterable by the breath of life (prāṇa), and its union with the couple having been established, an example is adduced to illustrate the *aforesaid* all-gratifying attribute of that couple. As in the creation. . ., so the couple existing in the innate soul realizes the all-gratifying power of the letter Om.

7. आपयिता ह वै कामानां भवति य एतदेवं विद्वानक्षरमुद्गीथमुपास्ते।।

He verily becomes the gratifier of desires, who, knowing it thus, adores the undecaying Udgītha.

To show that the adored (Udgītha) of this letter also partakes of its merits, it is said; "He verily becomes the gratifier of the desires" of his *yajamāna*,[10] (employer) who adores this letter, this all-granting Udgītha; *i.e.*, he procures for himself the aforesaid recompense;[11] thus the Śruti; "With whatsoever object it is adored, that is fulfilled."

8. तद्वा एतदनुज्ञाक्षरं यद्धि किंचानुजानात्योमित्येव तदाहैषा एव समृद्धिर्यदनुज्ञा समर्धयिता ह वै कामानां भवति य एतदेवं विद्वानक्षरमुद्गीथमुपास्ते।।

Verily this is an injunctive term. Whatever is enjoined, Om is surely repeated; hence this injunction is called Prosperity. He verily becomes the gratifier of desires, and promoter of prosperity who, knowing all this, adores the undecaying Udgītha.

Om is also prosperity. How ? "Verily this" (the subject of discourse) "is an injunctive term,"—*Anujñākṣaram,* from *anujñā* and *akṣara; anujñā* signifying "injunction," "order," *and ultimately* the letter Om. How come it to be an injunction explains the Śruti : "Whatever is enjoined" or assented to, by the learned or wealthy regarding learning or wealth, it is done by saying "Om"; thus in the Veda, "thirty-three" is assented to by Om.[12] In wordly affairs likewise when one is addressed with such words as, "I appropriate this wealth of yours," Om is his assent. The letter Om is called "Prosperity" for injunction and prosperity are *here* equivalent; from the latter being the origin, source or root of the former. The prosperous alone can pass the word of command. "Om," wherefore is that letter possessed of *the attribute of* prosperity. By the adoration of the prosperous Udgītha he partakes of its quality and promotes the desires of his employer, who knowing it thus adores, etc.

9. तेनेयं त्रयी विद्या वर्तते ओमित्याश्रावयत्योमिति शꣳस-
त्योमित्युद्गायत्येतस्यैवाक्षरस्यापचित्यै महिम्ना रसेन।।

Through its greatness and effects is the three-fold knowledge maintained; for the worship of this letter is Om recited, Om exclaimed, Om chanted.

The letter Om is now eulogized for its adorableness, and as an inducement to its worship.

How ? By that same letter the three-fold knowledge, comprising the Ṛg-Veda and the rest, is maintained, *i.e.,* the ceremonies enjoined therein; for recitations and other processes of the Vedas cannot maintain the threefold, knowledge themselves [*i.e.,* the Vedas,] whereas it is plain that the ceremonies do. How ? It is evident from the premises "Om is recited! Om is exclaimed! Om is chanted" that the Soma Yāga [sacrifice of the moon plant] is alluded to, the rites whereof are for the worship of this letter, the emblem of the Divine Soul, the adoration of which is the worship of the Deity's Self; thus in the Bhagavad-Gītā : "Mankind attain excellence by adoring him through their respective works." What are "its greatness and effects" ? By the "greatness" of Om is implied the existence of priests, institutors of sacrifices, and their wives; and by its "effects," oblations of *fermented* corn, barley or the like. Sacrifices and burnt offerings are performed through this letter; thereby is the sun maintained; from the sun proceed life and aliment, through the instrumentality of heat and rain; through life and aliment, are sacrifices performed. It is therefore said [in the text] through the greatness and effect of this letter, etc.

That it might not appear that ceremonies are due to those only who are proficient in the knowledge of "Om," the Śruti proceeds :

10. तेनोभौ कुरुतो यश्चैतदेवं वेद यश्च न वेद। नाना तु विद्या
चाविद्या च यदेव विद्यया करोति श्रद्धयोपनिषदा तदेव
वीर्यवत्तरं भवतीति खल्वेतस्यैवाक्षरस्योपव्याख्यानं भवति।।

Both those who are versed in the letter thus *described,* and those who are not, alike perform *ceremonies* through this *letter.* Knowledge and ignorance are unlike each other. What is performed through knowledge, through faith, through Upaniṣad, is more effectual. This verily is the description of the letter.

"Both, those who are versed in the letter thus" described, and those who are proficient in mere ritual performances, but know not its exact nature, "perform" ceremonies. Since both are entitled to fruition from their capability in ritual works, of what import then is a knowledge of the exact nature of this letter, it being evident that *the succession of cause and effect is invariable and altogether irrespective of the knowledge of such succession; thus,* the use of myrobolams causes purgation to all, whether apprized of its effects or otherwise? But that cannot apply here; for "knowledge and ignorance are unlike each other," *i.e.,* they are distinct in their natures, *and cannot lead to a similar fruition.*

Is the knowledge of the letter Om as a component of ceremony, and its knowledge as the quintessence, the all-gratific and the prosperous, the same ? No. Since the latter knowledge is additional to knowing it has a mere part of ceremony, it is reasonable that the fruition thereof should be greater; just as in worldly affairs, in the sale of a ruby or other jewel, *for instance,* a jeweller from his superior knowledge obtains advantages over a forester *(śabara);* so a work performed "through knowledge," *i.e.,* with a consciousness of its nature—"through faith," with a confidence in its results,—"through Upaniṣad," with a devotion or an earnest application of the mind,—"is more effectual" *than otherwise; i.e.,* when unaccompanied with adequate knowledge, it does not produce great results. Works with knowledge having been declared "more effectual," it is to be inferred that works without knowledge are *also* effectual, *but only in a positive degree;* for the ignorant are not *wholly* disentitled to works, as it is to be found, in the ANUṢAṢTI chapter of the *Ṛg-Veda* that even ignorant men can officiate *as priests.*

The adoration of this letter as the quintessence, as the all gratifiers, or, as the prosperous is all the same, there being no difference in the effort necessary for its performance;—multiplicity of attributes merely denotes varied means of adoration.

This is the description of the letter under discussion, called the Udgītha.

SECTION II

1. देवासुरा ह वै यत्र संयेतिर अभये प्राजापत्यास्तद्ध देवा उद्गीथमाजह्रुरनेनैनानभिभविष्याम इति ॥

Wherefore indeed the Devas (Gods) and the Asuras (demons),

the offspring of Prajāpati, contended. Thereof the *Devas* collected the Udgītha, *saying*, hereby we will overcome the Asuras.

"Wherefore indeed, etc." The "Devas" are faculties which are enlightened (regulated) by this Śāstra; *the word being derived from* div, to "illuminate," "enlighten," "manifest". The Asuras are opposed to the former; they are faculties devoted to enjoyment of self in all its vital functions and are naturally the types of darkness. The indeclinables ह and वै are introduced to indicate connection. "Wherefore," *i.e.,* with the object of depriving each other of their objects of desire, the Devas and Asuras "contended," contested ; the rood यत् to "exert," to "endeavour" with the prefix सम् meaning to fight, to "contest," to "contend". The Asuras or the dark passions common to all animated creatures, being naturally disposed to overcome those faculties which have the light of the Śastra for their guide, and again, the Devas or faculties enlightened by the Śāstra, being opposed to the former, the wars of the Devas and Asuras, *i.e.,* their mutual contention, for supremacy, are constant from eternity within the breast[13] of every creature.

This contest is here narrated by the Śruti in the form of a tale, in order to develop a knowledge of the cause of virtue and vice, and of the purity of life.[14] Both the Devas and the Asuras are the offspring of Prajāpati. Prajāpati is the designation of a soul proficient in knowledge and ceremonies; thus says a Śruti, "Verily the soul is the *Uktha;* he is the great Prajāpati."[15] knowledge and natural propensities being opposed to each other, through proceeding from the same source they are likened to the discordant sons of one parent, of whom, in order to acquire supremacy, the Devas "collected" commenced the "Udgītha," or ceremonies connected with the recitation of the Udgītha, that is, they commenced the ceremonies *jotiṣtoma*, etc.—the commencement of the Udgītha itself being impracticable, the object of the ceremony being to have success over their antagonists : "hereby we will overcome the Asuras."

2. ते ह नासिक्यं प्राणमुद्गीथमुपासांचक्रिरे तꣳहासुराः पाप्मना विविधुस्तस्मात्तेनोभयं जिघ्रति सुरभि च दुर्गन्धि च पाप्मना ह्येष विद्धः ॥

They adored breath as the Udgītha; the Asuras contaminated it with sin; hence it smells both fetor and aroma, being verily contaminated by sin.

Wishing to commence the Udgīthaic ceremony, the Devas adored breath or *nāsikya prāṇa* [nasal air or nasal life]—so called from the nostrils being the place of its origin,—the original source and reciter of the Udgītha, and possessing sensibility and the power of inhaling, under the belief of its being the Udgītha, that is to say, they adored the letter Om, called the Udgītha, as breath. Nor was this being wrong and adopted at the expense of truth for in reality the letter Om is adored. "You have said" [argues an opponent], "that they commenced works connected with the Udgītha,[16] how can you now maintain that they adored Om as breath ?" There is no inconsistency in this; for in the Udgīthaic ceremony, its performer, *i.e.*, the soul looked upon as the Om—the representative of a part or portion of the Udgītha—being declared as the object of adoration—and no distinct object being propounded—and that act of itself being a ceremony [the expression] "They commenced ceremony" is appropriate. The *Asuras*, naturally of dark disposition, contaminated, pierced, penetrated, tainted the chanter of the Devas, the resplendent nasal air with the sin which proceedeth from themselves; [or in other words] breath elated by the desire to inhale sweet odours, lost its sense of discriminations,[17] and in consequence of this fault, was tainted by sin, and therefore is it said, "the Asuras contaminated it with sin." Because the Asuras tainted breath with sin, therefore doth the breath of creatures impelled by sin, inhale bad odours : and hence do mankind smell both stench and perfume, being "contaminated by sin". The word "both" [उभय here used] is objectless, just as in the passage : "Let him expiate whose oblations both of dawn and twilight are defiled" ;[18] the Śruti itself elsewhere on a similar occasion says, "that by which it inhales obnoxious (smell) in vice."

3. अथ ह वाचमुद्गीथमुपासांचक्रिरे ताꣳहासुराः पाप्मना विविधुस्तस्मात्तयोभयं वदति सत्यं चानृतं च पाप्मना ह्येष विद्धः॥

They then adored speech as the Udgītha; the Asuras contaminated it with sin; hence it expresses both truth and untruth, being verily contaminated by sin.

4. अथ ह चक्षुरुद्गीथमुपासांचक्रिरे तद्धासुराः पाप्मना विविधुस्तस्मात्तेनोभयं पश्यति दर्शनीयं चादर्शनीयं च पाप्मना ह्येतद्विद्धम्॥

They then adored vision as the Udgītha; the Asuras contaminated it with sin; hence it views objects both [such as are] worthy and [such as are] not worthy of observation, being verily contaminated by sin.

5. अथ ह श्रोत्रमुद्गीथमुपासांचक्रिरे तद्धासुराः पाप्मना विविधुस्तस्मात्तेनोभयꣳ शृणोति श्रवणीयं चाश्रवणीयं च पाप्मना ह्येतद्विद्धम्॥

Next they adored audition as the Udgītha; the Asuras contaminated it with sin; hence it hears both what are worthy of audition and what are not, being verily contaminated by sin.

6. अथ ह मन उद्गीथमुपासांचक्रिरे तद्धासुराः पाप्मना विविधुस्तस्मात्तेनोभयꣳसंकल्पयते संकल्पनीयं चासंकल्पनीयं च पाप्मना ह्येतद्विद्धम्।।

Next they adored mind as the Udgītha; the Asuras contaminated it with sin, and hence it wills both good and evil, being verily contaminated by sin.

In order to establish the adorableness of the chief vital air, the Śruti here engages to prove its [sole] purity, and with that view, vision and the other vital functions (devatās, gods) are successively discussed, and forsaken as contaminated by sin proceeding from the Asuras. Those not recited, such as perception, taste and the like, are to be taken in the same light with those that are a different Śruti having said : "thus, indeed, these Devatās (faculties) were pierced by sin."

7. अथ ह य एवायं मुख्यः प्राणस्तमुद्गीथमुपासांचक्रिरे तꣳहासुरा ऋत्वा विदध्वंसुर्यथाश्मानमाखणमृत्वा विध्वꣳसेत।।

They then adored that which is the chief vital air, as the Udgītha; the Asuras approached it, and were destroyed as [is an earthen ball-hit] against an impregnable rock.

Breath and the rest being contaminated *by vice,* and the idea of their being worthy of adoration being thus renounced, they next adored that which is the chief vital air, and which abides in the mouth, as the Udgītha. It, the Asuras, approached as before, and on wishing [to contaminate it with sin] were immediately destroyed. As in the (physical) world an earthen ball thrown against a stone to break it, breaks itself and is destroyed without in the least affecting the stone, so were the Asuras destroyed : that which cannot be dug (Khana) with a spade or the like, nor even broken by an axe, is *Akhana*—impregnable.

Thus the chief vital air is [proved to be] pure, being unsubjugated by carnal passions.

8. एवं यथाश्मानमाखणमृत्वा विध्वꣳसत एवꣳहैव स विध्वꣳसते य एवंविदि पापं कामयते यश्चैनमभिदासति स एषोऽश्माखणः।।

Thus, verily, as an earthen ball is destroyed when hit against an impregnable rock, so doth he perish who wishes to contaminate with vice, him who thus knoweth [the chief vital air], as also he who injures him. He is as the impregnable rock.

The Śruti now proceeds to propound the reward of knowing the chief vital air thus. "As an earthen ball is destroyed," etc., is given as an example. "So doth he perish," is destroyed, "who desires to contaminate with vice," unbecoming actions, as also he who injures, abuses, vilifies, or chastises him "who knoweth the chief vital air" to be thus, as herein related—*i.e.*, perish in a like manner, he, the knower of the chief vital air, being—like unto an impregnable rock,—unsubjugable. Breath and the chief vital air are both modifications of air, how then doth one become liable to contamination by sin and not the other ? This is not inconsistent. Breath by its location in an impure place, becomes contaminated while the other from its superior position remains pure and uncontaminated. As an axe [or other instrument] is made subservient to use when in the hands of a proficient person, and not otherwise, so breath, ministered by impure odour becomes polluted and not the other.

9. नैवैतेन सुरभि न दुर्गन्धि विजानात्यपहतपाप्मा ह्येष तेन यदश्नाति यत्पिबति तेनेतरान् प्राणानवत्येतमु एवान्ततोऽवित्त्वोत्क्रामति व्याददात्येवान्तत इति॥

Through it, man inhales not odours, sweet or foul, being itself immaculate. Whatever is drunk or eaten by it supports the rest of the vital powers. At the last moment, deprived of support, they depart, and make men gape at the time of their death.

As the chief vital air is not contaminated by vice, so it does not inhale fetor or aroma, and men perceive odour through the organ of smell only. The effect of vice not being perceivable in the chief vital air, it is said to be that by which sin is "destroyed," consumed, demolished, (अपहतपाप्मा), and this destroyer of sin itself is pure. The organs of smell and the rest are selfish in their disposition, inasmuch as they are addicted to their own peculiar gratifications; not so life, which seeks the good of all.

How so ? Thus. Whatever men eat or drink through vital life supporteth and nourisheth breath and the rest of the organs, and they are preserved thereby, and life necessarily becomes all-supporting and pure. If it be questioned how the food and drink of the chief vital air maintain the rest, it is said, "at the last moment," at the time of death, deprived of support" [food and drink] they depart; that is, the organs of sense depart from or forsake the body, the functions of eating and drinking being impracticable without life, and the death of the orgnas follows as a matter of course. The disrelish of the chief vital air for food at the time of the death is evident, hence the gaping, which constitutes a characteristic of death from want of food.

10. तꣳहाङ्गिरा उद्गीथमुपासांचक्र एवाङ्गिरसं मन्यतेऽङ्गानां यद्रसः॥

Āṅgira adored it, the Udgītha, hence verily it is called *Āngirasa*, [or] the essence of all the organs [Angas].

Āṅgira adored it, etc. [This verse has been differently rendered by Śaṅkara. According to him Baka, son of Dalbhya as hereafter related, adored the chief vital air possessing the nature of Āṅgira, which verily is the Udgītha.

The most abvious meaning is as given above. Śaṅkara was aware of this, but says that the word ĀṄGIRA though in the nominative should be construed as if it were in the dative, and in support of this, adduces instances from the Vedas in which the nominative has been thus used.

11. तेन तꣳह बृहस्पतिरुद्गीथमुपासांचक्र एतमु एव बृहस्पतिं मन्यंते वाग्घि बृहती तस्या एष पतिः॥

Lo, Bṛhaspati adored it, the Udgītha, hence verily it is called Bṛhaspati ; speech in *Bṛhatī* [a form of metre] whereof it is the source [pati].

12. तेन तꣳहायास्य उद्गीथमुपासांचक्र एतमु एवायास्यं मन्यन्त आस्याद्यदयते॥

Āyāsya also adored it, the Udgītha, hence it is called Āyāsya; [or] that which proceeds from the mouth [Āsya].

13. तेन तꣳह बको दाल्भ्यो विदांचकार॥ स ह नैमिषीयानामुद्गाता बभूव स ह स्मैभ्यः कामानागायति॥

So, did Baka, son of Dalbhya, know it, and glorify it for the gratification of the desires of the sages of Naimiṣa, for whom he officiated as a chanter [of the Sāma Veda].

14. आगाता ह वै कामानां भवति य एतदेवं विद्वानक्षरमुद्गीथमुपास्त इत्यध्यात्मम्॥

He who, knowing it thus, adores this undecaying Udgītha,

becomes the (most successful) solicitor [of boons]. This is spiritual [worship].

Section III

1. अथाधिदैवतं य एवासौ तपति तमुद्गीथमुपासीतोद्यन्वा एष प्रजाभ्य उद्गायति उद्यꣳस्तमोभयमपहन्त्यपहन्ता ह वै भयस्य तमसो भवति य एवं वेद॥

Next (the worship of the Udgītha) as connected with gods: He who dispenseth heat is the Udgītha. Let him be adored. For rising he singeth for welfare of the creation rising he dispelleth the dread of gloom. He, who knows him thus, becomes a destroyer of the fear of gloom.

The Udgītha being adorable in different ways, "Next," subsequent to the narration of its inherent [lit. mental] worth, the Śruti commences the adoration of the Udgītha as connected with deities. "He," the sun who dispenseth heat, should be adored as that Udgītha, that is the Udgītha should be adored as the sun. The phrase "that Udgītha" denotes certain letters, how is it to be applied to the sun ? It is said "rising" *(Udyan)*, ascending he singeth for the creation, that is, for the growth of food for the creation. Did he not rise, grains, such as wheat, would not attain to maturity, consequently he singeth as do the chanters at a sacrifice—that is, as the chanters at a sacrifice, reciting the Udgītha, pray for the abundance of food, so doth the sun. Moreover ascending above the horizon, he destroyeth the dread of the animated creation and nocturnal gloom. He who knows the sun as herein described, becomes the destroyer both of the dread of birth and death, and its cause, gloom, which is ignorance.

2. समान उ एवायं चासौ चोष्णोऽयमुष्णोऽसौ स्वर इतीममाचक्षते स्वर इति प्रत्यास्वर इत्यमुं तस्माद्वा एतमिमममुं योद्गीथमुपासीत॥

Verily this [the sun] and that [the chief vital air] are alike; this is warm as well as that; this may be called transitive (स्वर) ; that is transitive and retransitive; therefore let this and that be adored as the Udgītha.

3. अथ खलु व्यानमेवोद्गीथमुपासीत यद्वै प्राणिति स प्राणो यदपानिति सोऽपानोऽथ यः प्राणापानयोः सन्धिः स व्यानो यो व्यानः सा वाक् तस्मादप्राणन्ननपानन्वा-चमभिव्याहरति ।।

Moreover, let Vyāna be adored as the Udgītha. That [function] by which (breath) is respired in *Prāṇa,* that by which [it] is inspired in *Apāna,* and the interval of the two is *Vyāna,* which is speech. Therefore speech is articulated irrespective of inspiration and expiration.

Moreover, etc. The worship of the Udgītha in a different form is now to be related. *Vyāna,* a vital action of life is to be adored as the Udgītha. Now for its nature. The function by which man "respires," breathes through his mouth or the nostrils, is called *Prāṇa;* that by which he "inspires," inhales, is *Apāna* or the function of inspiration. We next come to that which is the interval between the inhalation and exhalation aforesaid; a distinct function called *Vyāna,* but it is not the same which is described by the Sāṅkhyas. But why forsake these Prāṇa and Apāna, and assiduously apply to Vyāna? Because, of its functional superiority; and what is that functional superiority is next described : "Whatever is Vyāna is speech," that is, the function of Vyāna is speech. Thus the vocal function being dependant on Vyāna, men articulate without any reference to inspiration or respiration.

4. या वाक्सर्क्तस्मादप्राणन्ननपानन्नृचमभिव्याहरति यर्क्तत्साम तस्मादप्राणन्ननपानन्साम गायति यत्साम स उद्गीथस्तस्माद-प्राणन्ननपानन्नुद्गायति ।।

That which is speech is Ṛk, therefore do [men] articulate the Ṛk without inspiring or respiring. That which is Ṛk is Sāma, hence is it chanted without inspiring or respiring. That which is Sāma, is Udgītha, hence is it chanted without reference to inspiration or respiration.

Again, Ṛk is only a form of speech, which includes the Sāma, of which letter the Udgītha is but a form, *consequently* they are articulated without reference to inspiration or respiration, by the assistance of Vyāna alone.

5. अतो यान्यन्यानि वीर्यवन्ति कर्माणि यथाग्नेर्मन्थनमाजेः सरणं दृढस्य धनुष आयमनमप्राणन्ननपानꣳस्तानि करोत्येतस्य हेतोर्व्यानमेवोद्गीथमुपासीत ।।

Moreover, all other mighty actions, such as the production of fire by friction, running a course, or stringing a strong bow, are performed without reference to inspiration or respiration, therefore is the Vyāna worshipped as the Udgītha.

Nor is articulation alone the function of Vyāna, other mighty actions requiring great exertions, "such as the production of fire by friction, running a course, stringing by bending a strong bow," men perform without either inspiring or respiring: consequently Vyāna is superior to the function of either Prāṇa or Apāna, and inasmuch as adoration to the great is proper, being highly efficacious as adoration to a king, it is advanced to be an object of worship.

6. खलूद्गीथाक्षराण्युपासीतोद्गीथ इति प्राण एवोत्प्राणेन ह्युत्तिष्ठति वाग्गीर्वाचो ह गिर इत्याचक्षतेऽन्नं थमन्ने हीदꣳ सर्वꣳ स्थितम् ।।

Next verily let the letters of the [word] Udgītha be adored as the Udgītha. Respiration [Prāṇa] is "Ut," for men attain the power of rising from respiration; speech (Vāk) is "Gī," for vāk and gira, are said to be synonymous;—"tha" is aliment, for verily, every thing is supported by food [sthitam].

"Next," it is propounded that "verily let the letters of the Udgītha be adored," not the letters described in the chapter called the Udgītha, but the syllables of the word Udgītha; by adoring the syllable of a name the nominee is adored, just as Miśra so and so. "Prāṇa is *ut*" and this syllable ought to be believed as much. How Prāṇa is called *'ut'* is thus explained: for all *living beings* rise *(uttiṣthati)* while those that are without life rise not, and therefore they are identical. Speech is *gī*, for all honest men know speech by the word *gī*. Lastly, *tha* is aliment. All are sustained (स्थितं sthitam) by aliment [anna] and therefore there is *evident* similarity between the letter *tha* and aliment अन्न. The triple similarity here shown, in the Śruti will be (again) met with *as we proceed.*

7. द्यौरेवोदन्तरिक्षं गीः पृथिवी थमादित्य एवोद्वायुर्गीरग्निस्थꣳसा-मवेद एवोद्यजुर्वेदो गीः ऋग्वेदस्थं दुग्धेऽस्मै वाग्दोहं यो वाचो दोहोऽन्नवानन्नादो भवति य एतान्येवं विद्वानुद्गीथाक्षराण्यु-पास्त उद्गीथ इति ।।

The heaven *(dyau)* is Ut, the atmosphere [antarikṣa] is Gī, and the earth (pṛthivī) is Tha. The sun (Āditya) is Ut, the wind (Vāyu) is Gī, and fire (Agni) is Tha. The Sāma Veda is Ut, the Yajur Veda Gī, and the Ṛg Veda Tha. For him who, thus knowing, adores the letters of the Udgītha as the Udgītha, speech itself yields its wealth, and the adorer obtains alimental treasure and the power to consume the same.

8. **अथ खल्वाशीः समृद्धिरुपसरणानीत्युपासीत येन साम्ना स्तोष्यन्स्यात्तत्सामोपधावेत् ॥**

Now, then, that which yields desirable objects [*will be disclosed]*. What are worthy of meditation should be thus adored: the Sāma hymn by which *the adorer* is to glorify should be enquired into.

9. **यस्यामृचि तामृचं यदार्षेयं तमृषिं यां देवतामभिष्टोष्यन्स्यात्तां देवतामुपधावेत् ॥**

The Ṛk hymns in which they [the Sāma hymns] occur, the Sages, *who first promulgated them,* and the Devas glorified by those hymns, should also be reflected upon.

10. **येन छन्दसा स्तोष्यन्स्यात्तच्छन्द उपधावेद्येन स्तोमेन स्तोष्यमाणः स्यात्तꣳ स्तोममुपधावेत् ॥**

The metre with which he is to glorify, the praise with which he is to eulogize.

11. **यां दिशमभिष्टोष्यन्स्यात्तां दिशमुपधावेत् ॥**

And the quarter facing which he is to eulogize, should also be reflected upon.

12. **आत्मानमन्तत उपसृत्य स्तुवीत कामं ध्यायन्नप्रमत्तोऽभ्याशो ह यदस्मै स कामः समृध्येत यत्कामः स्तुवीतेत यत्कामः स्तुवीतेति ॥**

Lastly, approaching his own spirit, and calmly reflecting on one's object, let him eulogize. With whatever object he singeth—verily with whatever object he singeth—fruition doth immediately follow.

Having thus successively eulogized the Sāma hymn and the like, let his own self be meditated upon, eulogized in meditation, meditating also upon, the desires *(which lead to action)*; "without excitement," *i.e.*, without error as to voice or in the enunciation of sibilants or consonants. For him who thus knows, fruition immediately follows. What fruition? That which one wisheth; the repetition implies earnestness.

Section IV

1. ॐमित्येतदक्षरमुद्गीथमुपासीतोमिति ह्युद्गायति तस्योपव्याख्यानम् ॥

Om, this letter should be adored, Om is recited. Its description.

2. देवा वै मृत्योर्बिभ्यतस्त्रयीं विद्यां प्राविशꣳस्ते छन्दोभिरच्छादयन्यदेभिरच्छादयꣳस्तच्छन्दसां छन्दस्त्वम् ॥

The Devas, dreading death, adopted the three-fold knowledge of the Vedas. They shielded themselves with psalms. The psalms are called chandas, because the Devas shielded *(acchādayan)* themselves therein.

3. तानु तत्र मृत्युर्यथा मत्स्यमुदके परिपश्येदेवं पर्यपश्यदृचि साम्नि यजुषि। ते नु वित्त्वोर्ध्वा ऋचः साम्नो यजुषः स्वरमेव प्राविशन् ॥

As *Fishermen* look at a fish in water so did Death behold them in the Ṛk, Yajus and Sāma hymns. They, apprised of it, forsaking the Vedas, of a truth betook to the asylum of Voice.— *Svara.*

"As *Fishermen* look at fish, in" shallow water with a view to ascertain how they may be secured, either by hook or by drawing out the water, so Death, with a like object, beheld "them," the Devas, immersed in ceremonies, *i.e.,* he ascertained that they may be secured when their rites together with their effects *which are equally impermanent* shall be consumed. Where did he observe the Devas ? "In Ṛk Sāma and Yajus"—*i.e.,* engaged in ceremonies achievable by those Vedas. "They," the Devas, having their intellect refined by their attachment to the rituals of the Vedas, learnt the object of Death. Apprised of it, they, forsaking the ceremonies achievable by the three Vedas whereby they despaired of being defended, betook to the asylum of the letter possessed of immortality and security called *Svara, i.e.,* they devoted themselves to the adoration of Om. The word एव "of a truth" not only signalizes the act, but excludes all ritural performances save the adoration of Om.

4. यदा वा ऋचमाप्नोत्योमित्येवातिस्वरत्येवꣳसामैवं यजुरेष उ स्वरो यदेतदक्षरमेतदमृतमभयं तत्प्रविश्य देवा अमृता अभया अभवन्॥

In reciting the Ṛk hymns Om is articulated *(Svarati),* so in the Yajus and Sāma, therefore, indeed, is this letter [the Udgītha] possessing immortality and safety, *called* SVARA. Adopting its support the gods became immortal and secure.

How the letter Om is deducible from the word Svara, is thus explained : "In reciting the hymns of the Ṛk, Yajus, and Sāma Vedas Om is articulated, *(Svarati)* therefore it is SVARA, the letter possessing immortality and security," Adopting its support the Devas obtained immortality and safety, the attributes of that support.

5. स य एतदेवं विद्वानक्षरं प्रणौत्येतदेवाक्षरꣳस्वरममृतमभयं प्रविशति तत्प्रविश्व यदमृता देवास्तदमृतो भवति॥

He who, knowing it thus, praiseth this letter, obtains the immortal and secure letter Svara, and obtaining it, like unto the Devas, becomes immortal.

Like the gods, he who, knowing this letter possessed of immortality and safety, "praiseth" it (by praise adoration is indicated) obtains it and attains immortality like unto the gods; for as the Deity is not actuated by the same feeling which makes a mortal monarch differently regard his guests according to intimacy, etc., the reward of the adoration is (alike) in all cases, neither more nor less than what the gods obtained.

SECTION V

1. अथ खलु य उद्गीथः स प्रणवो यः प्रणवः स उद्गीथ इत्यसौ वा आदित्य उद्गीथ एष प्रणव ओमिति ह्येष स्वरन्नेति॥

Verily that which is Udgītha, is Praṇava, and the Praṇava is the Udgītha. The Āditya in truth is the Udgītha—the Praṇava, for it moves resounding Om.

2. एतमु एवाहमभ्यगासिषं तस्मान्मम त्वमेकोऽसीति ह कौषीतकिः पुत्रमुवाच रश्मीꣳस्त्वं पर्यावर्तयाद्बहवो वै ते भविष्यन्तीत्यधिदैवतम्॥

"Verily I sang *in praise* of the sun," said Kauṣītaki, to his son, "therefore have I thee alone. Know the rays[19] and thou shalt obtain a numerous progeny." This *is the adoration of Om as* related to physical powers.

"Verily I sang in praise of the sun" *i.e.,* "I meditated on the sun and its rays as the same, 'therefore' have I thee alone for my son," said Kauṣītaki, son of Kuṣītaka, to his son. Do you know them to be different, and "thou shalt obtain a numerous progeny ".

3. अथाध्यात्मं य एवायं मुख्यः प्राणस्तमुद्गीथमुपासीतोमिति ह्येष स्वरन्नेति॥

Next as connected with the Spirit. Verily the chief life is to be adored as the Udgītha, for, resounding Om, it proceedeth.

The adoration of Om as connected with the spirit is next described. The chief life is to be adored, for it, like the sun, resounding the word of command, Om, sets speech and the other organs to their duty. No body ever hears life *actually* resounding Om, the sense therefore is that it enjoins to *each its duty.*

4. एतमु एवाहमभ्यगासिषं तस्मान्मम त्वमेकोऽसीति ह कौषीतकिः पुत्रमुवाच प्राणाꣳस्त्वं भूमानमभिगायताद्बहवो वै मे भविष्यन्तीति॥

"Verily I sang in praise of that," [the chief life] said Kauṣītaki to his son, "Do thou sing in praise of it as manifold, praying for numerous progeny."

5. अथ खलु य उद्गीथः स प्रणवो यः प्रणवः स उद्गीथ इति होतृषदनाद्धैवापि दुरुद्गीथमनुसमाहरतीत्यनुसमाहरतीति॥

He verily, who knows the Udgītha, to be the Praṇava and the Praṇava to be the Udgītha, reconciles by the rituals of the Hotā, the errors of the Udgātā,—verily reconciles the errors of the Udgātā.

Having identified the Udgītha with the Praṇava, its advantages are next related, "Rituals of the Hotā," [lit *Hotṛṣadana,]* the place or seat of the Hotā, but as the place cannot produce the effects, the rituals are menat : "the errors of the Udgāta," the errors which the Udgātā commits in reciting the Udgītha, he reconciles, as medicines reconcile offending humours.

SECTION VI

1. इयमेवर्गग्निः साम तदेतदेतस्यामृच्यध्यूढꣳ साम तस्मादृच्य-
ध्यूढꣳसाम। गीयत इयमेव साग्निरमस्तत्साम॥

This [earth] verily is the Ṛk, and fire Sāma. The Sāma rests on the Ṛk, and therefore doth the chanter of the Sāma Veda call the Ṛk the upholder of the Sāma. Verily the earth is SĀ, and fire AMA, whence comes Sāma.

Having in the preceding sections described the adoration of Om for the attainment of particular objects, the Śruti now begins to relate a form of adoration which gratifies all desires. "This verily is the Ṛk," etc. This earth is verily the Ṛk, *i.e.,* the earth and fire are to be identified with the Ṛk and the Sāma, because, says the Śruti, the igneous Sāma rests on, or is supported by, the terrene Ṛk ; (the point of resemblance being that as the Sāma is included in the Ṛk, so is fire contained in the earth, or because there is slight difference between them, the letters of the Sāma being indicative of the earth and fire;) nor are fire and the earth different, for they are always connected with each other like unto the Ṛk and Sāma.

2. अन्तरिक्षमेवर्ग्वायुः साम तदेतदेतस्यामृच्यध्यूढꣳ साम
तस्मादृच्यध्यूढꣳ साम गीयतेऽन्तरिक्षमेव सा वायुरमस्तत्साम॥

Verily the sky is Ṛk, and the wind Sāma. The Sāma rests on the Ṛk, therefore doth the chanter of the Sāma Veda, call Ṛk the upholder of the Sāma. Verily the sky is SĀ, and wind AMA whence comes Sāma.

How ? The earth is Sā, the first half of the word Sāma, and fire the other half—Ama, and necessarily the two words together form the Sāma; nor are they mutually different, for lie unto the Ṛk and the Sāma they have constant connection with each other, therefore are they said to be a *compound* of the Ṛk and the Sāma. Some say that this verse establishes that the two constituents of साम (Sāma) should be revered as indicative of the earth and fire.

3. द्यौरेवर्गादित्यः साम तदेतदेतस्यामृच्यध्यूढꣳ साम तस्मा-
दृच्यध्यूढꣳ साम गीयते द्यौरेव सादित्योऽमस्तत्साम॥

Verily the heaven (Dyau) is Ṛk and the Sun, Sāma. The Sāma rests on the Ṛk, therefore doth the reciter of the Sāma Veda, etc., etc., as before.

"Verily the heaven is the Ṛk," etc., as before.

4. नक्षत्राण्येवर्क् चन्द्रमाः साम तदेतदेतस्यामृच्यध्यूढꣳ साम
तस्मादृच्यध्यूढꣳ साम गीयते नक्षत्राण्येव सा चन्द्रमा
अमस्तत्साम॥

Verily the Stars are Ṛk and the moon is Sāma, the Sāma rests, etc., etc., as before.

The moon is the lord of stars, hence is it likened to the Sāma.

5. अथ यदेतदादित्यस्य शुक्लं भाः सैवर्गथ यन्नीलं परः
कृष्णं तत्साम तदेतदेतस्यामृच्यध्यूढꣳ साम तस्मादृच्यध्यूढꣳ
साम गीयते॥

The whiteness of the sun is Ṛk, and its darkness—deep darkness—is Sāma. The latter rests on the former, therefore doth the reciter of the Sāma Veda call the Ṛk the upholder of the Sāma.

"The whiteness of the sun," that is the luminous rays of the sun, constitute the Ṛk, and the "darkness—the deep darkness"—which is only visible to those who know the Sāstras, constitutes the Sāma.

Hence the different rays of the sun from the *Sā* and *Ama.*

6. अथ यदेवैतदादित्यस्य शुक्लं भाः सैव साथ यन्नीलं
परः कृष्णं तदमस्तत्सामाथ य एषोऽन्तरादित्ये हिरण्मयः
पुरुषो दृश्यते हिरण्यश्मश्रुर्हिरण्यकेश आप्रणखात्सर्व
एव सुवर्णः॥

The brightness of the sun, that is, the white light of the sun, is Sā; that which is back—very back—is Ama, whence comes Sāma. That resplendent male of golden hair and whiskers, whose whole *body even* unto the nails is of gold, whom we behold in the interior of the sun.

"The brightness of the sun," etc., "Golden". As it is not consistent for the Deity, whose joints are formed of the Ṛk and Sāma to be made of actual gold, nor can vice be consistently attributed to gold, therefore to talk of its absence is absurd—farther, it is evident the object under discussion is not formed of metal, it necessarily follows, that the expression gold metaphorically implies brilliancy—elsewhere the same construction follows. He who dwells (शयानात्) in an abode, पुरि, or He who fills (पूरयति) the universe with his own soul, is the Male or Puruṣa; who is "visible" only to those whose eyes are withdrawn from worldly objects, whose hearts are contented, and who have undergone the discipline appropriate to a religious scholar (Brahmacarya). As it is possible for a resplendent being to have black hairs and whiskers—it is here expressly pointed out "golden whiskers, golden hairs," etc., *i.e.*, they too are brilliant.

7. तस्य यथा कप्यासं पुण्डरीकमेवमक्षिणी तस्योदिति नाम स एष सर्वेभ्यः पाप्मभ्य उदित उदेति ह वै सर्वेभ्यः पाप्मभ्यो य एवं वेद।।

Whose eyes are like unto lotuses, red as the orb of the rising god of day, is called Ut. He verily is above [Udgātā]—all sin. He indeed ascends above all sin, who knows Him thus.

Of this Male, whose whole body is golden, there is some distinction in the eyes. They are red like unto lotuses which are bright, as the parts around the postial calosities of the monkey; Kapyāsa from Kapi monkey, and Āsa to sit. Here the comparison is not unworthy, being between the lotuses and the parts around the calosities. Of him is this qualitative named Ut. How ? Qualitative, because, having exceeded (Udgātā) all sin together with its effects it becomes Ut. He who knows him of the name of Ut, as herein described, rises above all sin : ह and वै are expletives.

8. तस्यर्क् च साम च गेष्णौ तस्मादुद्गीथस्तस्मात्त्वेवोद्गातैतस्य हि गाता स एष ये चामुष्मात्प्राञ्चो लोकास्तेषां चेष्टे देवकामानां चेत्यधिदैवतम्।।

The Ṛk and the Sāma are his joints, hence is He the Udgītha, and therefore in chanting the Udgītha, doth the chanter become Udgātā, for he sings in praise of Ut. He rules over all the regions above the sun, and over all who desire the abode of gods. Thus far on the adoration of the Deity with reference to physical powers.

To point out that the Male is the Udgītha, as are the sun and the rest, it is said as follows :

The Ṛk and the Sāma which have been likened to the earth and Agni are His joints, for verily He is the soul of all, being the lord (ईश) of those who desire recompense, they may be His joints, also for His being the cause of all. Whereas He who is called Ut., has the Ṛk and Sāma for His joints, therefore is He the Udgītha, here [somewhat] indirectly expressed, as gods delight in indirect allusions. "Therefore" for this reason, for reciting the Ut, he is called Udgātā.

That god called Ut is the lord of all who reside in regions above the yonder sun, and is the protector of all, for says a *mantra :* "He upholds the earth as well as the heaven. He is the lord of what is longed for by gods."

Thus hath been related the description of the venerable Udgītha as connected with physical powers.

SECTION VII

1. तथाध्यात्मं वागेवर्क् प्राणः साम तदेतदेतस्यामृच्यध्यूढꣳ साम तस्मादृच्यध्यूढꣳ साम गीयते वागेव सा प्राणोऽमस्तत्साम ॥

Now with reference to self. Speech is Ṛk, and Life, Sāma. On that [speech alias] Ṛk rests the [life alias] Sāma, therefore is the Ṛk said to be the upholder of the Sāma. Speech is SĀ, and life Ama, whence Sāma.

2. चक्षुरेवर्गात्मा साम तदेतदेतस्यामृच्यध्यूढꣳ साम तस्मादृच्यध्यूढꣳ साम गीयते चक्षुरेव सात्मामस्तत्साम ॥

The eyes are Ṛk, and their reflection, Sāma. On the [eyes alias] Ṛk rests the [reflection alias] Sāma, therefore is the Ṛk said to be the upholder of the Sāma. The eyes are SĀ and the reflection Ama, whence Sāma.

3. श्रोत्रमेवर्ङ्मनः साम तदेतदेतस्यामृच्यध्यूढꣳ समा तस्मादृच्यध्यूढꣳ साम गीयते श्रोत्रमेव सा मनोऽमस्तत्साम ॥

The ears are the Ṛk, and the mind Sāma. On those [ears alias]

Ṛk rests the [mind alias] Sāma, therefore is the Ṛk said to be the upholder of the Sāma. The ears SĀ and the mind Ama, whence Sāma.

4. अथ यदेतदक्ष्णः शुक्लं भाः सैवर्गथ यन्नीलं परः कृष्णं तत्साम तदेतदेतस्यामृच्यध्यूढꣳसाम तस्मादृच्यध्यूढꣳसाम गीयते। अथ यदेवैतदक्ष्णः शुक्लं भाः सैव साथ यन्नीलं परः कृष्णं तदमस्तत्साम॥

Next, that which is the white light of the eyes is Ṛk, and its black—deep black—rays are the Sāma. On that [white light alias] the Ṛk rests [the black rays alias] the Sāma, therefore is the Ṛk said to be the upholder of the Sāma. Now the white light of the eyes is SĀ, and that which is black—very black—is Ama, whence Sāma.

5. अथ य एषोऽन्तरक्षिणी पुरुषो दृश्यते सैवर्क्तत्साम तदुक्थं तद्यजुस्तद्ब्रह्म तस्यैतस्य तदेव रूपं यदमुष्य रूपं यावमुष्य गेष्णौ तौ गेष्णौ यन्नाम तन्नाम॥

Next, the Male which is seen in the interior of the eyes is the Ṛk and the Sāma. He is the Uktha, He the Yajus, He Brahman. His figure is the figure of Brahman; the joints of the one are the joints of the other, and the name of the one that of the other.

6. स एष ये चैतस्मादर्वाञ्चो लोकास्तेषां चेष्टे मनुष्यकामानां चेति तद्य इमे वीणायां गायन्त्येतं ते गायन्ति तस्मात्ते धनसनयः॥

He is the lord of all that are within the scope of the eyes and of those who long for worldly advancement. Whatever songs are sung with the accompaniment of Vīnā are due to Him; He is the lord of wealth.

7. अथ य एतदेवंविद्वान्साम गायत्युभौ स गायति सोऽमुनैव स एष ये चामुष्मात्पराञ्चो लोकास्ताꣳश्चाप्नोति देवकामाꣳश्च॥

He, who knowing all these, sings in praise of the Sāma, verily sings in praise of both. Through that he obtains a hereafter and the regions of the gods.

8. अथानेनैव ये चैतस्मादर्वाञ्चो लोकास्तांश्चाप्नोति मनुष्यकामांश्च तस्मादु हैवंविदुद्गाता ब्रूयात् ॥

And through this, all the regions below his sight and all worldly prospects. Therefore should the singer of the Udgītha, who knows all this, say [unto those who know not] :

9. कं ते काममागायानीत्येष ह्येव कामगानस्येष्टे य एवं विद्वान्साम गायति साम गायति ॥

"[Say,] what are thy wishes ? I shall pray for the same." He, who knowing all this, sings in praise of the Sāma becomes a sovereign solicitor of boons.

Section VIII

1. त्रयो होद्गीथे कुशला बभूवुः शिलकः शालावत्यश्चैकितायनो दाल्भ्यः प्रवाहणो जैवलिरिति ते होचुरुद्गीथे वै कुशलाः स्मो हन्तोद्गीथे कथां वदाम इति ॥

Verily, three [persons] were skilled in the Udgītha : Śilaka, son os Śalāvat; Caikitāyana, the progeny of Dalbha; and Pravāhaṇa, son of Jīvala. They said [to each other], "We are proficient in the Udgītha, and are prepared to reveal its knowledge [if it pleaseth you]."

The Udgītha being adorable in various ways, an excellent form of adoration is here narrated, and towards its better illucidation, a tradition recited. The word "three" is not used with reference to the mass of mankind, but to three individuals of a particular assembly, for Uṣasti, Janaśruti, Kaikeya, and others are well known to have been proficient likewise.

2. तथेति ह समुपविविशुः स ह प्रवाहणो जैवलिरुवाच भगवन्तावग्रे वदतां ब्राह्मणयोर्वदतोर्वाचꣳ श्रोष्यामीति ॥

Saying this, they seated themselves. Pravāhaṇa, son of Jīvala, said : "You, Venerable Sirs, both of you begin the discourse, that I may listen to such Brāhmaṇa speakers."

From the expression "both of you Brāhmaṇa speakers," it is evident that Pravāhaṇa was a Kṣatriya.

3. स ह शिलकः शालावत्यश्चैकितायनं दाल्भ्यमुवाच हन्त त्वा पृच्छानीति पृच्छेति होवाच॥

Of them, Śilaka, son of Śalāvat, thus addressed Caikitāyana, the progeny of Dalbha : "If it pleaseth you, I shall ask some questions." "Be it so," said the other.

4. का साम्नो गतिरिति स्वर इति होवाच स्वरस्य का गतिरिति प्राण इति होवाच प्राणस्य का गतिरित्यन्नमिति होवाचान्नस्य का गतिरित्याप इति होवाच॥

[Śilaka enquired]. "What is the asylum of the Sāma?" "Voice" [replied Caikitāyana]. "What of voice ?" "Breath." "Of Breath ?" "Aliment." "Of Aliment ?" "Water."

5. अपां का गतिरित्यसौ लोक इति होवाचामुष्य लोकस्य का गतिरिति न स्वर्गं लोकमतिनयेदिति होवाच स्वर्गं वयं लोकꣳ सामाभिसंस्थापयाम स्वर्गसꣳस्तावꣳ हि सामेति॥

"Of Water ?" "That sphere." "And of that sphere ?" "We shall not exceed the heavens, for on them we rest the Sāma, which is likened to the heavens in its eulogy."

6. तꣳह शिलकः शालावत्यश्चैकितायनं दाल्भ्यमुवाचाप्रतिष्ठितं वै किल ते दाल्भ्य साम यस्त्वेतर्हि ब्रूयान्मूर्धा ते विपतिष्यतीति मूर्धा ते विपतेदिति॥

Then did Śilaka, son of Śalāvat address Chaikitāyana, the progeny of Dalbha : "Verily, irreverent is thy Sāma. O Dālbhya, [when you describe it to be so august] were one [who fully understands it] to say, 'Let thy head fall off [thy neck]'; it would verily so happen."

i.e., Not so venerable as you describe it to be, when you say we should stop our enquiry with it, and proceed no further.

7. हन्ताहमेतद्भगवत्तो वेदानीति विद्धीति होवाचामुष्य लोकस्य का गतिरित्ययं लोक इति होवाचास्य लोकस्य का गतिरिति न प्रतिष्ठा लोकमतिनयेदिति होवाच प्रतिष्ठां वयं लोकꣳ सामाभिसꣳस्थापयामः प्रतिष्ठासꣳस्तावꣳहि सामेति॥

"Then I should like to know it better from you, Venerable Sir." "Bẹ it so," said the other. "What [say you] is the asylum of that sphere ?" "This sphere," said [Śilaka, alluding to the earth]. "And what is the asylum of this sphere ?" "We should not exceed this receptacle, for on it we rest the Sāma, whence it is eulogized as *the* receptacle."

The earth by its sacrifices, charity and burnt-offerings affords subsistence to the upper sphere, whence, says the Śruti, "The offerings [of mankind] become the livelihood of the gods." It is [further] evident that the earth is the receptacle of all living beings, and it is therefore not inconsistent to say that it is receptacle of the Sāma.

8. तꣳ ह प्रावहणो जैवलिरुवाचान्तवद्वै किल ते शालावत्य साम यस्त्वेतर्हि ब्रूयान्मूर्धा ते विपतिष्यतीति मूर्धा ते विपतेदिति हन्ताहमेतद्भगवत्तो वेदानीति विद्धीति होवाच॥

Unto him said Pravāhaṇa, son of Jīvala : "Impermanent is thy Sāma, O son of Śalāvat, and [when thou describest it as otherwise] were one to say 'Let thy head fall of thy neck,' forthwith would it drop down." "Let me then learn it of thee O Venerable Sir." "Be it so," responded the other.

Section IX

1. अस्य लोकस्य का गतिरित्याकाश इति होवाच सर्वाणि ह वा इमानि भूतान्याकाशादेव समुत्पद्यन्त आकाशं प्रत्यस्तं यन्त्याकाशो ह्येवैभ्यो ज्यायानाकाशः परायणम्॥

"What is the end of this sphere ?" The sky, said the other, [and continued] "all these creations proceed from, and end in, the sky. The sky is the senior of all these, it is the great receptacle.

The other, having thus obtained permission, enquired : "Of this sphere what is the end ?" To him Pravāhaṇa said : "The sky." The word "sky" [Ākāsa] means the "Great Soul" [God]. For we will [elsewhere] hear [Chap. VII]. "The sky [Brahman] is the prime cause of all objects possessing a name and a form. The creation is Its work, and in It do the elements submerge." It will also be said [hereafter] : "He created light, in Him doth light subside."

2. स एष परोवरीयानुद्गीथः स एषोऽनन्तः परोवरीयो हास्य भवति परोवरीयसो ह लोकाञ्जयति य एतदेवं विद्वान्परोवरीयाꣳ समुद्गीथमुपास्ते ।।

It is the most excellent Udgītha, it is endless. He, who knowing thus, adores the most excellent Udgītha, attains to most excellent regions, and his [life] becomes most excellent."

The most excellent Udgītha means the Udgītha endowed with the Deity, or the Great Soul.

3. तꣳहैतमतिधन्वा शौनक उदरशाण्डिल्यायोक्त्वोवाच यावत्त एनं प्रयाजमुद्गीथं वेदिष्यन्ते परोवरीयो हैभ्यस्तावदस्मिँल्लोके जीवनं भविष्यति ।।

Atidhanvā, son of Śaunaka, having thus explained it [the Udgītha] to Udaraśāṇḍilya, observed : The career of such of your descendants as will know the Udgītha thus, will continue most excellent in this world.

4. तथामुष्मिँल्लोके लोक इति स य एतमेवं विद्वानुपास्ते परोवरीय एव हास्यास्मिँल्लोके जीवनं भवति तथामुष्मिँल्लोके लोक इति लोके लोक इति ।।

"As also hereafter" : therefore the career of those who, knowing thus, adore [the Udgītha] will become most excellent in this world, as also in worlds to come,—verily in worlds to come.

SECTION X

1. मटचीहतेषु कुरुष्वाटिक्या सह जाययोषस्तिर्ह चाक्रायण इभ्यग्रामे प्रद्राणक उवास ।।

Uṣasti, son of Cakra, with his virgin wife, forsaking Kuru, lived in great distress in Ibhyagrāma [a village inhabited by an elephant-driver].

2. स हेभ्यं कुल्माषान्खादन्तं बिभिक्षे तꣳहोवाच नेतोऽन्ये विद्यन्ते यश्च ये म इम उपनिहिता इति॥

Of him [the elephant-driver whilst] eating some vile beans,[20] he begged [for food]. Unto him, said the elephant-driver : "I have none other than what you see before me."

3. एतेषां मे देहीति होवाच तानस्मै प्रददौ हन्तानुपानमित्युच्छिष्टं वै मे पीतꣳस्यादिति होवाच॥

"Give me of the same," replied he. The elephant-driver gave him thereof, and also offered him some drink. Uṣasti said : "[Were I to take that] I would swallow the remnant of another's drink."

4. न स्विदेतेऽप्युच्छिष्टा इति न वा अजीविष्यमिमां न खादन्निति होवाच कामो म उदपानमिति॥

"Is not that also an offal ?" [replied the elephant-driver, alluding to the beans.] "I cannot live without-eating that," said Uṣasti, "but drink I can command at pleasure.

5. स ह खादित्वातिशेषाञ्जायाया आजहार साग्र एव सुभिक्षा बभूव तान्प्रतिगृह्य निदधौ॥

Having eaten thereof, he presented the remainder to his wife. She had before partaken [of the same, and therefore] took it and laid it by.

6. स ह प्रातः संजिहान उवाच यद्बतान्नस्य लभेमहि लभेमहि धनमात्राꣳ राजासौ यक्ष्यते स मा सर्वैरार्त्विज्यैर्वृणीतेति॥

On the [following] morning, rising from his bed, he [the husband] exclaimed : "Alas! If I could [now] obtain a little food, I could earn some wealth. A king is performing a sacrifice in the neighbourhood, he would surely employ me to perform all its functions."

7. तं जायोवाच हन्त पत इम एव कुल्माषा इति तान्खादित्वामुं यक्षं विततमेयाय॥

To him said his wife : "Here are the beans, [take them] and, eating thereof, quickly proceed to the sacrifice."

8. तत्रोद्गातॄ नास्तावे स्तोष्यमाणानुपोपविवेश स ह प्रस्तोतारमुवाच।।

Arrived there, he took his seat at the place of sacrifice[21] before the chanters of the Udgītha, and then thus addressed the chanters of praise:

9. प्रस्तोतर्या देवता प्रस्तावमन्वायत्ता तां चेदविद्वान्प्रस्तोष्यसि मूर्धा ते विपतिष्यतीति।।

"O chanters of praise [प्रस्तोतृ], should ye eulogize him who is the presiding deity of all praise without knowing his nature,[22] your heads would be lopped off."

10. एवमेवोद्गातारमुवाचोद्गातर्या देवतोद्गीथमन्वायत्ता तां चेदविद्वानुद्गास्यसि मूर्धा ते विपतिष्यतीति।।

Then [turning] to the chanters of the Udgītha, [Udgātāra,] said : "O ye changers of the Udgītha, should ye chant [in praise of] Him who is the presiding deity of the Udgītha your heads would verily be lopped off."

11. एवमेव प्रतिहर्तारमुवाच प्रतिहर्तर्या देवता प्रतिहारमन्वायत्ता तां चेदविद्वान्प्रतिहरिष्यसि मूर्धा ते विपतिष्यतीति ते ह समारतास्तूष्णीमासांचक्रिरे।।

And then thus addressed he to the chanters of the Pratihāra, saying, "and ye, O chanters of the Pratihāra, should ye chant [in praise of] Him who is the presiding deity of all Pratihāras without knowing his nature, your heads would surely be lopped off." They, [in dread of losing their heads] resigning their duty, sat in silence.

9-11. [After the words] "should ye eulogize Him who is the presiding deity of all praise," [the expression] *in my presence* [is understood,] for otherwise the ignorant would not at all be entitled to perform ceremonies; which is not the meaning here, for we see it otherwise stated in divers parts of the Vedas.

Section XI

1. अथ हैनं यजमान उवाच भगवन्तं वा अहं विविदिषाणी-
त्युषस्तिरस्मि चाक्रायण इति होवाच॥

Then said the institutor of the sacrifice unto him : "I wish to know thee, O Lord." "I am Uṣasti, son of Cakra," replied the other.

2. स होवाच भगवन्तं वा अहमेभिः सर्वैरार्त्विज्यैः पर्यैषिषं
भगवतो वा अहमवित्त्यान्यानवृषि॥

He [the king] rejoined : "I searched for thee, O Lord, to officiate [at this sacrifice], but finding thee not, engaged others.

3. भगवाꣳस्त्वेव मे सर्वैरार्त्विज्यैरिति तथेत्यथ तर्ह्येत एव
समतिसृष्टाः स्तुवतां यावत्त्वेभ्यो धनं दद्यास्तावन्मम दद्या
इति तथेति ह यजमान उवाच॥

[Do] thou, O Lord, [perform] the several parts of my sacrifice ?" "Be it so," replied the other; "let these men, with my sanction, recite the hallelujah. Do thou give me the wealth which thou wouldst have given unto them." "Even be it so," said the institutor of the sacrifice.

4. अथ हैनं प्रस्तोतोपससाद प्रस्तोतर्या देवता प्रस्तावमन्वायत्ता
तां चेदविद्वान्प्रस्तोष्यसि मूर्धा ते विपतिष्यतीति मा
भगवानवोचत्कतमा सा देवतेति॥

Next, verily, the chanters of praise approached him, [and said]: "You have said unto us, O venerable Sir, 'O chanters of praise, should ye eulogize Him who is the presiding deity of all praise, your heads would be lopped off'; will you now tell us who is that Deity ?"

5. प्राण इति होवाच सर्वाणि ह वा इमानि भूतानि
प्राणमेवाभिसंविशन्ति प्राणमभ्युज्जिहते सैषा देवता
प्रस्तावमन्वायत्ता तां चेदविद्वान्प्रास्तोष्यो मूर्धा ते
व्यपतिष्यत्तथोक्तस्य मयेति॥

"Life," replied the other. "Verily all these created objects merge into Life,[23] and from it are they developed ; it is the Deity who presides over all praises. Had ye eulogized Him without knowing ḥis nature, your heads would surely have been lopped off, as I said unto ye."

6. अथ हैनमुद्गातोपससादोद्गातर्या देवतोद्गीथमन्वायत्ता तां चेदविद्वानुद्गास्यसि मूर्धा ते विपतिष्यतीति मा भगवानवो-चत्कतमा सा देवतेति॥

Next did the Udgātās approach him, and thus address : "You have said unot us, O venerable Sir, 'should ye reciters of the Udgītha, chant in praise of him who is the presiding deity of all praise, your heads would surely be lopped off.' [Will you now tell us] who is that Deity ?"

7. आदित्य इति होवाच सर्वाणि ह वा इमानि भूतान्या-दित्यमुच्चैः सन्तं गायन्ति सैषा देवतोद्गीथमन्वायत्ता तां चेदविद्वानुदगास्यो मूर्धा ते व्यपतिष्यत्तथोक्तस्य मयेति॥

"The sun [Āditya]," said the other. "Verily all these created objects sing in praise of the sun as the highest object; he is the Deity who presides over the Udgītha. Had ye chanted the Udgītha in his praise without knowing him, your heads would surely have been lopped off, as I said unto ye."

8. अथ हैनं प्रतिहर्तोपससाद प्रतिहर्तर्या देवता प्रतिहारमन्वायत्ता तां चेदविद्वान्प्रतिहरिष्यसि मूर्धा ते विपतिष्यतीति मा भगवानवोचत्कतमा सा देवतेति॥

Next came untc him the Pratihartās and thus addressed : "You have said unto us, O venerable Sir, 'should ye chant the Pratihāra in praise of him who is the presiding Deity of all Pratihāras, O reciters of the Pratihāra, without knowing his nature, your heads would surely be lopped off.' [Will you now tell us,] who is that Deity ?"

9. अन्नमिति होवाच सर्वाणि ह वा इमानि भूतान्यन्नमेव प्रतिहरमाणानि जीवन्ति सैषा देवता प्रतिहारमन्वायत्ता तां चेदविद्वान्प्रत्यहरिष्यो मूर्धा ते व्यपतिष्यत्तथोक्तस्य मयेति तथोक्तस्य मयेति॥

"Aliment [Anna]," said the other; "all these created beings live by the consumption of food; it is the Deity president of the Pratihāras; had ye chanted the Pratihāras without knowing Him, you heads would surely have been lopped off, as I said unto ye."

Section XII

1. अथातः शौव उद्गीथस्तद्ध बको दाल्भ्यो ग्लावो वा मैत्रेयः स्वाध्यायमुद्वव्राज॥

Next the canine Udgītha.[24] Verily, Baka, son of Dalbha or [alias] Glāva, son of Mitrā, had gone forth to study the Vedas.

Baka was the son of Dalbha, but having been adopted by Mitrā, obtained the patronymic [or rather matronymic] of Maitreya and the name Glāva. . . He had "gone forth" to a lonely spot near a sheet of water, with a view to study in retirement.

2. तस्मै श्वा श्वेतः प्रादुर्बभूव तमन्ये श्वान उपसमेत्योचुरन्नं नो भगवानागायत्वशनायाम वा इति॥

[In mercy] to him appeared a white dog. Other dogs[25] approached it and said, "O Lord, pray for abundance of food for us; we wish to consume the same."

Pleased by his study of the Vedas and knowing his object, a god—or a sage, assuming the shape of a dog—a white dog, in mercy to the sage [Baka] "appeared," became manifest . . . The most reasonable construction appears to be that the chief vital air, together with speech and others, which are nourished by the aliment of that chief, pleased with the study of the sage, in mercy to him assumed the shape of dogs.

3. तान्होवाचेहैव मा प्रातरुपसमीयातेति तद्ध बको दाल्भ्यो ग्लावो वा मैत्रेयः प्रतिपालयांचकार॥

To them said the white dog : "Come ye here unto me to-morrow morning." At the appointed time did Baka, son of Dalbha—[alias] Glāva, son of Mitrā—act up to the injunction.

4. ते ह यथैवेदं बहिष्पवमानेन स्तोष्यमाणाः सꣳरब्धाः सर्पन्तीत्येव मासससृपुस्ते ह समुपविश्य हिंचक्रुः॥

As those who wish to pray through the Bahishpavamāna,

[hymns,] collecting together, proceed [to their work], so did they [the little dogs] come together and, taking their seats, bark out :

5. ओ३मदा३मों३पिबा३मो३देवो वरुणः प्रजापतिः सविता३न्न-
मिहा२हरदन्नपते२न्नमिहाहरा३हरो३मिति ।।

"Om! Let us eat. Om! Let us drink. Om! may the resplendent sun, who showers on us rain and supports all animated beings, grant us food. O Lord of food, deign to bestow food unto us; do deign to grant us food!"

SECTION XIII

1. अयं वाव लोको हाउकारो वायुर्हाइकारश्चन्द्रमा अथकार
आत्मेहकारोऽग्निरीकारः ।।

Verily, this earth is the particle HĀ Ū,[26] the wind HĀ i, and the moon ATHA; the soul is IHA, and fire Ī.

2. आदित्य ऊकारो निहव एकारो विश्वेदेवा औहोइकारः
प्रजापतिर्हिंकारः प्राणः स्वरोऽन्नं या वाग्विराट् ।।

The sun [is] Ū; the hymns of welcome [Nihava] E; the Viśvedevas the ĀUHOI; Prajāpati is HIṄ; Life is SVARA; Aliment is YĀ; Speech is VIRĀṬ;

3. अनिरुक्तस्त्रयोदशस्तोभः संचरो हुंकारः ।।

And, thirteenthly, the Anirukta or undecided hymns are the indistinct particle HUṁ.

4. दुग्धेऽस्मै वाग्दोहं यो वाचो दोहोऽन्नवानन्नादो भवति य
एतामेवं साम्नामुपनिषदं वेदोपनिषदं वेद इति ।।

Unto him speech grants its blessings, and he becomes the milker of speech and the owner and consumer of aliments who knows—verily knows—this Upaniṣad of the Sāma Veda,[27] as herein described.

Foot Notes

1. Om, when considered as one letter uttered by the help of one articulation, is the symbol of the Supreme Spirit. It is derived from the radical अव to preserve, with the affix मन "One letter (Om) is the emblem of the Most High". *Manu,* ii, 83. "This one letter, Om is the emblem of the Supreme Being." *Bhagavad-Gītā.* It is true that this emblem conveys two sounds, that of *O* and *m,* nevertheless it is held to be one letter in the above sense; and we meet with instances even in the ancient and modern languages of Europe that can justify such privileges and Q, W, X, in English and others. But when considered as a trilateral word consisting of अ (a), उ (u), म् (m), Om implies the three Vedas, the three states of human nature, the three divisions of the universe, and the three deities. Brahmā, Viṣṇu, and Śiva, agents in the creation, preservation, and destruction of this world; or, properly speaking, the three principal attributes of the Supreme Being personified as Brahmā, Viṣṇu, and Śiva. In this sense it implies, in fact, the universe controlled by the Supreme spirit—Rāmmohun Roy.
2. अक्षर immutable, imperishable, undecayable; and also a letter of the alphabet. "That which passes not away is declared to be the syllable Om thence called Akṣara." Manu, ii, 84.
3. Lit. "part," "member," प्रतिक.
4. Name of that portion of the Sāma Veda (second Chapter) which comprehends the hymns recited at the sacrifice of the moon plant (Soma yāga). *Vide* Stevenson's Sāma Veda.
5. The Udgītha hymns are chanted at the Soma yāga, and Om, being an essential member of those hymns, is called, in the commentary, कर्म्माङ्गावयव.
6. By the terms *ota* and *prota* the commentator alludes to the repeated origin and dissolution of the earth from and into, water.
7. The produce of annuals.
8. Bohlingk's Pānini, chap. V, Sec. 3, Rule 93.—Vol. II, p. 359.
9. A portion of the Yajur Veda.
10. An employer of priests at a sacrifice, the person who institutes its performance, and pays its expense.
11. Śaṅkara argues that if he can procure the gratification of the desires of his employer, he must of course be able to gratify his own wishes.

12. An allusion to a Vedic tradition. YĀJÑAVALKYA having been asked by ŚĀKALYA as to how many gods there were, said: "Thirty-three." Śākalya assented by saying, "Om."
13. Li.. body.
14. We ought, we think, to render here, the word *prāṇa* by soul, for Śaṅkara evidently had his eye on the *mukhya prāṇa* "chief life" or "vital air," of the 6th verse when he penned this line.
15. Sāma Veda.
16. Verse 1st.
17. The sense is that the benefit of inhaling good odour was common to all.—ĀNANDAGIRI.
18. *I.e.*, as in the passage quoted, the word "both" does not render it necessary that the oblations of *both* dawn and twilight should be simultaneously defiled, so here the inhalation of *either* fetor or aroma is intended.
19. In the original the word is used in the singular number.
20. Phasealus mas.
21. Lit. the place where gods are eulogized, प्रस्ताव.
22. Lit. him.
23. At the time of the dissolution of the earth, adds the commentary.
24. That is the Udgītha as recited by a dog.
25. Little white dogs, adds the commentator.
26. Songs of all nations avail largely of inarticulate sounds for the development of melody. Each of the Vedas has its appropriate harmonic sounds : those of the Sāma Veda, given above, are freely used in chanting the Sāma hymns : but instead of being placed at the end of a Stanza like the Tol di rol of old English songs, they are introduced promiscuously in every part of the hymns. Whenever a word happens to be lengthened out to double or treble time, it is followed by one or more Hā i, Hā u, or some such phonetic particles.
27. Or the hymns of the Sāma Veda, explains Śaṅkara.

SECOND CHAPTER

SECTION I

1. ॐ समस्तस्य खलु साम्न उपासनꣳसाधु यत्खलु साधु तत्सामेत्याचक्षते यदसाधु तदसामेति ।।

Om ! Verily the adoration of the entire Sāma is proper. Whatever is proper is Sāma; and whatever is improper is not Sāma.

2. तदुताप्याहुः साम्नैनमुपागादिति साधुनैनमुपगादित्येव तदाहुरसाम्नैनमुपागादित्यसाधुनैनमुपागादित्येव तदाहुः ।।

Hence it is generally said : "He went to him [to a king] with Sāma," meaning that he proceeded becomingly, and "he went to him without Sāma," *i.e.,* he proceeded unbecomingly.

"To him," *i.e.,* to a king or the like by whom propriety of conduct might be rewarded, and its want reprehended.

3. अथोताप्याहुः साम नो बतेति यत्साधु भवति साधु बतेत्येव तदाहुरसाम नो बतेति यदसाधु भवत्यसाधु बतेत्येव तदाहुः ।।

It is also said when any good happens, "Sāma has happened unto us," meaning, "Good has happened unto us," and when any evil happens, "Asāma has happened unto us," meaning that evil has happened.

4. स य एतदेवं विद्वान्साधु सामेत्युपास्तेऽभ्याशो ह यदेनꣳसाधवो धर्मा आ च गच्छेयुरुष च नमेयुः ।।

Unto him, who knowing this adores the Sāma whose characteristic is propriety, the most proper acts and religion become feasible and easily accessible.

SECTION II

1. लोकेषु पञ्चविधꣳसामोपासीत पृथिवी हिंकारोऽग्निः प्रस्तावोऽन्तरिक्षमुद्गीथ आदित्यः प्रतिहारो द्यौर्निधनमित्यूर्ध्वेषु॥

The five-formed Sāma should be adored [by identifying it] with the regions from below upwards, [thus] : the earth as HIṄKĀRA the fire (Agni) as PRASTĀVA, the Ether [Antarikṣa] as UDGITHA, the sun, [Āditya] as PRATIHĀRA, and the heavens as NIDHANA.

2. अथावृत्तेषु द्यौर्हिंकार आदित्यः प्रस्तावोऽन्तरिक्षमुद्गीथोऽग्निः प्रतिहारः पृथिवी निधनम्॥

And also from above downwards : [thus]; the heaven [Dyau] as HIṄKĀRA, the sun as PRASTĀVA, Ether [Antarikṣa] as UDGĪTHA, the fire [Agni] as PRATIHĀRA, and earth as NIDHANA.

3. कल्पन्ते हास्मै लोका ऊर्ध्वाश्चावृत्ताश्च य एतदेवं विद्वाँल्लोकेषु पञ्चविधꣳसामोपास्ते॥

Unto him these regions from below upwards, and from above downwards, become accessible, who, knowing thus, adores the five-formed Sāma [by identifying it] with these regions.

SECTION III

1. वृष्टौ पञ्चविधꣳसामोपासीत पुरो वातो हिंकारो मेघो जायते स प्रस्तावो वर्षति स उद्गीथो विद्योतते स्तनयति स प्रतिहारः॥

In rain should the five-formed Sāma be adored; the forward wind as HIṄKĀRA, whatever cloud collects as PRASTĀVA, the raining [itself] as UDGĪTHA, the lightning and rolling of clouds as PRATIHĀRA.

2. उद्गृह्णाति तन्निधनं वर्षति हास्मै वर्षयति ह य एतदेवंविद्वान्वृष्टौ पञ्चविधꣳसामोपास्ते॥

and the cessation of the rain as NIDHANA. He who knowing

thus, adores the five-formed Sāma by identifying it with rain, can command the rain to fall [at his pleasure], and for him doth rain pour [forth its treasures].

SECTION IV

1. सर्वास्वप्सु पञ्चविधꣳसामोपासीत मेघो यत्संप्लवते स हिंकारो यद्वर्षति स प्रस्तावो याः प्राच्यः स्यन्दन्ते स उद्गीथो याः प्रतीच्य स प्रतिहारः समुद्रो निधनम्।।

In the waters [of this earth] should the five-formed Sāma be adored : the clouds which collect together into dense masses as HIṄKĀRA, that which falls [in drops] as PRASTĀVA, those waters which flow to the east as UDGITHA, those to the west as PRATIHĀRA, and the ocean as NIDHANA.

2. न हाप्सु प्रैत्यप्सुमान्भवति य एतदेवंविद्वान्सर्वास्वप्सु पञ्चविधꣳसामोपास्ते।।

He who, knowing thus, adores the five-formed Sāma by identifying it with the waters, falleth not into water, and becomes the lord of the same.

SECTION V

1. ऋतुषु पञ्चविधꣳ सामोपासीत वसन्तो हिंकरो ग्रीष्मः प्रस्तावो वर्षा उद्गीथः शरत्प्रतिहारो हेमन्तो निधनम्।।

In the seasons should the five-formed Sāma be adored : the spring as HIṄKĀRA, the summer as PRASTĀVA, the autumn as UDGITHA, the dewy-season [Śarat] as PRATIHĀRA and the winter as NIDHANA.

2. कल्पन्ते हास्मा ऋतव ऋतुमान्भवति य एतदेवं विद्वानृतुषु पञ्चविधꣳसामोपास्ते।।

For him are the seasons designed who adores the five-formed Sāma in the seasons : he is the lord of the seasons.

Section VI

1. पशुषु पञ्चविधꣳसामोपासीताजा हिंकारोऽवयः प्रस्तावो गाव उद्गीथोऽश्वाः प्रतिहारः पुरुषो निधनम्।।

In the beasts [of the field] should the five-formed Sāma be adored : the goats as HIṄKĀRA, the sheep as PRASTĀVA, the cows as UDGITHA, the horses as PRATIHĀRA and man as NIDHANA.

2. भवन्ति हास्य पशवः पशुमान्भवति य एतदेवं विद्वान्पशुषु पञ्चविधꣳसामोपास्ते।।

To him belong the beasts of the field who, knowing all this, adores the five-formed Sāma in the beasts.

Section VII

1. प्राणेषु पञ्चविधं परोवरीयः सामोपासीत प्राणो हिंकारो वाक्प्रस्तावश्चक्षुरुद्गीथः श्रोत्रं प्रतिहारो मनो निधनं परोवरीयाꣳसि वैतानि।।

In the vital airs, should the five-formed, the noble and venerable Sāma be adored : respiration [Prāṇa] as HIṄKĀRA, speech as PRASTĀVA, the eyes as UDGITHA, the ears as PRATIHĀRA, and the mind as NIDHANA; they are all noble and venerable.

2. परोवरीयो हास्य भवति परोवरीयसो ह लोकाञ्जयति य एतदेवं विद्वान्प्राणेषु पञ्चविधं परोवरीयः सामोपास्त इति तु पञ्चविधस्य।।

Verily his life becomes noble and venerable, and he triumphs over noble and venerable regions, who, knowing all this, adores the five-formed, the noble and venerable Sāma in the vital airs. This much about the five-formed Sāma.

Section VIII

1. अथ सप्तविधस्य वाचि सप्तविधꣳ सामोपसीत यत्किंच वाचो हुमिति स हिंकारो यत्प्रेति स प्रस्तावो यदेति स आदिः ।।

Now [the adoration] of the seven-formed [Sāma will be disclosed]. In speech is the seven-formed [Sāma to be adored]. Of words [the adjunct] Hum is Hiṅkāra, [the prefix] Pra [प्र] is Prastāva, [the prefix] Ā [आ] is Ādi.

2. यदुदिति स उद्गीथो यत्प्रतीति स प्रतिहारो यदुपेति स उपद्रवो यन्नीति तन्निधनम् ।।

[The prefix] Ut [उत्] is Udgītha, [the prefix] Prati [प्रति] is Pratihāra, [the prefidx] Upa [उप] is Upadrava, and [the prefix] Ni [नि] is Nidhāna.

3. दुग्धेऽस्मै वाग्दोहं यो वाचो दोहोऽन्नवानन्नादो भवति य एतदेवं विद्वान्वाचि सप्तविधꣳसामोपास्ते ।।

Unto him speech yields its treasure, and he becomes the lord and consumer of aliment, who, thus knowing, adores the seven-formed Sāma in speech.

Section IX

1. अथ खल्वमुमादित्यꣳसप्तविधꣳ सामोपासीत सर्वदा समस्तेन साम मां प्रति मां प्रतीति सर्वेण समस्तेन साम ।।

Next verily should yonder sun be adored [as identified] with the seven-formed Sāma. It is always equal [sama सम] and is therefore [called] Sāma. Every body says, "[it looks] towards me, [it looks] towards me" : [thus equally] perceived by all, [it is called] Sāma.

2. तस्मिन्निमानि सर्वाणि भूतान्यन्वायत्तानीति विद्यात्तस्य यत्पुरोदयात्स हिंकारस्तदस्य पशवोऽन्वायत्तास्तस्मात्ते हिं कुर्वन्ति हिंकारभाजिनो ह्येतस्य साम्नः।।

Know that on it depend all these [visible] objects. Its pre-ascension is Hiṅkāra, on it depend all animals, and hence do they growl [हिंकुर्वन्ति at that hour]. They are, with the Sāma, co-sharers of the Hiṅkāra.

3. अथ यत्प्रथमोदिते स प्रस्तावस्तदस्य मनुष्या अन्वायत्तास्तस्मात्ते प्रस्तुतिकामाः प्रशꣳसाकामाः प्रस्तावभाजिनो ह्येतस्य साम्नः।।

Next, its first ascent is Prastāva. On it are men dependants, for they are desirous of [Praise], Prastuti. They are, with the Sāma, co-sharers of the Prastāva.

4. अथ यत्सङ्गववेलायाꣳ स आदिस्तदस्य वयाꣳस्यन्वायत्तानि तस्मात्तान्यन्तरिक्षेऽनारम्भणान्यादायात्मानं परिपतन्त्यादिभाजीनि ह्येतस्य साम्नः।।

Next, that hour of its ascent when cows associate with their calves[1] is Ādi; on it depend birds who unsupported fly about in the air, in praise of the Supreme. They are, with the Sāma, co-sharers of the Ādi.

5. अथ यत्संप्रति मध्यन्दिने स उद्गीथस्तदस्य देवा अन्वायत्तास्तस्मात्ते सत्तमाः प्राजापत्यानामुद्गीथभाजिनो ह्येतस्य साम्नः।।

Next, the time when it arrives at mid-day is Udgītha. On it depend gods [Devas], therefore are these good beings among the sons of Prajāpati, co-sharers, with the Sāma, of the Udgītha.

6. अथ यदूर्ध्वं मध्यंदिनात्प्रागपराह्णात्स प्रतिहारस्तदस्य गर्भा अन्वायत्तास्तस्मात्ते प्रतिहृता नावपद्यन्ते प्रतिहारभाजिनो ह्येतस्य साम्नः।।

Next, the time when it passes beyond the meridian is Pratihāra. On it depend the Garbhas; therefore are they kept attached and fall not. They are co-sharers, with the Sāma, of the Pratihāra.

7. अथ यदूर्ध्वमपराह्णात्प्रागस्तमयात्स उपद्रवस्तदस्यारण्या अन्वायत्तास्तस्मात्ते पुरुषं दृष्ट्वा कक्षः श्वभ्रमित्युपद्रवन्त्यु-पद्रवभाजिनो ह्येतस्य साम्नः॥

Next, the transition from mid-day to afternoon is Upadrava. On it depend wild animals who fly [upadravanti] from the sight of man, to [seek] shelter in deserts. They are co-sharers, with the Sāma, of the Upadrava.

8. अथ यत्प्रथमास्तमिते तन्निधनं तदस्य पितरोऽन्वायत्तास्त-स्मात्तान्निदधति निधनभाजिनो ह्येतस्य साम्न एवं खल्वमुमादित्यः सप्तविधः सामोपास्ते॥

Next, the first twilight is Nidhana. To it are the Pitṛs attached, and therefore are oblations offered to the manes at that hour. They are co-sharers, with the Sāma, of the Nidhana : Thus verily should the seven-formed Sāma be adored [as identified] with yonder sun.

Section X

1. अथ खल्वात्मसंमितमतिमृत्यु सप्तविधःसामोपासीत हिंकार इति त्र्यक्षरं प्रस्ताव इति त्र्यक्षरं तत्समम्॥

Next, verily the seven-formed Sāma, which is above death like unto the soul, should be adored. Hiṅkāra, [हिङ्कार includes] three letters, [so] doth Prastāva [प्रस्ताव] include three letters, therefore are they equal.

The sun is death, for it puts a limit to the earth by dividing time into day, night, and the like. To overcome it is this adoration of the Sāma revealed. "Next verily," *i.e.,* after the adoration of the Sāma relating to the sun [which likewise relates to] death, another form of adoration of the Sāma comprehending seven members, is to be described.

2. आदिरिति द्व्यक्षरं प्रतिहार इति चतुरक्षरं तत इहैकं तत्समम्॥

[The word] Ādi [आदि includes] two letters, and [the word]

Pratihāra प्रतिहार four letters, of which [latter] one letter [being added to the former] they become equal.

The letter Om is called Ādi.

3. उद्गीथ इति त्र्यक्षरमुपद्रव इति चतुरक्षरं त्रिभिस्त्रिभिः समं भवत्यक्षरमतिशिष्यते त्र्यक्षरं तत्समम्॥

[The word] Udgītha [उद्गीथ includes] three letters, and [the word] Upadrava, [उपद्रव] four; the three [of the former] with the three [of the latter] are equal, leaving one letter redundant; [which being assumed] to be three, they [all become] equal.

Though one, as it is an Akṣara [अक्षर which includes three letters] it becomes three.

4. निधनमिति त्र्यक्षरं तत्सममेव भवति तानि ह वा एतानि द्वाविंशतिरक्षराणि॥

[The word] Nidhana, [निधन includes] three letters, and therefore it is equal [with the rest]. These well-known terms thus verily [include] twenty-two letters.

5. एकविंशत्यादित्यमाप्नोत्येकविंशो वा इतोऽसावादित्यो द्वाविंशेन परमादित्याज्जयति तन्नाकं तद्विशोकम्॥

The twenty-first is the sun [Āditya], for it is the twenty-first from this earth. By the twenty-second that which is above the sun, might be triumphed; it is heaven [नाक] exempt from pain and grief.

Because the Āditya is reckoned the twenty-first from this sphere, for says a Śruti : "The twelve months, the five seasons, the three regions and twenty-first the sun." "That which is above the sun" what is it ? Heaven, Nāka : *ka* pleasure with the privative prefix *a* meaning "pain," and *na* "not," *i.e.*, where pain existeth not.

6. आप्नोतीहादित्यस्य जयं परो हास्यादित्यजयाज्जयो भवति य एतदेवं विद्वानात्मसंमितमतिमृत्यु सप्तविधं सामोपास्ते सामोपास्ते॥

He obtaineth the conquest of the sun, and that which is above the conquest of the sun, who, knowing all this, adores—verily adores—the seven-formed which is above death, and like unto the soul.

Section XI

1. मनो हिंकारो वाक्प्रस्तावश्चक्षुरुद्गीथः श्रोत्रं प्रतिहारः प्राणो निधनमेतद्गायत्रं प्राणेषु प्रोतम्॥

The mind is Hiṅkāra, speech Prastāva, the eyes Udgītha, the ears Pratihāra, and Prāṇa Nidhana : [thus] is this Gāyatra[2] Sāma connected with life [Prāṇa].

2. स य एवमेतद्गायत्रं प्राणेषु प्रोतं वेद प्राणी भवति सर्वमायुरेति ज्योग्जीवति महान्प्रजया पशुभिर्भवति महान्कीर्त्या महामनाः स्यात्तद्व्रतम्॥

He, who knows the Gāyatra to be thus connected with Prāṇa, becomes possessed of life [Prāṇa], enjoys the full limit of existence, his career becomes refulgent,[3] he becometh great in dependants and cattle, and great in noble deeds ; and his duty is to be noble-minded.

"Becomes possessed of Prāṇa," *i.e.,* all his organs retain their proper powers. "Attain the full limit of existence." "The full limit of man's existence is a hundred years," says the Śruti.

Section XII

1. अभिमन्थति स हिंकारो धूमो जायते स प्रस्तावो ज्वलति स उद्गीथोऽङ्गारा भवन्ति स प्रतिहार उपशाम्यति तन्निधनः संशाम्यति तन्निधनमेतद्रथन्तरमग्नौ प्रोतम्॥

The generation [of fire by friction] is Hiṅkāra, the smoke which issues [therefrom] is Prastāva, the flame is Udgītha; whatever charcoal forms is Pratihāra, the blowing out [of the flame] is Nidhana, and its entire cessation [also] is Nidhana. [Thus] is the Rathantara Sāma connected with fire[4] [Agni].

2. स य एवमेतद्रथन्तरमग्नौ प्रोतं वेद ब्रह्मवर्चस्यन्नादो भवति सर्वमायुरेति ज्योग्जीवति महान्प्रजया पशुभिर्भवति महान्कीर्त्या न प्रत्यङङ्ग्निमाचामेन्न निष्ठीवेत्तद्व्रतम्॥

He, who knows the Rathantara thus connected with fire [Agni], attains the glory available by the study and practice of the Vedas, a superior power of digestion, and enjoys the full limit of existence; his career becomes refulgent, he becomes great in dependants and cattle, and great in noble deeds;—and his duty is not to eat or spit before a fire.

SECTION XIII

1. उपमन्त्रयते स हिंकारो ज्ञपयते सप्रस्तावः स्त्रिया सह शेते स उद्गीथः प्रतिस्त्री सह शेते स प्रतिहारः कालं गच्छति तन्निधनं पारं गच्छति तन्निधनमेतद्वामदेव्यं मिथुने प्रोतम्।।

One summons—that is a Hiṅkāra. He makes request—That is a Prastāva. Together with the woman he lies down—that is an Udgītha. He lies upon the woman—that is a Pratihāra. He comes to the end—That is a Nidhana. He comes to the finish—That is a Nidhana. This is the Vāmadevya Sāma as woven upon copulation.

2. स य एवमेतद्वामदेव्यं मिथुने प्रोतं वेद मिथुनीभवति मिथुनान्मिथुनात्प्रजायते सर्वमायुरेति ज्योग्जीवति महान्प्रजया पशुभिर्भवति महान्कीर्त्या न कांचन परिहरेत्तद्व्रतम्।।

He who knows thus this Vāmadevya Sāma as woven upon copulation comes to copulation, procreates himself from every copulation, reaches a full length of life, lives long, becomes great in offspring and in cattle, great in fame. One should never abstain from any woman. That is his rule.

SECTION XIV

1. उद्यन्हिंकार उदितः प्रस्तावो मध्यन्दिन उद्गीथोऽपराह्णः प्रतिहारोऽस्तं यन्निधनमेतद्बृहदादित्ये प्रोतम्।।

The dawn is Hiṅkāra, the ascent [of the sun] Prastāva, the mid-day Udgītha, the afternoon Pratihāra, and the disappearance Nidhana. [Thus] is the Bṛhat [Sāma] connected with the sun [Āditya].

2. स य एवमेतद्बृहदादित्ये प्रोतं वेद तेजस्व्यन्नादो भवति सर्वमायुरेति ज्योग्जीवति महान्प्रजया पशुभिर्भवति महान्कीर्त्या तपन्तं न निन्देत्तद्व्रतम्।।

He who knows the Bṛhat [Sāma] to be thus connected with Āditya, becomes a mighty consumer of aliment, enjoys the full limit of existence, his career becomes refulgent, he becomes great in dependants and cattle, and great in noble deeds; and his duty is not to calumniate the sun.

Section XV

1. अभ्राणि संप्लवन्ते स हिंकारो मेघो जायते स प्रस्तावो वर्षति स उद्गीथो विद्योतते स्तनयति स प्रतिहार उद्गृह्णाति तन्निधनमेतद्वैरूपं पर्जन्ये प्रोतम्।।

The vapours collect, it is Hiṅkāra, the clouds overcast [the sky], it is Prastāva; it rains, it is Udgītha; the lightning flashes and the thunder rolls, they are Pratihāra; the ascent [of vapours] is Nidhana. [Thus is] the Vairūpa[5], [Sāma] connected with the clouds.

2. स य एवमेतद्वैरूपं पर्जन्ये प्रोतं वेद विरूपाꣳश्च सुरूपाꣳश्च पशूनवरुन्धे सर्वमायुरेति ज्योग्जीवति महान्प्रजया पशुभिर्भवति महान्कीर्त्या वर्षन्तं न निन्देत्तद्व्रतम्।।

He who knows the Vairūpa Sāma, thus connected with the clouds, obtains both well-formed and ugly cattle, and the full limit of existence; his career becomes refulgent; he becomes great in dependants and cattle, and great in noble deeds;—and his duty is not to calumniate the rain-pouring clouds.

Section XVI

1. वसन्तो हिंकारो ग्रीष्मः प्रस्तावो वर्षा उद्गीथः शरत्प्रतिहारो हेमन्तो निधनमेतद्वैराजमृतुषु प्रोतम्।।

The spring is Hiṅkāra, the summer Prastāva, the autumn

Udgītha, the dewy-season Pratihāra, and the winter Nidhana. [Thus] is the Vairāja [Sāma] connected with the seasons.

2. स य एवमेतद्वैराजमृतुषु प्रोतं वेद विराजति प्रजया पशुभिर्ब्रह्मवर्चसेन सर्वमायुरेति ज्योग्जीवति महान्प्रजया पशुभिर्भवति महान्कीर्त्यर्तूंन्न निन्देत्तद्व्रतम्।।

He who knows the Vairāja [Sāma] thus connected with the seasons, becomes magnificent in dependants, cattle and Vedic glory, obtains the full limit of existence, his career becomes glorious, and he becomes great in dependants and cattle, and great in noble deeds;—and his duty is not to calumniate the seasons.

SECTION XVII

1. पृथिवी हिंकारोऽन्तरिक्षं प्रस्तावो द्यौरुद्गीथो दिशः प्रतिहारः समुद्रो निधनमेताः शक्वर्यो लोकेषु प्रोताः।।

The earth is Hiṅkāra, space [Antarikṣa] is Prastāva, the heaven Udgītha, the sides Pratihāra, and the ocean Nidhana. [Thus] are the Śakvari Sāma hymns connected with the stations.

2. स य एवमेताः शक्वर्यो लोकेषु प्रोता वेद लोकी भवति सर्वमायुरेति ज्योग्जीवति महान्प्रजया पशुभिर्भवति महान्कीर्त्या लोकान्न निन्देत्तद्व्रतम्।।

He who knows the Śakvari [Sāma hymns] to be thus connected with the stations, obtaineth the wealth of those stations, and the full limit of existence; his career becomes glorious, he becomes great in dependants and cattle, and great in noble deeds; and his duty is not to calumniate the stations.

SECTION XVIII

1. अजा हिंकारोऽवयः प्रस्तावो गाव उद्गीथोऽश्वाः प्रतिहारः पुरुषो निधनमेता रेवत्यः पशुषु प्रोताः।।

The goats are Hiṅkāra, the sheep Prastāva, the cows Udgītha, the horses Pratihāra, and man Nidhana; [thus] are the Revatya [Sāma hymns] connected with animals.

2. स य एवमेता रेवत्यः पशुषु प्रोता वेद पशुमान्भवति सर्वमायुरेति ज्योग्जीवति महान्प्रजया पशुभिर्भवति महान्कीर्त्या पशून्न निन्देत्तद्व्रतम्।।

He who knows the Revatya [Sāma hymns] to be thus connected with animals, becomes the lord of animals, enjoys the full limit of existence, his career becomes glorious, he becomes great in dependants and cattle, and great in noble deeds; and his duty is not to calumniate animals.

SECTION XIX

1. लोम हिंकारस्त्वक्प्रस्तावो माꣳसमुद्गीथोऽस्थि प्रतिहारो मज्जा निधनमेतद्यज्ञायज्ञीयमङ्गेषु प्रोतम्।।

The hair of the body is Hiṅkāra, the skin Prastāva, the flesh Udgītha, the bones Pratihāra, and the marrow Nidhana. [Thus] are the Yajnā-Yajnīya [Sāma hymns] connected with the body.

2. स य एवमेतद्यज्ञायज्ञीयमङ्गेषु प्रोतं वेदाङ्गी भवति नाङ्गेन विमूर्च्छति सर्वमायुरेति ज्योग्जीवति महान्प्रजया पशुभिर्भवति महान्कीर्त्या संवत्सरं मज्ज्ञो नाश्नीयात्तद्व्रतं मज्ज्ञो नाश्नीयादिति वा।।

He, who knows the Yajnā-Yajnīya [Sāma hymns] to be thus connected with the body, obtains a perfect body which never becomes defective, enjoys the full limit of existence, his career becomes glorious, he becomes great in dependants and cattle, and great in noble deeds, and his duty is not to eat meat for a year, or not to eat meat at all.

SECTION XX

1. अग्निर्हिंकारो वायुः प्रस्ताव आदित्य उद्गीथो नक्षत्राणि प्रतिहारश्चन्द्रमा निधनमेतद्राजनं देवतासु प्रोतम्।।

Agni [fire] is Hiṅkāra, the wind Prastāva, the sun Udgītha, the stars Pratihāra, and the moon Nidhana. [Thus] are these Rājana [Sāma hymns] connected with gods [devatās].

2. स य एवमेतद्राजनं देवतासु प्रोतं वेदैतासामेव देवताना॰ सलोकता॰ सार्ष्टिता॰ सायुज्यं गच्छति सर्वमायुरेति ज्योग्जीवति महान्प्रजया पशुभिर्भवति महान्कीर्त्या ब्राह्मणान्न निन्देत्तद्व्रतम्।।

He, who knows the Rājana [Sāma hymns] to be thus connected with the gods, obtains habitation, wealth,[6] body, similar unto what appertain to these gods; he enjoys the full limit of existence, his career becomes glorious, he becomes great in dependants and cattle, and great in noble deeds; and his duty is not to calumniate Brāhmaṇas.

SECTION XXI

1. त्रयी विद्या हिंकारस्त्रय इमे लोकाः स प्रस्तावोऽग्निर्वायुरादित्यः स उद्गीथो नक्षत्राणि वयाꣳसि मरीचयः स प्रतिहारः सर्पा गन्धर्वाः पितरस्तन्निधनमेतत्साम सर्वस्मिन्प्रोतम्।।

The threefold knowledge constitutes the Hiṅkāra; the three regions[7] form the Prastāva; Agni, Vāyu and Āditya are the Udgītha; the stars, the feathered tribe and the rays [of lights] form the Pratihāra, and the serpent race, the Gandharvās and the manes are Nidhana. Thus is the Sāma connected with all.

2. स य एवमेतत्साम सर्वस्मिन्प्रोतं वेद सर्व॰ ह भवति।।

He who thus knows the Sāma connected with all [objects] becomes [the lord of] all

3. तदेष श्लोकः। यानि पञ्चधा त्रीणि त्रीणि तेभ्यो न ज्यायः परमन्यदस्ति।।

Therefore is the verse : "there is nothing greater than the five-fold three."

"There-of," *i.e.*, on this subject there is a verse. "Fivefold," *i.e.*,

Hiṅkāra, Prastāva and the rest; "three," the three-fold knowledge, the three regions, and the three gods, Agni, Vāyu and Āditya.

4. यस्तद्वेद स वेद सर्वं सर्वा दिशो बलिमस्मै हरन्ति सर्वमस्मीत्युपासीत तद्व्रतं तद्व्रतम्।।

He , who knows this, understands every thing; unto him all the different quarters [of the earth] render tribute; his duty—his duty—is to entertain the belief that "I am all".

SECTION XXII

1. विनर्दि साम्नो वृणे पशव्यमित्यग्नेरुद्गीथोऽनिरुक्तः प्रजापतेर्निरुक्तः सोमस्य मृदु श्लक्ष्णं वायोः श्लक्ष्णं बलवदिन्द्रस्य क्रौञ्चं बृहस्पतेरपध्वान्तं वरुणस्य तान्सर्वानेवोपसेवेत वारुणं त्वेव वर्जयेत्।।

[A chanter said] "I wish for the taurine-toned Sāma hymn, the canticle of Agni, which contributes to the weal of animals." The hymns of the *anirukta* tone belong to Prajāpati; those of the *nirukta* tone to Soma; those of the mild sweet tone to Vāyu; those of the sweet high-pitched tone to Indra; those of the tone resembling the voice of the crane to Bṛhaspati, and to Varuṇa, those of the tone of a broken piece of bell-metal : they are all to be practised; the hoarse toned alone are to be avoided.[8]

2. अमृतत्वं देवेभ्य आगायानीत्यागायेत्स्वधां पितृभ्य आशां मनुष्येभ्यस्तृणोदकं पशुभ्यः स्वर्गं लोकं यजमानायान्नमात्मन आगायानीत्येतानि मनसा ध्यायन्नप्रमत्तः स्तुवीत।।

[The hymns] are to be sung [with the wish] : "Let me sing for the immortality of the gods. For [the due offering of] oblations to the manes, for the [fulfillment of the] desires of mankind, for securing grass and water to animals, heaven to the institutors of sacrifices, and aliment for self, let me sing." Thinking thus without excitement let them be sung.

3. सर्वे स्वरा इन्द्रस्यात्मानः सर्व ऊष्माणः प्रजापतेरात्मानः सर्वे स्पर्शा मृत्योरात्मानस्तं यदि स्वरेषूपालभेतेन्द्रः शरणं प्रपन्नो अभूवं स त्वा प्रतिवक्ष्यतीत्येनं ब्रूयात्।।

The vowels [swaraḥ] constitute the body of Indra, the sibilants and ha [Ūṣmāṇaḥ] that of Prajāpati, and the consonants [sparśaḥ] that of Death. Should any body revile him [who is a reciter of these] he should say, "I take protection of Indra, he will give thee a meet reply."

4. अथ यद्येनमूष्मसूपालभेत प्रजापतिः शरणं प्रपन्नोऽभूवं स त्वा प्रति पेक्ष्यतीत्येनं ब्रूयादथ यद्येनःस्पर्शेषूपालभेत मृत्युः शरणं प्रपन्नोऽभूवं स त्वा प्रतिधक्ष्यतीत्येनं ब्रूयात्।।

Should any revile him about the sibilants and ha, he should say : "I take protection of Prajāpati, he will ground thee down"; and should any revile him about the consonants, he should say : "I take protection of Death, he will hurl thee into flames."

5. सर्वे स्वरा घोषवन्तो बलवन्तो वक्तव्या इन्द्रे बलं ददानीति सर्वे ऊष्माणोऽग्रस्ता अनिरस्ता विवृता वक्तव्यौः प्रजापते-रात्मानं परिददानीति सर्वे स्पर्शा लेशेनानभिनिहिता वक्तव्या मृत्योरात्मानं परिहराणीति।।

The vowels are to be recited with sound and force, saying : "I take the strength of Indra." The sibilants and ha are to be sounded internally, but not uttered out [of the mouth], and yet distinctly, saying : "to Prajāpati, I resign my life." The consonants are to be repeated slowly and distinctly, saying : "from Death, I extricate my life."

Section XXIII

1. त्रयो धर्मस्कन्धा यज्ञोऽध्ययनं दानमिति प्रथमस्तप एव द्वितीयो ब्रह्मचार्याचार्यकुलवासी तृतीयोऽत्यन्तमात्मानमा-चार्यकुलेऽवसादयन्सर्व एते पुण्यलोका भवन्ति ब्रह्मसंस्थोऽमृतत्वमेति।।

Three-fold is the division of Duty. Sacrifice, study and charity constitute the first; Penance is the second, and Residence by a Brahmacārin exclusively in the house of a tutor is the third. Al those [who attend to these duties] attain virtuous regions; the believer in Brahman alone attains to immortality.

In order to develop the adoration of Om, [this Śruti] begins with : "threefold is the division of Duty." But it must not be supposed that the adoration of Om or the Udgītha as forming a part of the Sāma Veda, secures the effect to be propounded, for that which cannot be had by the adoration of the whole of the Sāma Veda, *i.e.*, immortality, may be secured by the adoration of Om [as the emblem of the Deity], hence it is only in praise of Om that the Śruti begins as aforesaid.

"Threefold is the division of Duty," *i.e.*, Religion or Duty is divided into three classes and what they are is next described. "Sacrifice" [Yajña] or the offering of oblations to fire, etc.,—"Study," of the Ṛk and the other Vedas according to rule,—"and charity," or the donation of alms according to one's resources, beyond the boundary of the altar, to parties not seeking for the same,—constitute the first branch or division of religious duty. Since this class of duties relates to house-holders, and is performable by them [alone], it may be called the duty of house-holders. The expression "first" (प्रथम:) means one [or the first of a series,] and not the commencement of duty, for we hear of the "second," and the third [in succession]. "The second is Penance," [तप: Tapas], *i.e.*, the performance of Kṛcchra, Cāndrāyana and such other Penances, or asceticism, or the adoption of the life of a hermit, without relying on Brahman [for reliance on Brahman ensures immortality], constitutes the second division. Residence under the roof of a tutor, "Exclusively," *i.e.*, all life through, in the exercise of the duties of a Brahmacārin, constitutes the third division of duty. The use of the expression "exclusively" indicates that the residence must be all life through, for otherwise a mere sojourn at the house of a tutor, for the study of the Vedas, does not secure [a future translation to] virtuous regions. "All those," *i.e.*, the three orders of men, through the virtuous works aforesaid, "attain virtuous regions," . . . Lastly, the undescribed hermit, he who exclusively abides in Brahman,—he alone obtains immortality, which is a stage of being distinct from the virtuous regions, and constitutes existence without end, and not the secondary immortality of the Devas [which is but temporary], as is evident from its being reckoned under a different class. Had it been merely a superior gradation of the former, it would not have been described separately. From its being disjoined from the rest, it is evident that immortality without end is intended.

The allusion here to the rewards due to the different orders of men is intended to eulogize the odoration of Om, and not to lay down any rule on the subject. To say that it has two-fold object of eulogizing and laying down a rule regarding rewards, would be to admit a divided meaning, [which is inadmissible, in as much as a word can have but one meaning at a time] : hence, after reciting the rewards described in the Smṛtis, to say that the rewards of worshipping Om is immortality, is to eulogize the same. Just as by saying "the service of Pūrnavarma secures food and raiment, whilst that of Rājavarma ensures a kingdom" [the superior advantages of the latter are pointed out in comparison with the former, and no merit of the former described]; such is the case in the above.

The Praṇava is the truthful Supreme Brahman being its emblem. From the Vedic declaration "This letter verily is the Supreme," the Kaṭha Upaniṣad hath declared that "its adoration ensures immortality".

Some [commentators] maintain that men of the four different orders of life, who have no pretensions to knowledge, from the fruit of their works, obtain, without any distinction, virtuous regions, as is evident from the expression : "all those attain virtuous regions," and the hermit is not excluded therefrom. The knowledge and the religious acts and observances of the hermit amount in fact to penance, and so has the Śruti included it by saying, 'Penance is the second'—hence," they continue, "it follows that whoever among the four orders of men adopts the adoration of Om, *i.e.*, becomes devoted to Brahman attains immortality, every one of them without distinction being fit to perform such adoration, and none being forbidden; besides all of them having opposite opportunities, during the intervals of their respective duties, to engage themselves in such devotion." The word Brahmasaṁstha, devotion to Brahman, they further aruge "is not, like the words wheat or hog, exclusively indicative of a particular object,—the hermit. It is a compound term formed of two words Brahman and Devotion, and that which has an etymological signification cannot be an arbitrary term at the same time. All orders of men can devote themselves to Brahman. Wherever there is a devotion to Brahman, there may we apply the compound term, and it would be improper to confine its meaning only to the hermit who devotes himself to the same. Further, the mere performance of the duties enjoined to hermits, does not ensure immortality, for that would make all allusion to knowledge redundant. Nor can it be said that knowledge in the state of hermitage alone ensures immortality for there is no special efficacy of the duties enjoined to men of any of the four orders. Should it be said that the virtuous works enjoined to the different orders of men when accompanied by knowledge ensures immortality, still it would apply to all the four orders [and have no special reference in behalf of any particular one.] There is no such ordinance, that none but the hermit alone, when he has acquired knowledge, should attain immortality; on the contrary all the Upaniṣads maintain that 'knowledge [alone] ensures liberation'. Hence whoever among the four orders of men devotes himself to Brahman will enjoy immortality".

But such is not the case, for the knowledge which leads to ceremonial rites, and that which manifests the Supreme cause of all, are dissimilar and discordant [and therefore cannot co-exist in the same individual].

The knowledge which indicates a difference between agents, actions, and objects, is the cause whence proceedeth the ceremonial injunction: "Do this and do that not," and that cause hath not its origin in any Śāstra, for it is manifest in all animated beings. While the knowledge which syaeth, "the truth is verily one without a second," "all this is the divine soul," "all this is Brahman," proceedeth from the Śāstra, and cannot become manifest without in the first place destroying the disjunctive knowledge[9] of agents, actions, and objects, which is the prime cause of all ceremonial injunction, for the knowledge which disjoins and that which identifies are opposed to each other. Just as the erroneous conception of two moons cannot co-exist together with a knowledge of the unity of the moon, knowledge and ignorance being discordant and unable to abide together; even so is the case with the knowledge of the Deity. Such being the case, he in whom the disjunctive knowledge which leads to ceremonial rites, is overcome by the non-dual knowledge originating from the maxims, "The truth is verily one without a second": "He is truth" : "All the difference of created objects are unreal" : retires from all ceremonial rites, from their cause being overcome; and he is said to be abiding in Brahman, and exempt from ceremony. Such a state is not attainable by any but a hermit, (Parivraṭ)

He, whose disjunctive knowledge has not been overcome, who sees differently, hears differently, reflects differently, understands differently, and believes that the performances of such and such [ceremonies] will secure for him such and such [results], and believing, acts accordingly, cannot resign himself in Brahman, for he relies on a false understanding of there being a distinction where the distinction is purely verbal. In him, who has overcome the disjunctive knowledge by knowing it to be false, the idea of certain objects being fit for ceremonies, and the propriety of his performing them therefore as a matter of duty, cannot exist, like the idea of the sky having a dark substratum to one conscient of the nature of the sky. If you say that after the disjunctive knowledge is overcome, ceremonies [still] continue [dominate] as before, all ordinances relating to Unitarian knowledge become falsified, [whereas] they are, like the ordinances relating to forbidden food, venerable, all the Upaniṣads being infavour of them. It might be argued that then you destroy the authority of the ceremonial ordinances. But such is not the case; their authority remains in all its integrity and exercises its full force on those whose disjunctive knowledge is not overcome, like the effect of dreams on one who is still asleep. Nor are they destroyed by the neglect of the learned to abide by them,—seeing that ordinances regarding optional ceremonies[10] have not been destroyed. As the non-performance of optional ceremonies by those who know that "optional ceremonies are improper," does not destroy them, for they are performed by others who long for enjoyment, so the neglect of all ceremonies by those knowers of Brahman who are resigned in Brahman, does not [necessarily] do away with all ordinances relating to them, for the ignorant in Brahman continue to submit thereto. It cannot be said, that because those who, renouncing the duties of house-holders, adopt asceticism, still continue to eat and drink , the knowers of Brahman should not give up their oblations to fire, etc., for in an enquiry as to duty, the instances of particular individuals do not hold good. Magic for a malevolent purpose is forbidden, yet should any practise it, that will be no precedent for him who injures not his enemies, to practise the same. Disjunctive knowledge as the cause of ceremonies being destroyed, there remains no incentive to the offering of oblations to fire and the like, while to the hermit hunger is a sufficient incentive for food. If you say, the dread of evil from the non-performance of ceremonies is a sufficient incentive, such is not the cause; for those who have the disjunctive knowledge are [alone] subject to that evil. I have already said, those whose disjunctive knowledge is not overcome by true or identifying knowledge, are the appropriate subjects for the performance of ceremonies. The neglect of duty brings evil on him who is bound to its performance not on him who is not required to perform the same; such as the omission by a house-holder of duties of a Brahmacārin.

Can it not be said that in whatever station of life a man obtains a knowledge of the unity [of all objects], therein he becomes a hermit ? No; because [in those stations of life] he retains his disjunctive knowledge of self and matters relating unto him,[11] and ceremonies are the special requisites of those stations. "Now [after having acquired a wife] I shall perform ceremonies," says the Śruti, and hence [it is evident that] he who, renouncing all selfish ideas, has adopted asceticism, is a hermit, and not the house-holder and the rest.

If it be said that the knowledge resulting from the Unitarian maxims having overcome the disjunctive knowledge which results from ceremonial ordinances, there is no necessity for a hermit to abide by religious restrainsts and observances. We reply, that for those who are apt to forego their Unitarian knowledge, from the effects of hunger and the like, they are appropriate; for they prevent such aberration. Nor would that authorise the performance, on their part, of forbidden actions, for that is debarred even previous to the attainment of that knowledge :

he who falls in a well or a thorny bush at night does not go thereto during sunshine. From all these it is established that the ascetic alone who has abjured ceremonial rites, is devoted to Brahman. What has been said [by my antagonists] about men of all the four stations of life who have not attained true knowledge, migrating to higher regions, is true; but their remark "that by penance (tapas) asceticism is implied," is incorrect. Because the ascetic alone is likely to be devoted to Brahman, and we have already established that he is not included among the other orders. In regard to the conscient of the Unitarian knowledge penance ceaseth alone with sacrificial rites, penance being enjoined to him only whose disjunctive knowledge is not overcome. Thereby we have (further) replied to the opinion which maintains that reliance on Brahman, at intervals of the performance of ceremonies, is admissible, and that none are debarred therefrom; likewise to the opinion regarding the uselessness of knowledge by showing that the ascetic unconnected with ceremony is (alone) possessed of (the true) knowledge.

The remark about Brahmasaṁstha (devoted to Brahman) not being a crude word like java or varāha, (wheat or hog,) and a simple equivalent of Parivrāt, has been responded to, by shewing that the Brahmasaṁstha alone is entitled to be devoted to Brahman, and none else. What has been said about crude words not admitting of a derivative meaning, is not correct, seeing that *gṛhastha, takṣa, parivrājaka,* and others do admit of such meaning. *Gṛhastha*, or he who lives in a house, *takṣa*, who chisels wood, *parivrāt*, he who is homeless, or passes his time in rambling about from place to place, are all derivative terms, and yet we see the first and the last, without foregoing their derivative signification, are used in the crude form in regard to the two different classes of the house-holders and the ascetics, and the middle, in regard to the caste of carpenters, and cannot be applied in every case where the derivative attributes may be indicated; that being opposed to general usage. Now with reference to the word Brahmasaṁstha, it is applicable only to that ascetic who has relinquished all ceremonial observances and their attributes, who has exceeded the [first three] orders of life, and who is styled a Paramahaṁsa : for to him is assigned the recompense of super-eminent immortality, as we hear [in the text]. He alone is the true ascetic [parivrāṭ] of the Vedas, and not he who wears the Brāhmanical thread, or carries the pilgrim's staff, or the beggar's platter. "He has cast off his crown-lock, he is without emblem, without compassion" : says a Śruti. "To them who have surpassed all orders of life, he explained the pre-eminent and immaculate truth" : says the Svetāsvatara Upaniṣad. "He neither praiseth nor saluteth": maintain the Smṛtis. "Therefore do the Yatis, who have attained true knowledge, perform no ceremonies"; "Therefore is he the knower of true religion; he is without emblem and without any manifest characteristic": also say the Smṛtis.

"What the followers of the Sānkhya maintain to be exemption from ceremonies, is false, for they believe in the truth of the impression which shews a difference between ceremonies, their performers and their recompenses; and the exemption from agency in ceremonial works which would follow from the Buddhist doctrine of nothingness, is likewise false, for the maintainer of the doctrine proves his own reality. Independence from ceremony which the ignorant from indolence maintain, is also worthless, for in him the idea of agency is not overcome by proof. From these arguments it is evident that asceticism, which results from a forsaking of all ceremonial observances, and from a devotion to Brahman, is true only of him whose Unitarian knowledge is established by the proofs of the Vedānta. Thereby if a house-holder were to obtain that knowledge, asceticism would be true of him. May he not, by thus gaining asceticism, be guilty of neglecting the house-hold fire ? He is the destroyer of the champions of the gods who bloweth out the house-hold fire": says the Śruti. No. Such neglect following from Unitarian knowledge the result is the same as in the case of accidental blowing out [from an innundation, falling in of a house or the like : "[For him who knoweth the trugh] the virtue [lit, fieriness] of Agni passeth away"; says the Śruti [seq; chap. vi, sec. 4, verse 1], and hence the house-holder becomes not liable to any sin from such asceticism.

2. प्रजापतिर्लोकानभ्यतपत्तेभ्योऽभितप्तेभ्यस्त्रयी विद्या संप्रास्त्रवत्तामभ्यतपत्तस्या अभितप्ताया एतान्यक्षराणि संप्रास्त्रवन्त भूर्भुवःस्वरिति।।

Prajāpati reflected on mankind; from it, the reflected, issued forth the threefold knowledge; her reflected on it : from it, the reflected, proceeded the [three letters, Bhūḥ, Bhuvaḥ and Svaḥ]!

Prajāpati may mean Virāṭ [son of Brahmā] or Kaśyapa [son of Marīci].

3. तान्यभ्यतपत्तेभ्योऽभितप्तेभ्य ॐकारः संप्रास्त्रवत्तद्यथा शङ्कुना सर्वाणि पर्णानि संतृण्णान्येवमोंकारेण सर्वा वाक् संतृण्णोंकार एवेदꣳ सर्वमोंकार एवेदꣳ सर्वम्।।

On them, he reflected; from them, the reflected, issued forth Om. As leaves are attached to their stalks, so is speech[12] connected with Om ! Verily all this is Om ! verily all this is Om !

SECTION XXIV

1. ब्रह्मवादिनो वदन्ति यद्वसूनां प्रातःसवनᳲ रुद्राणां माध्यन्दिनᳲ सवनमादित्यानां च विश्वेषां च देवानां तृतीयसवनम्॥

The knowers of the Veda declare the morning ceremony to belong to the Vasus, that of the mid-day to Rudras and that of the afternoon to the Suns and the Viśvedevas.

What is known as the morning ceremony is subject to the Vasus, and this region [the earth], which is connected with that ceremoney is likewise subject to them. To the Rudras the lords of the mid-day ceremony, is the middle region or sky subject, and to the Suns[13] and the Viśvedevas, lords of the afternoon ceremony, belongs the third region or heaven.

2. क्व तर्हि यजमानस्य लोक इति स यस्तं न विद्यात्कथं कुर्यादथ विद्वान्कुर्यात्॥

Where then is the region for the institutor of sacrifice ? How can he, who knoweth not that [the reply to this query] perform [ceremonies] ? Now he who knoweth should perform [the same].

The last clause is eulogistic of the Sāma, and does not exclude the ignorant from the performance of ceremonies.

3. पुरा प्रातरनुवाकस्योपाकरणाज्जघनेन गार्हपत्यस्योदङ्मुख उपविश्य स वासवᳲ सामाभिगायति॥

Before the reading of the matin chant [prataranuvāk] he [the institutor of sacrifice], sitting down behind the house-hold fire [gārhapatya agni], with his face to the north, singeth the Sāma hymn relating to the Vasus.

4. लो ३ कद्वारमपावा ३ र्णु ३ ३ पश्येम त्वा वयᳲरा ३ ३ ३ ३ ३ हुं ३ आ ३ ३ ज्या ३ यो ३ आ ३ २ १ १ १ इति॥

"Unfold the gates of this earth, that we may behold thee for our supremacy."

5. अथ जुहोति नमोऽग्नये पृथिवीक्षिते लोकक्षिते लोकं मे यजमानाय विन्दैष वै यजमानस्य लोक एतास्मि॥

6. अत्र यजमानः परस्तादायुषः स्वाहापजहि परिघमित्युक्त्वो-
त्तिष्ठति तस्मै वसवः प्रातःसवनꣳ संप्रयच्छन्ति ।।

Then doth he offer the oblation to the fire [saying] : "Salutations be to Agni, he the receptacle of the earth, and the support of regions. [Oh ye] secure a region for me, who am an institutor of sacrifice ! This is the region of the institutor of sacrifice. I, institutor of sacrifice, will secure it after death. May this oblation prove acceptable ! Cast aside the bar." And then he riseth. For him do the Vasus fulfil the morning ceremony.

7. पुरा माध्यन्दिनस्य सवनस्योपाकरणाज्जघनेनाग्नीध्रीय-
स्योदङ्मुख उपविश्य स रौद्रꣳसामाभिगायति ।।

Before the commencement of the mid-day ceremony, sitting behind Āgnīdhrīya fire, and facing the north, he singeth the Sāma in praise of the Rudras [saying] :

8. लो ३ कद्वारमपाश ३ र्णू ३ ३ पश्येम त्वा वयं वैरा ३
३ ३ ३ ३ हुं ३ आ ३ ३ ज्या ३ यो ३ आ ३ २ १
१ १ इति ।।

"Unfold the gates of [yonder] region, that we may behold thee for our full supremacy."

9. अथ जुहोति नमो वायवेऽन्तरिक्षक्षिते लोकक्षिते लोकं
में यजमानाय विन्दैष वै यजमानस्य लोक एतास्मि ।।

10. अत्र यजमानः परस्तादायुषः स्वाहाऽपजहि परिघमित्युक्त्वोत्तिष्ठति
तस्मै रुद्रा माध्यन्दिनꣳ सवनꣳ संप्रयच्छन्ति ।।

Then doth he offer the oblation, saying : "I salute the Winds, who abideth in the sky and are the supports of regions. [Oh ye] secure a region for me who am an institutor of sacrifice ! This verily is the region of the institutor of sacrifice. I, institutor of sacrifice, will secure it after death. May this oblation prove acceptable ! Cast aside the bars." And then he riseth. For him do the Rudras fulfil the mid-day ceremony.

11. पुरा तृतीयसवनस्योपाकरणाज्जघनेनाहवनीयस्योदङ्मुख उपविश्य स आदित्यꣳ स वैश्वदेवꣳ सामाभिगायति।।

Before the commencement of the afternoon ceremony, sitting behind the Āhavanīya fire, with his face to the north he singeth the Sāma in praise of the Suns and the Viśvedevas [saying]:

12. लो ३ कद्वारमपावा ३ र्णू ३ ३ पश्येम त्वा वयꣳस्वारा ३ ३ ३ ३ ३ हुं ३ आ ३ ३ ज्या ३ यो ३ आ ३ २ १ १ १ इति।।

13. आदित्यमथ वैश्वदेवं लो ३ कद्वारमपावा ३ र्णू ३ ३ पश्येम त्वा वयꣳ साम्रा ३ ३ ३ ३ ३ हुं ३ आ ३ ३ ३ यो ३ आ ३ २ १ १ १ इति।।

"Unfold the gates of [yonder] region that we may behold thee for our heavenly supremacy !" Thus much for the Suns; and then to the Viśvedevas; "Unfold the gates of yonder region, that we may behold thee for our absolute supremacy !"

14. अथ जुहोति नमः आदित्येभ्यश्च देवेभ्यो दिविक्षिद्भ्यो लोकक्षिद्भ्यो लोकं मे यजमानाय विन्दत।।

Then doth he offer the oblation saying : "I salute the Suns and the Viśvedevas, the dwellers of heaven and the supporters of regions. Secure that region for me, who am an institutor of sacrifice.

15. एष वै यजमानस्य लोक एतास्म्यत्र यजमानः परस्तादायुषः स्वाहाऽपहतपरिघमित्युक्त्वोत्तिष्ठति।।

"That is verily the region for the institutor of sacrifice. I, institutor of sacrifice, shall come thereto after death. May this oblation prove acceptable ! Cast aside the bars," saying this he riseth.

16. तस्मा आदित्याश्च विश्वे च देवास्तृतीयं सवनꣳ संप्रयच्छन्त्येष ह वै यज्ञस्य मात्रां वेद य एवं वेद य एवं वेद।।

For him do the Suns and Viśvedevas fulfil the afternoon ceremony. He understands the real purport of ceremonies, who knoweth this—verily, he who knoweth this [understands the real purport of ceremonies].

Foot Note

1. *i.e.*, at the hour when after milking, cowherds allow kine to, suckly their young.
2. A particular chapter of the Sāma Veda, so called from its verses being composed in the Gāyatrī metre.
3. *i.e.*, "Beneficent to his kind," says Ānandagiri.
4. At the time of generating fire by friction it is usual to recite hymns from the Rathantara chapter of the Sāma Veda in praise of Agni, therefore are they said to be connected with each other.—Ānandagiri.
5. A form of the Sāma hymns.
6. Śaṅkara says, that the word *or* (वा) is understood after "wealth," and the meaning is, the adorer obtains habitation, wealth *or* body like unto that of the gods, according to his wish.
7. Heaven, earth and sky.
8. These evidently relate to the seven tones of a gamut. The taurine and the ardine tones appear, from the subjoined verse of Nārada, to be equivalent to the B and D of the English music; the rest we have not been able to ascertain. If our conjecture be right, the five-formed Sāma would include all those hymns which embrace five tones, and the seven-formed those which are sung on the full gamut.

   षड्जं रौति मयूरो हि गावो नर्दन्ति ऋषभम्।
   अजा विरौति गान्धारं क्रोञ्चा नर्दति मध्यमम्।।
9. भेदज्ञान The knowledge or instinct by which physical objects are perceived as distinct and independent of each other, is called disjunctive because it disjoins or sets apart the Vedāntic truth, that the whole universe is an emanation of the Deity.
10. Ceremonies are divided into four classes : 1st, those which house-holders are bound to perform every day, Diurnal [Nitya]. 2nd, Occasional, such as on the birth of a child, etc. [Naimittika]. 3rd, Optional, or such as are performed for the attainment of some specific object (Kāmya,) 4th, Expiatory [Prāyaschitta.]
11. Such as the propriety of putting on the Brahminical thread and the like.—Ānandagiri.
12. Lit. All words.
13. The Vedas enumerate 12 suns.

THIRD CHAPTER

SECTION I

1. ॐ असौ वा आदित्यो देवमधु तस्य द्यौरेव तिरश्चीनवंशोऽन्तरिक्षमपूपो मरीचयः पुत्राः॥

Hari, Om ! Verily the sun is the honey of the gods. The heaven is the arched bamboo, [whence hangeth pendant] the atmosphere [like a] hive, the vapours [floating therein] are the eggs.

2. तस्य ये प्राञ्चो रश्मयस्ता एवास्य प्राच्यो मधुनाड्य ऋच एष मधुकृत ऋग्वेद एव पुष्पं ता अमृता आपस्ता वा एता ऋचः॥

On the sun the eastern beams are the eastern honey cells; the Ṛk-hymns are the manufacturers of honey; [the ceremonies enjoined by] the Ṛg-Veda from the flowers, and the fluids [used in their performance] are nectars. Verily those Ṛk-hymns.

3. एतमृग्वेदमभ्यतपंस्तस्याभितप्तस्य यशस्तेन इन्द्रियं वीर्यमन्नाद्यं रसोऽजायत॥

Reflected on the ceremonies of the Ṛg-Veda. From them, the reflected, proceeded forth fame, splendour, sensations, power, aliment and such like essences.

4. तद्व्यक्षरत्तदादित्यमभितोऽश्रयत्तद्वा एतद्यदेतदादित्यस्य रोहितं रूपम्॥

They flowed and rested around the sun. Verily, thence proceedeth the redness of the sun.

SECTION II

1. अथ चेऽस्य दक्षिणा रश्मयस्ता एवास्य दक्षिणा मधुनाड्यो यजूꣳष्येव मधुकृतो यजुर्वेद एव पुष्पं ता अमृता आपः।।

Now, its southern beams are verily the southern honey-cells; [therein] the Yajur-hymns are the honey-makers; [the ceremonies enjoined by] the Yajur-Veda form the flowers; and the fluids [used in their performance] are nectars.

2. तानि वा एतानि यजूꣳष्येतं यजुर्वेदमभ्यतपत्तस्याभितप्तस्य यशस्तेज इन्द्रियं वीर्यमन्नाद्यꣳरसोऽजायत।।

Verily those Yajur-hymns reflected on the [ceremonies, enjoined by the] Yajur-Veda. From them, the reflected proceeded forth fame, splendour, sensations, power, aliment and such like essences.

3. तद्व्यक्षरत्तदादित्यमभितोऽश्रयत्तद्वा एतद्यदेतदादित्यस्य शुक्लꣳरूपम्।।

They flowed and rested around the sun. Thence, verily proceedeth the whiteness of the sun.

SECTION III

1. अथ येऽस्य प्रत्यञ्चो रश्मयस्ता एवास्य प्रतीच्यो मधुनाड्यः सामान्येव मधुकृतः सामवेद एव पुष्पं ता अमृता आपः।।

Next, its western beams are verily the western honey-cells; [therein] in Sāma hymns are the honey-makers; [the ceremonies enjoined by] the Sāma-Veda from the flowers, and the fluids [used in their performance] are nectars.

2. तानि वा एतानि सामान्येतꣳ सामवेदमभ्यतपꣳस्तस्याभितप्तस्य यशस्तेज इन्द्रियं वीर्यमन्नाद्यꣳ रसोऽजायत।।

Verily those Sāma-hymns reflected on the [ceremonies enjoined by the] Sāma-Veda. From them, the reflected, issued forth fame, splendour, sensations, power, aliment and such like essences.

3. तद्व्यक्षरत्तदादित्यमभितोऽश्रयत्तद्वा एतद्यदेतदादित्यस्य परं कृष्णꣳरूपम्॥

They flowed and rested around the sun. Thence, verily, proceedeth the dark coloured rays of the sun.

SECTION IV

1. अथ येऽस्योदञ्चो रश्मयस्ता एवास्योदीच्यौ मधुनाड्योऽथर्वाङ्गिरस एव मधुकृत इतिहासपुराणं पुष्पं ता अमृता आपः॥

Now, the northern rays are verily the northern honey-cells; [therein] the Atharvāṅgirasa hymns are the honey-makers; [the ceremonies enjoined by] the Itihāsa and the Purāṇa[1] form the flowers, and the fluids [used in their performance] are nectars.

2. ते वा एतेऽथर्वाङ्गिरस एतदितिहासपुराणमभ्यतपꣳस्तस्याभितप्तस्य यशस्तेज इन्द्रियं वीर्यमन्नाद्यꣳ रसोऽजायत॥

They, the Atharvāṅgirasa, reflected on the Itihāsa and the Purāṇa. From them, the reflected, proceeded forth fame, splendour, sensations, power, aliment and such like essences.

3. तद्व्यक्षरत्तदादित्यमभितोऽश्रयत्तद्वा एतद्यदेतदादित्यस्य परं कृष्णꣳरूपम्॥

They flowed and rested around the sun. Thence verily proceedeth the very dark rays of the sun.

SECTION V

1. अथ येऽस्योर्ध्वा रश्मयस्ता एवास्योर्ध्वा मधुनाड्यो गुह्या एवादेशा मधुकृतो ब्रह्मैव पुष्पं ता अमृता आपः॥

Next, the upward rays are verily the upper honey, cells; there the secret ordinances are the honey-markes; Brahman[2] is the flower, and its fluids are nectars.

2. ते वा एते गुह्या आदेशा एतद्ब्रह्माभ्यतपꣳस्तस्याभितप्तस्य यशस्तेज इन्द्रियं वीर्यमन्नाद्यꣳरसोऽजायत।।

They, the secret ordinances, reflected on Brahman. From it, the reflected, issued forth fame, splendour, sensations, power, aliment and such like essences.

3. तद्व्यक्षरत्तदादित्यमभितोऽश्रयत्तद्वा एतद्यदेतदादित्यस्य मध्ये क्षोभत इव।।

They flowed and rested around the sun. Verily thence proceedeth the delusive opalescence in the centre of the sun.[3]

4. ते वा एते रसानाꣳ रसा वेदा हि रसास्तेषामेते रसास्तानि वा एतान्यमृतानाममृतानि वेदा ह्यमृतास्तेषामेतान्यमृतानि।।

They, the different rays of the sun, are the essences of essences; the Vedas are the essences, and thereof are they the essences; —they are the nectars of nectars : the Vedas are nectars, and thereof are they the nectars.

SECTION VI

1. तद्यत्प्रथमममृतं तद्वसव उपजीवन्त्यग्निना मुखेन न वै देवा अश्नन्ति न पिबन्त्येतदेवामृतं दृष्ट्वा तृप्यन्ति।।

Thereof the first named nectar is enjoyed by the Vasus with Agni at their head, Verily the Devas neither eat nor drink [of the same], they [only] gratify themselves by its sight.

2. त एतदेव रूपमभिसंविशन्त्येतस्माद्रूपादुद्यन्ति।।

They are quieted by the sight of those rays,[4] they are excited thereby.[5]

3. स य एतदेवमृतं वेद वसूनामेवैको भूत्वाऽग्निनैव मुखेनैतदेवामृतं दृष्ट्वा तृप्यति स य एतदेव रूपमभिसंविशत्येतस्माद्रूपादुदेति।।

He, who thus knoweth the nectar, becoming one of the Vasus,

and reflecting on the nectar with Agni before him, enjoyeth content. He is quieted by those rays; he is excited thereby.

4. स यावदादित्यः पुरस्तादुदेता पश्चादस्तमेता वसूनामेव तावदाधिपत्यꣳस्वाराज्यं पर्येता॥

He obtaineth the entire dominion of the Vasus which extends from the rising of the sun [in the east] to its setting [in the west].

SECTION VII

1. अथ यद्द्वितीयममृतं तद्रुद्रा उपजीवन्तीन्द्रेण मुखेन न वै देवा अश्नन्ति न पिबन्त्येतदेवामृतं दृष्ट्वा तृप्यन्ति॥

Now, the second mentioned nectar is enjoyed by the Rudras, with Indra at their head. Verily the Devas neither eat nor drink [of the same], they [only] gratify themselves by its sight.

2. त एतदेव रूपमभिसंविशन्त्येतस्माद्रूपादुद्यन्ति॥

They are soothed by that appearance [of the sun], and by it are they excited.

3. स य एतदेवममृतं वेद रुद्राणामेवैको भूत्वेन्द्रेणैव मुखेनैतदेवामृतं दृष्ट्वा तृप्यति स एतदेव रूपमभिसंविशत्येतस्माद्रूपादुदेति॥

He, who knoweth the nectar thus, becoming one of the Rudras and reflecting on the same with Indra before him, enjoyeth content. That appearance doth pacify him, and thereby is he excited.

4. स यावदादित्यः पुरस्तादुदेता पश्चादस्तमेता द्विस्तावद्दक्षिणत उदेतोत्तरतोऽस्तमेता रुद्राणामेतावदाधिपत्यꣳ स्वाराज्यं पर्येता॥

He obtaineth the dominion of the Rudras, which extends from the rising of the sun in the south to its setting in the north,—a period double that within which it riseth in the east and setteth in the west.

SECTION VIII

1. अथ यत्तृतीयममृतं तदादित्या उपजीवन्ति वरुणेन मुखेन न वै देवा अश्नन्ति न पिबन्त्येतदेवामृतं दृष्ट्वा तृप्यन्ति ।।

Now, the third nectar is enjoyed by the Ādityas, with Varuṇa at their head. Verily the Devas neither eat nor drink [of the same], they [only] gratify themselves by its sight.

2. त एतदेव रूपमभिसंविशन्त्येतस्माद्रूपादुद्यन्ति ।।

They are soothed by that appearance of the sun, and by it are they excited.

3. स य एतदेवममृतं वेदादित्यानामेवैको भूत्वा वरुणेनैव मुखेनैतदेवामृतं दृष्ट्वा तृप्यति स एतदेव रूपमभिसंविशत्ये-तस्माद्रूपादुदेति ।।

He, who knoweth the nectar thus, becoming one of the Ādityas, with Varuṇa before him, enjoyeth content. That appearance of the sun doth sooth him, and thereby is he excited.

4. स यावदादित्यो दक्षिणत उदेतोत्तरतोऽस्तमेता द्विस्तावत्पश्चादुदेता पुरस्तादस्तमेतादित्यानामेव तावदाधिपत्यं स्वाराज्यं पर्येता ।।

He obtaineth the entire dominion of the Ādityas, which extends from the rising of the sun behind to its setting before, —a period double that within which it riseth in the south and sets in the north.

SECTION IX

1. अथ यच्चतुर्थममृतं तन्मरुत उपजीवन्ति सोमेन मुखेन अश्नन्ति न पिबन्त्येतदेवामृतं दृष्ट्वा तृप्यन्ति ।।

Now, the fourth nectar is enjoyed by the Maruts with Soma at their head. Verily, the Devas neither eat nor drink [of the same], they [only] gratify themselves by its sight.

2. त एतदेव रूपमभिसंविशन्त्येतस्माद्रूपादुद्यन्ति ।।

They are verily soothed by that appearance of the sun, and by it are they excited.

3. स य एतदेवममृतं वेद मरुतामेवैको भूत्वा सोमेनैव मुखेनैतदेवामृतं दृष्ट्वा तृप्यति स एतदेव रूपमभिसंविश-त्येतस्माद्रूपादुदेति।।

He, who knoweth the nectar thus, becoming one of the Maruts, and reflecting on that nectar with Soma before him, enjoyeth content. He is soothed by that appearance of the sun, and by it is he excited.

4. स यावदादित्यः पश्चादुदेता पुरस्तादस्तमेता द्विस्तावदुत्तरत उदेता दक्षिणतोऽस्तमेता मरुतामेव तावदाधिपत्यः स्वाराज्यं पर्येता।।

He obtaineth the entire dominion of the Maruts, which extends from the rising of the sun in the north to its setting in the south,—a period double that within which it riseth behind and setteth before.

SECTION X

1. अथ यत्पञ्चमममृतं तत्साध्या उपजीवन्ति ब्रह्मणा मुखेन न वै देवा अश्नन्ति न पिबन्त्येतदेवामृतं दृष्ट्वा तृप्यन्ति।।

Now, the fifth nectar is enjoyed by the Sādhyas with Brahman [Om] at their head. Verily the Devas neither eat nor drink [of the same], they [only] gratify themselves by its sight.

2. त एतदेव रूपमभिसंविशन्त्येतस्माद्रूपादुद्यन्ति।।

They are verily soothed by that appearance of the sun, and by it are they excited.

3. स य एतदेवममृतं वेद साध्यानामेवैको भूत्वा ब्रह्मणैव मुखेनैतदेवामृतं दृष्ट्वा तृप्यति स एतदेव रूपमभिसंविश-त्येतस्माद्रूपादुदेति।।

He, who knoweth the nectar thus, becoming one of the Sādhyas and reflecting on that nectar with Brahman before him, enjoyeth content. Verily he is soothed by that appearance [of the sun], and by it is he excited.

4. स यावदादित्य उत्तरत उदेता दक्षिणतोऽस्तमेता द्विस्तावदूर्ध्वमुदेतार्वागस्तमेता साध्यानामेव तावदाधिपत्यꣳ स्वाराज्यं पर्येता॥

He obtaineth the entire dominion of the Sādhyas which extends from the rising of the sun above to its setting below,—a period double that in which he riseth in the north and setteth in the south.

. . . The duration of the sun in the different spheres (as described here) is apparently opposed to the doctrine of the Purāṇas. The followers of those records maintain that the periods of the sun's rising and setting in the four different spheres of Indra, Yama, Varuṇa and Soma are equal, the extent of the orbit of the sun above the Mānasottara mountain and around the mount Meru being equal. The discrepancy, however, has been explained by sages. Fach of the different spheres (as set forth) is destroyed at a period double that of its preceding one. The rising of the sun means the time during which it remains visible to the residents of any one of those shperes, and the setting is when it is invisible, there being actually no rising or setting of that luminary. In the absence of inhabitants in those shperes there will be no sunrise or sunset there, though the sun may become visible therefrom.

SECTION XI

1. अथ तत ऊर्ध्व उदेत्य नैवोदेता नास्तमेतैकल एव मध्ये स्थाता तदेष श्लोकः॥

Next, beyond that, appearing above, He neither riseth nor setteth, but remaineth alone in the centre. Thereof is the verse :

2. न वै तत्र न निम्लोच नोदियाय कदाचन। देवास्तेनाहꣳ सत्येन मा विराधिषि ब्रह्मणेति॥

"No; of a truth there is neither rising nor setting. [Bear ye witness] O Gods, that I may say nothing contradictory of that truthful Brahman !"

3. न ह वा अस्मा उदेति न निम्लोचति सकृद्दिवा हैवास्मै भवति य एतामेव ब्रह्मोपनिषदं वेद॥

For him there is neither rising nor setting of the sun—for him there is one eternal day,—who possesseth this knowledge of Brahman.

4. तद्धैतद्ब्रह्मा प्रजापतय उवाच प्रजापतिर्मनवे मनुः प्रजाभ्यस्तद्धैतदुद्दालकायारुणये ज्येष्ठाय पुत्राय पिता ब्रह्म प्रोवाच॥

Verily that knowledge was explained by Brahmā to Prajāpati, and by Prajāpati to Manu, and by Manu to his descendants. This knowledge of Brahman was explained to one of the descendants Uddālaka Āruṇi, an eldest son, by his father.

5. इदं वाव तज्ज्येष्ठाय पुत्राय पिता ब्रह्म प्रब्रूयात्प्रणाय्याय वान्तेवासिने॥

This knowledge of Brahman should verily be explained by a father to his eldest son or to a worthy disciple;

6. नान्यस्मै कस्मैचन यद्यप्यस्मा इमामद्भिः परिगृहीतां धनस्य पूर्णां दद्यादेतदेव ततो भूय इत्येतदेव ततो भूय इति॥

But to none else. Were none to give this sea-girt sphere with all its treasures to the instructor, [in exchange of this knowledge] the latter would still be greater—greater by far [in value than the sphere].

Section XII

1. गायत्री वा इदꣳ सर्वं भूतं यदिदं किंच वाग्वै गायत्री वाग्वा इदꣳ सर्वं भूतं गायति च त्रायते च॥

Verily all this creation is Gāyatri. Speech is Gāyatri; by speech is all this creation recited and preserved.

2. या वै सा गायत्रीयं वाव सा येयं पृथिव्यस्याꣳ हीदꣳ सर्वं भूतं प्रतिष्ठितमेतामेव नातिशीयते॥

That Gāyatrī is verily this earth. And on this earth are all creatures sustained; that they exceed not.

3. या वै सा पृथिवी यं वाव सा यदिदमस्मिन्पुरुषे शरीरमस्मिन्हीमे प्राणाः प्रतिष्ठिता एतदेव नातिशीयन्ते।।

That which is the earth is likewise the boy of the animated creation. In that body are the animal functions sustained; that they exceed not.

4. यद्वै तत्पुरुषे शरीरमिदं वाव तद्यदिदमस्मिन्नन्तः पुरुषे हृदयमस्मिन्हीमे प्राणाः प्रतिष्ठिता एतदेव नातिशीयन्ते।।

That which is the body is likewise the heart which is within it. In it are the animal functions sustained; that they exceed not.

5. सैषा चुतष्पदा षड्विधा गायत्री तदेतदृचाभ्यनूक्तम्।।

That Gāyatrī is verily composed of four feet, and possesseth six characteristics. Regarding it has this verse been recited :

Speech, being earth, body, heart and life, are the six characteristics of Gāyatrī. Or because each of its feet has six letters.

6. तावानस्य महिता ततो ज्यायाꣳश्च पुरूषः। पादोऽस्य सर्वा भूतानि त्रिपादस्यामृतं दिवीति।।

"They [the creations] constitute the glories of the Gāyatri; to which is the soul [Puruṣa[6]] superior. He has the creation for his first foot, and his own immortal self [7] constitutes the other three."

7. यद्वै तद्ब्रह्मेतीदं वाव तद्योऽयं बहिर्धा पुरुषादाकाशो यो वै स बहिर्धा पुरुषादाकाशः।।

That Brahman [*i.e.,* the being indicated in the Gāyatrī] is verily the space which[8] surroundeth mankind.

8. अयं वाव स योऽयमन्तः पुरुष आकाशो यो वै सोऽन्तः पुरुष आकाशः।।

That which surroundeth mankind is of a truth the space which existeth within mankind.

9. अयं वाव स योऽयमन्तर्हृदय आकाशस्तदेतत्पूर्णमप्रवर्ति पूर्णमप्रवर्तिनीꣳ श्रियं लभते य एवं वेद।।

That which existeth within mankind is of a truth the space which existed within the heart. It is omnipresent and eternal. He who knoweth this attains eternal and all-sufficient treasures.

Section XIII

1. तस्य ह वा एतस्य हृदयस्य पञ्च देवसुषयः स योऽस्य प्राङ्सुषिः स प्राणस्तच्चक्षुः स आदित्यस्तदेतत्तेजोऽन्नाद्यमित्युपासीत तेजस्व्यन्नादो भवति य एवं वेद।।

For that [space which is] within the heart there are five gates to heaven. Thereof the eastern gate is breath [Prāṇa]; which is vision and that is Āditya [the sun]. That [Prāṇa] is to be adored as the consumer of aliment and all glorious. Glorious and an [able] consumer of aliment doth he become who knoweth it thus.

2. अथ योऽस्य दक्षिणः सुषिः स व्यानस्तच्छ्रोत्रं स चन्द्रमास्तदेतच्छ्रीश्च यशश्चेत्युपासीत श्रीमान्यशस्वी भवति य एवं वेद।।

Next, the southern aperture is Vyāna, which is audition, and that is the Moon. Believing it to be prosperity and fame let it be worshipped. He who knoweth it so, attaineth celebrity and prosperity.

3. अथ योऽस्य प्रत्यङ्सुषिः सोऽपानः सा वाक् सोऽग्निस्तदेतद्ब्रह्मवर्चसमन्नाद्यमित्युपासीत ब्रह्मवर्चस्व्यन्नादो भवति य एवं वेद।।

Next, the western aperture is Apāna, it is speech, which is fire [Agni]. Believing it to be Vedic glory and aliment let it be worshipped. He who knoweth it so, attaineth plenty and Vedic glory.

4. अथ योऽस्योदङ्सुषिः स समानस्तन्मनः स पर्जन्यस्तदेतत्कीर्तिश्च व्युष्टिश्चेत्युपासीत कीर्तिमान्व्युष्टिमान्भवति य एवं वेद।।

Next, that which is the northern aperture, is Samāna which is the mind, which is cloud. Believing it to be reputation and beauty, let it be worshipped. He who knoweth it so, attaineth reputation and beauty.

5. अथ योऽस्योर्ध्वः सुषिः स उदानः स वायुः स आकाशस्तदेतदोजश्च महाश्चेत्युपासीतौजस्वी महस्वान्भवति य एवं वेद।।

Next, that which is the upper aperture is Udāna; which is the wind, which is the sky. Believing it to be strength and glory let it be worshipped. He who knoweth it so, becomes glorious and mighty.

6. ते वा एते पञ्च ब्रह्मपुरुषाः स्वर्गस्य लोकस्य द्वाररपाः स य एतानेवं पञ्च ब्रह्मपुरुषान्स्वर्गस्य लोकस्य द्वारपान्वेदास्य कुले वीरो जायते प्रतिपद्यते स्वर्गं लोकं य एतानेवं पञ्च ब्रह्मपुरुषान्स्वार्गस्य लोकस्य द्वारपान्वेद।।

These five venerable[9] beings are the door-keepers of heaven. Heroes are born in his family who knoweth these five venerable beings to be door-keepers of heaven; he obtaineth heaven [for his reward] who knows these five venerable beings to be the door-keepers of heaven.

7. अथ यदतः परो दिवो ज्योतिर्दीप्यते विश्वतः पृष्ठेषु सर्वतः पृष्ठेष्वनुत्तमेषूत्तमेषु लोकेष्विदं वाव तद्यदिदमस्मिन्नन्तः पुरुषे ज्योतिस्तस्यैषा दृष्टिः।।

That which shines glorious above yonder heaven, above this world and above all others, large or small, is the same as that which shines within mankind. It is tangible [to all].[10]

8. यत्रैतदस्मिञ्छरीरे सꣳस्पर्शेनोष्णिमानं विजानाति तस्यैषा श्रुतिर्यत्रैतत्कर्णावपिगृह्य निनदमिव नदथुरिवाग्नेरिव ज्वलत उपश्रृणोति तदेतद्दृष्टं च श्रुतं चेत्युपासीत चक्षुष्यः श्रुतो भवति य एवं वेद य एवं वेद।।

For its warmth is felt in this body by touch. It is audible, for when the ears are closed, it is heard like the roar of a flaming fire, or that of a rolling car, or a bellowing ox. That tangible and audible glory is to be adored. He who knoweth—verily he who knoweth—this, becomes renowned and of handsome appearance.

SECTION XIV

1. सर्वं खल्विदं ब्रह्म तज्जलानिति शान्त उपसीताथ खलु क्रतुमयः पुरुषो यथा क्रतुरस्मिँल्लोके पुरुषो भवति तथेतः प्रेत्य भवति स क्रतुं कुर्वीत।।

All this verily is Brahman, for therefrom doth it proceed, therein doth it merge, and thereby is it maintained. With a quiet and controlled mind should it be adored. Man is a creature of reflection, whatever he reflects upon in this life, he becomes the same hereafter; therefore should he reflect [upon Brahman].

2. मनोमयः प्राणशरीरो भारूपः सत्यसंकल्प आकाशात्मा सर्वकर्मा सर्वकामः सर्वगन्धः सर्वरसः सर्वमिदमभ्यात्तोऽवाक्यनादरः।।

[Saying] "that which is nothing but mind, whose body is its life, whose figure is a mere glory, whose will is truth, whose soul is like space [*ākāśa,*] which performeth all things and willeth all things, to which belong all sweet odours and all grateful juices, which envelopes the whole of this [world], which neither speaketh nor respects any body.

3. एष म आत्मान्तर्हृदयेऽणीयान्व्रीहेर्वा यवाद्वा सर्षपाद्वा श्यामाकाद्वा श्यामाकतण्डुलाद्वा एष म आत्मान्तर्हृदये ज्यायान्पृथिव्या ज्यायानन्तरिक्षाज्ज्यायान्दिवो ज्यायानेभ्यो लोकेभ्यः।।

"Is the soul within me; it is lighter than a corn, or a barley, or a mustard, or a canary seed, or the substance within it. Such a soul is within me, as is greater than this earth, and greater than the sky, and greater than the heaven, and greater than all these regions [put together].

4. सर्वकर्मा सर्वकामः सर्वगन्धः सर्वरसः सर्वमिदमभ्यात्तोऽवाक्यनादर एष म आत्मान्तर्हृदय एतद्ब्रह्मैतमितः प्रेत्याभिसंभवितास्मीति यस्य स्यादद्धा न विचिकित्सास्तीति ह स्माह शाण्डिल्यः शाण्डिल्यः।।

"That which performeth all things, and willeth all things, to which belong all sweet odours and all grateful juices, which envelopes the whole of this [world], which neither speaketh nor respecteth any body, is the soul within me; it is Brahman; I shall obtain it after my transition from this world." He who believeth this, and hath no hesitation, will verily obtain the fruit of his reflection; so said Śāndilya—[the sage] Śāndilya.

Section XV

1. अन्तरिक्षोदरः कोशो भूमिर्बुध्नो न जीर्यति दिशो ह्यस्य स्रक्तयो द्यौरस्योत्तरं बिलꣳ स एष कोशो वसुधानस्तस्मि-न्विश्वमिदꣳ श्रितम् ।।

Of that sheath [the Soul] the sky is the ventricle and the earth is the rood; it never decayeht; the quarters of the universe are its corners, and the heaven is its upper aperture; it is the receptacle of wealth, and upon it is the universe supported.

2. तस्य प्राची दिग्जुहूर्नाम सहमाना नाम दक्षिणा राज्ञी नाम प्रतीची सुभूता नामोदीचली तासां वायुर्वत्सः स य एतमेवं वायुं दिशां वत्सं वेद न पुत्ररोदꣳरोदिति सोऽहमेतमेवं वायुं दिशां वत्सं वेद मापुत्ररोदꣳ रुदम् ।।

Its eastern quarter is called Juhu, its southern quarter Sahamānā, its western quarter Rājñī, and its northern quarter Subhutā; the winds of those quarters are their offspring. He who [wishing for long life for his children] knows the winds to be the offspring of the quarters, hath never to weep for his children. "I know the winds to be the offspring of the quarters, therefore have I had never to weep for my children.

The performers of sacrifice offer their oblations (juhoti) facing the east, therefore is that quarter called Juhū; the vicious suffer (sahante) the fruit of their actions in the abode of Yama in the south, therefore is that quarter called Sahāmān; the west is called Rājñī, because, it is the empire of king (Rājā), Varuṇa, or because, at twilight it becomes red (rāga). Wealthy beings (bhūtimat), such as Īśvara, Kubera, etc., reside in the north, hence it is called Sūbhutā.

3. अरिष्टं कोशं प्रपद्येऽमुनामुनामुना प्राणं प्रपद्येऽमुनामुनामुना भूः प्रपद्येऽमुनामुनामुना भुवः प्रपद्येऽमुनामुनामुना स्वः प्रपद्येऽमुनामुनामुना ।।

"Together with such and such and such, I take asylum of that undying sheath; with such and such and such I seek shelter of life. [Prāṇa]; with such and such and such I seek shelter of this earth [Bhūḥ]; with such and such and such I seek shelter of the sky [Bhuvaḥ]; with such and such and such I seek shelter of heaven [Svaḥ].

4. स यदवोचं प्राणं प्रपद्य इति प्राणो वा इदꣳ सर्वं भूतं यदिदं किंच तमेव तत्प्रापत्सि ।।

"By [the words] 'I seek shelter of Prāṇa' [life], I have said that I take asylum of the universal existence.

5. अथ यदवोचं भूः प्रपद्य इति पृथिवीं प्रपद्येऽन्तरिक्षं प्रपद्ये दिवं प्रपद्य इत्येव तदवोचम् ।।

"By what I have said by [the words] 'I seek shelter of Bhuḥ,' I mean that I take shelter of the earth, I take shelter of the sky, I take shelter of heaven."

6. अथ यदवोचं भुवः प्रपद्य इत्यग्निं प्रपद्ये वायुं प्रपद्य आदित्यं प्रपद्य इत्येव तदवोचम् ।।

"By what I have said by [the words] 'I take shelter of Bhūvaḥ,' I mean I seek shelter of Agni [fire], I seek shelter of Vāyu [wind], I seek shelter of Āditya [the sun]."

7. अथ यदवोचꣳ स्वः प्रपद्य इत्यृग्वेदं प्रपद्ये यजुर्वेदं प्रपद्ये सामवेदं प्रपद्य इत्येव तदवोचं तदवोचम् ।।

"By what I have said by [the words] 'I take shelter of Svaḥ,' I mean I take shelter of the Ṛg-Veda, I take shelter of the Yajur-Veda, I take shelter of the Sāma Veda."

SECTION XVI

1. पुरुषो वाव यज्ञस्तस्य यानि चतुर्विंशति वर्षाणि तत्प्रातःसवनं चतुर्विंशत्यक्षरा गायत्री गायत्रं प्रातःसवनं तदस्य वसवोऽन्वायत्ताः प्राणा वाव वसव एते हीदं सर्वं वासयन्ति॥

Verily man is Yajña [sacrifice]. The first twenty four years of his life constitute the morning ritual [Prātaḥ-savana]. The Gāyatrī includes 24 letters, and it is the Gāyatrī through which the morning riutal is performed. The Vasus are the presiding deities of dawn, and in man the vital airs verily represent the Vasus, for they preserve [vāsayanti] all.

2. तं चेदेतस्मिन्वयसि किंचिदुपतपेत्स ब्रूयात्प्राणा वसव इदं मे प्रातः सवनं माध्यन्दिनं सवनमनुसन्तनुतेति माहं प्राणानां वसूनां मध्ये यज्ञो विलोप्सीयेत्युद्धैव तत एत्यगदो ह भवति॥

At this age should any disease afflict him, he should say : "O vital Vasus, this is the season of my morning ritual, connect it with the mid-day sacrifice, that I, who am sacrifice [itself], may not be lost to the vital Vasus." Thus he escapes from disease, and verily becomes exempt from affliction.

3. अथ यानि चतुश्चत्वारिंशद्वर्षाणि तन्माध्यन्दिनं सवनं चतुश्चत्वारिंशदक्षरा त्रिष्टुप् त्रैष्टुभं माध्यन्दिनं सवनं तदस्य रुद्रा अन्वायत्ताः प्राणा वाव रुद्रा एते हीदं सर्वंरोदयन्ति॥

[The] next [period] to the forty-fourth year of his life constitutes the mid-day ritual. The Tristupa includes forty-four letters, and it is through the Tristupa that the mid-day sacrifice is performed. The Rudras are its presiding deities. In man the vital airs are the Rudras for they cause weeping,[11] [Rodayanti].

4. तं चेदेतस्मिन्वयसि किंचिदुपतपेत्स ब्रूयात्प्राणा रुद्रा इदं मे माध्यन्दिनं सवनं तृतीयसवनमनुसन्तनुतेति माहं प्राणानां रुद्राणां मध्ये यज्ञो विलोप्सीयेत्युद्धैव तत एत्यगदो ह भवति॥

At this age should any disease afflict him, he should say, "O vital Rudras, this is the season of mid-day ritual, connect it with the afternoon sacrifice, that I, who am sacrifice [itself], may not be lost to the vital Rudras." Thus he escapes from disease and becomes exempt from affliction.

5. अथ यान्यष्टाचत्वारिंशद्वर्षाणि तृतीयसवनमष्टाचत्वारिंशदक्षरा जगती जागतं तृतीयसवनं तदस्यादित्या अन्वायत्ताः प्राणा वावादित्या एते हीदं सर्वमाददते॥

[The] next [period] to the eighty-fourth year of his life constitutes the afternoon ritual. The Jagatī [metre] includes eighty-four letters, and it is through the Jagatī that the afternoon ceremony is performed. The Ādityas are its presiding deities. In man the vital airs are the Ādityas, for they receive [ādadate] all things.

6. तं चेदेतस्मिन्वयसि किंचिदुपतपेत्स ब्रूयात्प्राणा आदित्या इदं मे तृतीयसवनमायुरनुसन्तनुतेति माहं प्राणानामादित्यानां मध्ये यज्ञो विलोप्सीयेत्युद्धैव तत एत्यगदो हैव भवति॥

At this age should he be afflicted by any disease, he should say, "O vital Ādityas, this is the season of my afternoon ritual, connect it with the full term of my life, that I, who am sacrifice [itself], may not be lost to the vital Ādityas." Thus he escapes from disease and becomes exempt from affliction.

7. एतद्ध स्म वैतद्विद्वानाह महिदास ऐतरेयः स किं म एतदुपतपसि योऽहमनेन न प्रेष्यामीति स ह षोडशं वर्षशतमजीवत्प्र ह षोडशं वर्षशतं जीवति य एवं वेद॥

Verily knowing this Mahidāsa, son of Itara, said, "O ! why dost thou afflict me, for I shall not be destroyed by thee." He lived for one hundred and sixteen years. Verily he will live for one hundred and sixteen years who knoweth this.

SECTION XVII

1. स यदशिशिषति यत्पिपासति यन्न रमते ता अस्य दीक्षाः॥

His [of the individual typical of sacrifice] hunger, thirst, and want of pleasure constitute the pain which attends the performance of cermonies.

2. अथ यदश्नाति यत्पिबति यद्रमते तदुपसदैरेति।।

Whatever he eateth, whatever he drinketh, and whatever he enjoyeth, become unto him [like the reward which is available on the day of the] Upasad.[11]

3. अथ यद्धसति यज्जक्षति यन्मैथुनं चरति स्तुतशस्त्रैरेव तेदेति।।

Whatever he laugheth, whatever he eateth, and whatever he enjoyeth, become to him like unto [the] praises [of the Ṛk and Yajur-Veda].

4. अथ यत्तपो दानमार्जवमहिंसा सत्यवचनमिति ता अस्य दक्षिणाः।।

His penance, charity, sincerity, unenviousness and truthfulness constitute his reward [Dakṣiṇa].

5. तस्मादाहुः सोष्यत्यसोष्टेति पुनरुत्पादनमेवास्य तन्मरणमे-वास्यावभृथः।।

Therefore is it said, [both at the birth of a child and at the expression of the juice of the moon plant, in reply to the query] "Has she given birth ?" "yes, she has." His [of the being typical of ceremony] avabhṛtha [death] is the termination, so is the termination of the sacrifice called avabhṛtha.

6. तद्धैतद्घोर आङ्गिरसः कृष्णाय देवकीपुत्रायोक्त्वोवाचापिपास एव स बभूव सोऽन्तवेलायामेतत्त्रयं प्रतिपद्येताक्षित-मस्यच्युतमसि प्राणसंशितमसीति तत्रैते द्वे ऋचौ भवतः।।

Ghora, son of Angiras, having explained this [subject] to Kṛṣṇa son of Devakī, said : "He [who knoweth this] should, at the time of his death, repeat these three [Yajur Vedic mantras] : "O ! thou[13] art undecaying ! Thou art unchanging ! Thou art the true essence of life !" Hearing this he lost all desire for other knowledge, About it there are these two Ṛg-Vedic stanzas :

7. आदित्यव्रस्य रेतसो ज्योतिष्पश्यन्ति वासरं। परो यदिध्यते दिवा। उद्वयं तमसस्परि ज्योतिः पश्यन्त उत्तरꣳस्वः पश्यन्त उत्तरम्। देवं देवत्रा सूर्यमगन्म ज्योतिरुत्तममिति ज्योतिरुत्तममिति।।

"Sages, behold the glory of the first cause [as enveloping all like the day, and shedding radiance from the heaven above]."[14] "Having beheld that exquisite light, high above all darkness, and having beheld it also in our own hearts we attain to that god of gods and noblest of all lights the sun—the noblest of all lights."

SECTION XVIII

1. मनो ब्रह्मेत्युपासीतेत्यध्यात्ममथाधिदैवतमाकाशो ब्रह्मेत्युभयमादिष्टं भवत्यध्यात्मं चाधिदैवतं च।।

The mind should be adored as Brahman; this is intellectual [worship]. Next as relating to gods; the sky should be adored as Brahman. These are the two—intellectual and theological—forms of worship that have been ordained [by sages].

2. तदेतच्चतुष्पाद्ब्रह्म वाक् पादः प्राणः पादश्चक्षुः पादः श्रोत्रं पाद इत्यध्यात्ममथाधिदैवतमग्निः पादो वायुः पाद आदित्यः पादो दिशः पाद इत्युभयमेवादिष्टं भवत्यध्यात्मं चैवाधिदैवतं च।।

That [Brahman] hath four feet. Speech is one of its feet, life is one of its feet, vision is one of its feet, and audition is one of its feet. Thus much for the intellectual; next the theological : fire [Agni] is one of its feed, wind [Vāya] is one of its feet, sun [Āditya] is one of its feet, the quarters [Diśaḥ] are one of its feet. Thus the two—intellectual and theological forms of worship have been ordained.

3. वागेव ब्रह्मणश्चतुर्थः पादः सोऽग्निना ज्योतिषा भाति च तपति च भाति च तपति च कीर्त्या यशसा ब्रह्मवर्चसेन य एवं वेद।।

Speech is verily one of the four feet of Brahman. It radiates light and heat through the effulgence of Agni. Heat and light radiate from his works, from his fame and from his Vedic glory, who knoweth it thus.

[After explaining the meaning as above given, Śaṅkara adds] the consumption of inflammable article, such as oil or ghee, gives life and vigour to the organs of speech, hence it is said through Agni speech receives its light and heat. As a cow or a like quadruped moves on to where it wisheth on its four feet, so doth mind [here represented as Brahman] attain to its objects through the aid of speech, breath, vision and audition, hence the simile. Further, the feet of a quadruped are placed under its body, so are fire (Agni), air (Vāyu), the sun (Surya), and the quarters placed under the sky, and thence the comparison.

4. प्राण एव ब्रह्मणश्चतुर्थः पादः स वायुना ज्योतिषा भाति च तपति च भाति च तपति च कीर्त्या यशसा ब्रह्मवर्चसेन य एवं वेद।।

Breath is verily one of the four feet of Brahman. It radiates light and heat through the effulgence of Vāyu. Heat and light radiate from his works, from his fame and from his Vedic glory, who knoweth it thus.

5. चक्षुरेव ब्रह्मणश्चतुर्थः पादः स आदित्येन ज्योतिषा भाति च तपति च भाति च तपति च कीर्त्या यशसा ब्रह्मवर्चसेन य एवं वेद।।

Vision is verily one of the four feet of Brahman. It radiates light and heat through the effulgence of Āditya. Heat and light radiate from his works, from his fame and from his Vedic glory, who knoweth it thus.

6. श्रोत्रमेव ब्रह्मणश्चतुर्थः पादः स दिग्भिर्ज्योतिषा भाति च तपति च भाति च तपति च कीर्त्या यशसा ब्रह्मवर्चसेन य एवं वेद।।

Audition is verily one of the four feet of Brahman. It radiates heat and light through the effulgence of the quarters of the earth (Dik). Heat and light radiate from his works, from his fame and from his Vedic glory, who knoweth it thus.

SECTION XIX

1. आदित्यो ब्रह्मेत्यादेशस्तस्योपव्याख्यानमसदेवेदमग्र आसीत्तत्सदासीत्तत्समभवत्तदाण्डं निरवर्तत तत्संवत्सरस्य मात्रामशयत तन्निरभिद्यत ते आण्डकपाले रजतं च सुवर्णं चाभवताम्।।

The sun is described as Brahman;—its description—Verily at first all this was non-existent; that non-existence became existent; it developed,—it became an egg : it remained [quiet] for a period of one year; it burst into two; thence were formed two halves of gold and silver.

Having described the sun as a foot of Brahman, the Śruti now proceeds to describe it as Brahman, with the words : "the sun is described as Brahman." "Its description" is to be narrated for its eulogium. "Non-existent,"[15] *i.e.,* this earth before its development,[16] was of unmanifest name and form, and not actually non-existent, for [on the authority of the Śruti], "How can existence proceed from non-existence ?" Such deduction would be inadmissible. But it being distinctly laid down here that it was "non-existent," may it not be optional [with us to explain it one way or the other ?] No. Option applies to actions and not to facts. How [can you] then here [use the word] non-existent ? As I have already explained, being of unmanifest name and form, it is very like non-existence, though not actually so. The expression "verily" applies to the existence (*i.e.,* to the verb) and not to non-existence.

How [then this misuse of the term? It is no misuse]. We see the word *sat* is freely used to indicate the manifestation of the name and form of an object, and that manifestation being generally dependent upon the sun, in the absence of which the earth is enveloped in deep darkness and not visible, the expression is appropriate.

2. तद्यद्रजतꣳ सेयं पृथिवी यत्सुवर्णꣳ सा द्यौर्यज्जरायु ते पर्वता यदुल्बꣳ स मेघो नीहारो या धमनयस्ता नद्यो यद्वास्तेयमुदकꣳ स समुद्रः।।

Therefore the argentine half is the earth, and the golden half the heaven. The inner thick membrane [of the egg] became mountains, the thin one cloudy fog; the blood-vessels became rivers, and the fluid became the ocean; and lastly, what was born therefrom is the sun, Āditya.

3. अथ यत्तदजायत सोऽसावादित्यस्तं जायमानं घोषा उलूलवोऽनूदतिष्ठन्सर्वाणि च भूतानि च सर्वे च कामास्तस्मात्तस्योदयं प्रति प्रत्यायनं प्रति घोषा उलूलवोऽनूत्तिष्ठन्ति सर्वाणि च भूतानि सर्वे चैव कामाः ॥

On its birth arose loud shouts [or shouts of ulu-ulu] as well as all living beings and their desires. Hence on the rising and re-rising [day after day] of the sun arise shouts of ulu-ulu as well as all living beings and their desires.

4. स य एतमेवं विद्वानादित्यं ब्रह्मेत्युपास्तेऽभ्याशो ह यदेनं साधवो घोषा आ च गच्छेयुरुप च निम्रेडेरन्निम्रेडेरन् ॥

He [attaineth the glory of the sun] who, knowing this, adores the sun as Brahman, and grateful shouts soon arise in his behalf and contribute to his gratification,—veriiy they contribute to his gratification.

Foot Notes

1. This would indicate the existence of some Itihāsa, and Purāṇa, long anterior to the time when the extant compositions of those names were first compiled. We are, however, notwithstanding our veneration for those illustrious authors, as yet great sceptics to the dicta of Wilson and Burnouf who assign only 800 years to the oldest. Purāṇa, making the rest vary from three to five centuries.
2. By Brahman Praṇava or Om is meant, says Śaṅkara.
3. We are doubtful if "delusive opalescence" be a right rendering of "क्षोभत"
4. When the season of enjoyment is passed.
5. When the season of enjoyment returneth.
6. That which pervades all पूरणात् or abides in the heart—पुरिशयनात्.
7. The word is *divi,* (lit, glorious,) which in modern dictionaries is explained as heaven. Śaṅkara explains it as above.
8. The word in the original is *Ākas'a* आकाश. In common acceptation it means the sky, but the interpretation of Śaṅkara gives an idea as if it meant space. The difficulty of rendering the term, appositely gives a puerile air to the text.

9. Lit, Relating to Brahman.
10. Lit, दृष्टिः ocular proof. The commentator explains that the word may be used with reference to touch as an organ of perception
11. Human animosity being one of the chief causes of weeping.—*Śaṅkara.*
12. The day when the performers of a sacrifice are entitled to a drink of milk.
13. Addressing his soul as identified with the sun.
14. The words within the brackets are not quoted in the Sanskrit, text.
15. असत् asat, unreal, untrue, not being, from *sat,* true, being, with the negative prefix a अ.
16. Lit. "Utpatti," birth, creation.

FOURTH CHAPTER

SECTION I

1. ॐ जानश्रुतिर्ह पौत्रायणः श्रद्धादेयो बहुदायी बहुपाक्य आस स ह सर्वत आवसथान्मापयांचक्रे सर्वत एव मेऽत्स्यन्तीति।।

Om ! Of a truth there lived Jānaśruti, grandson of the son of Jānaśruti, the charitably disposed, the giver of large gifts, and the preparer of much food. He built houses everywhere that [people] from all sides might come and feast [therein].

2. अथ ह हꣳसा निशायामतिपेतुस्तद्धैष हꣳसो हꣳसमभ्युवाद हो होऽयि भल्लाक्ष भल्लाक्ष जानश्रुतेः पौत्रायणस्य समं दिवा ज्योतिराततं तन्माप्रसाङ्क्षीस्तत्त्वा मा प्रधाक्षीदिति।।

[Over his house] at night passed some geese,[1] the hindermost of which addressing the foremost, said. "Lo ! Lo ! Bhallākṣa, Bhallākṣa, [short-sighted] the glory of Jānaśruti, grandson of the son of Jānaśruti, is as widespreading as the heaven. Have nothing to do with him, so that his glory may not destroy thee."

3. तमु ह परः प्रत्युवाच कम्वर एनमेतत्सन्तꣳ सयुग्वानमिव रैक्वमात्थेति यो नु कथꣳ सयुग्वा रैक्व इति।।

To it said the other : "Who is he whom you compare with Raikva of the car ?" "And who is this Raikva of the car ?" enquired the first.

4. यथा कृतायविजितायाधरेयाः संयन्त्येवमेनꣳसर्वं तदभिसमेति यत्किंच प्रजाः साधु कुर्वन्ति यस्तद्वेद यत्स वेद स मयैतदुक्त इति।।

[The latter replied] "I allude to such a being to whom the fruits of all the good deeds of mankind become subservient in the same way in which all the minor numbers become due to him who hath secured the Kṛta or the highest cast of the dice, and those who know what he knows likewise secure [the same reward]."

5. यदु ह जानश्रुतिः पौत्रायण उपशुश्राव स ह संजिहान एव क्षत्तारमुवाचाङ्गारे ह सयुग्वानमिव रैक्कमात्थेति यो नु कथꣳ सयुग्वा रैक्क इति।।

Jānaśruti great-grandson of Janaśruti, listened to this. [In the morning] rising [from his bed while being eulogized by his bards] he thus addressed his herald : "O child, do you address me as if I were the Raikva of the car ? [I am not deserving of such praise]. O child, do you of a truth go and speak unto Raikva of the car [that I long to see him]." [Of him enquired the bard :] "and who is this Raikva of the car ?"

6. यथा कृतायविजितायाधरेयाः संयन्त्येवमेनꣳ सर्वं तदभिसमेति यत्किंच प्रजाः साधु कुर्वन्ति यस्तद्वेद यत्स वेद स मयैतदुक्त इति।।

[The latter replied] "I allude to such a being to whom the fruits of all the good deeds of mankind become subservient in the same way in which all the minor numbers become due to him who hath secured the Kṛta or the highest cast of the dice, and those who know what he knows likewise secure [the same reward]."

7. स ह क्षत्तान्विष्य नाविदमिति प्रत्येयाय तꣳ होवाच यत्रारे ब्राह्मणस्यान्वेषणा तदेनमर्च्छेति।।

The bard searched for him, and returning said, "I have found him not." Unto him, said [Jānaśruti], "Do ye go and look for him where the knowers of Brahman are to be met with.[2]

8. सोऽधस्ताच्छकटस्य पामानं कर्षमाणमुपोपविवेश तꣳ हाभ्युवाद त्वं नु भगवः सयुग्वा रैक्क इत्यहꣳ ह्यरा ३ इति ह प्रतिजज्ञे स ह क्षत्ताऽविदमिति प्रत्येयाय।।

He proceeded, and by one sitting beside a car and scratching his itches, sat down and said, "Art thou, O lord, Raikva of the car ?" "Yes, I am," said the other. "Now I know," [thought] the bard and retired.

SECTION II

1. तदुह जानश्रुतिः पौत्रायणः षट् शतानि गवां निष्कमश्वतरीरथं तदादाय प्रतिचक्रमे तꣳ हाभ्युवाद॥

Upon this Jānaśruti, the great-grandson of Janaśruti, taking with him six hundred head of cattle, a necklace and a chariot yoked with a pair of mules, repaired to him, and thus addressed.

2. रैक्वेमानि षट् शतानि गवामयं निष्कोऽयमश्वतरीरथो नु म एतां भगवो देवताꣳ शाधि यां देवतामुपास्स इति॥

"O Raikva, here [is a present] of six hundred head of cattle, a necklace, and a chariot yoked with a pair of mules [accept them, and deign], O Lord, to impart to me instruction on that deity whom thou adorest."

3. तमु ह परः प्रत्युवाचाह हारे त्वा शूद्र तवैव सह गोभिरस्त्विति तदुह पुनरेव जानश्रुतिः पौत्रायणः सहस्रं गवां निष्कमश्वतरीरथं दुहितरं तदादाय प्रतिचक्रमे॥

Unto his said the other, "Let these head of cattle and necklace and chariot remain with thee, O Śūdra." Hereupon, Jānaśruti, great-grandson of Janaśruti, taking a thousand head of cattle, a necklace, a chariot yoked with a pair of mules and his daughter, again returned to him.

. . . He [Jānaśruti] was a king, having a herald, as we learn [from the passage] : "He addressed to a herald," also from the fact of his repairing to a Brāhmaṇa for instruction, which would be inconsistent in a Śudra; how then did such an inapplicable expression as "O Śudra" proceed from Raikva? Sages have explained it thus. From the speech of the geese he was assailed by grief [śoka] hence Śudra; or because hearing [śrutvā] of Raikva's praise he ran [dravati] and therefoe Śudra; and the sage in order to show his omniscience used the expression "O Śudra" ; or it might be, because instead of trying to obtain knowledge by serving his tutor, he like a Śudra proceeded to gain instruction by pay for the same, and therefore is called a Śudra, although he was not of that caste. Others say, that annoyed with his small offer the sage rebuked him with the term Śudra.

4. तꣳ हाभ्युवाद रैक्वेदꣳ सहस्रं गवामयं निष्कोऽयमश्वतरीरथ इयं जायाऽयं ग्रामो यस्मिन्नास्सेऽन्वेव मा भगवः शाधीति।।

And said, "O Raikva, this [herd of a] thousand cows, this necklace, this chariot yoked with a pair of mules, this damsel, and this village in which thou dwellest [I beg to offer to thee : accept them and design] to impart to me instruction."

5. तस्या ह मुखमुपोद्गृह्णन्नुवाचाजहारेमाः शूद्रानेनैव मुखेनाला-पयिष्यथा इति ते हैते रैक्वपर्णानाम महावृषेषु यत्रास्मा उवास तस्मै होवाच।।

Knowing her, [the damsel,] to be the cause of his imparting instruction, [Raikva] said : "Hast thou brought her [for me], O Śudra? she will be the cause of my conversing with thee." Hence are these villages in this country of great virtue [mahāvṛṣa] where he lived, called Raikvaparṇa. Unto him explained he [the nature of the deity he adored].

SECTION III

1. वायुर्वाव संवर्गो यदा वा अग्निरुद्वायति वायुमेवाप्येति यदा सूर्योऽस्तमेति वायुमेवाप्येति यदा चन्द्रोऽस्तमेति वायुमेवाप्येति।।

The air [Vāyu] is verily the ultimatum [saṁvarga] of all. When a fire goes out, of a truth it merges into air [Vāyu]. When the sun doth disappear it verily mergeth into air, so doth the moon when it setteth.

2. यदाप उच्छुष्यन्ति वायुमेवापियन्ति वायुर्ह्येवैतान्सर्वान्संवृङ्क्त इत्यधिदैवतम्।।

When waters dry they vanish in air; the air verily consumeth all. Thus much relating to celestial objects.

3. अथाध्यात्मं प्राणो वाव संवर्गः स यदा स्वपिति प्राणमेव वागप्येति प्राणं चक्षुः प्राणꣳ श्रोत्रं प्राणं मनः प्राणो ह्येवैतान्सर्वान्संवृङ्क्त इति।।

Next as relating to self. Life is verily the ultimatum of all. When man sleepeth, speech mergeth into life, so doth vision merge into life, audition merge into life, and mind merge into life,—Life verily consumeth all.

4. तौ वा एतौ द्वौ संवर्गौ वायुरेव देवेषु प्राणः प्राणेषु।।

These are verily the two ultimata [saṁvarge] ; Vāyu among the celestial objects and life among the animal functions.

5. अथ ह शौनकं च कापेयमभिप्रतारिणं च काक्षसेनि परिविष्यमाणौ ब्रह्मचारी बिभिक्षे तस्मा उ ह न ददतुः।।

[Once] while Śaunaka of the race of Kapi, and Abhipratārin, son of Kakṣa-sena, were being served at their meals a Brahmacārin sought alms of them. Unto him they gave nothing.[3]

6. स होवाच महात्मनश्चतुरो देव एकः कः स जगार भुवनस्य गोपास्तं कापेय नाभिपश्यन्ति मर्त्या अभिप्रतारिन्बहुधा वसन्तं यस्मै वा एतदन्नं तस्मा एतन्न दत्तमिति।।

He said, "He [the Prajāpati] who swalloweth the venerable four,[4] and is the protector of the earth, O descendant of Kāpi, is not seen by mortals. O Abhipratārin, he exists in various forms. For him is food prepared, and him have you denied.[5]

7. तदु ह शौनकः कापेयः प्रतिमन्वानः प्रत्येयायात्मा देवानां जनिता प्रजानाꣳ हिरण्यदꣳ ष्ट्रो बभसोऽनसूरिर्महान्तमस्य महिमानमाहुरनद्यमानो यदनन्नमत्तीति वै वयं ब्रह्मचारिन्नेदमुपास्महे दत्तास्मै भिक्षामिति।।

Śaunaka, descendant of Kāpi, reflected within himself and returned [for answer] : "Life is the author of the gods and of the creation. His teeth are immutable; he is a great consumer; he is not unintelligent; his greatness is said to be extreme; none can consume him, and he consumeth all food. We, O Brahmācārin, adore such a Brahman." [Then turning to his servant, said]" Give him some alms."

8. तस्मा उ ह ददुस्ते वा एते पञ्चान्ये पञ्चान्ये दश संतस्तत्कृतं तस्मात्सर्वासु दिक्ष्वन्नमेव दशकृतꣳ सैषा विराडन्नादी तयेदꣳ सर्वं दृष्टꣳ सर्वमस्येदं दृष्टं भवत्यन्नादो भवति य एवं वेद॥

The servant] gave him [some]. These five and five [the two ultimata] make ten and they are a Kṛta [complete number]. Therefore the aliment in all the different quarters being ten, is a Kṛta. It [the complete number] is Virāt, the consumer of food. Through it, all this becomes visible. Unto him who knoweth–verily unto him who knoweth—this, all this [world] becomes visible, and he becomes a [great] consumer of food.

Section IV

1. सत्यकामो हं जाबालो जबाला मातरमामन्त्रयांचक्रे ब्रह्मचर्यं भवति विवत्स्यामि किंगोत्रोऽहमस्मीति॥

Satyakāma Jābālā enquired of his mother Jabālā : "I long to abide [by a tutor] as a Brahmacārin; of what gotra am I ?"

2. सा हैनमुवाच नाहमेतद्वेद तात यद्गोत्रस्त्वमसि बह्वहं चरन्ती परिचारिणी यौवने त्वामलभे साहमेतन्न वेद यद्गोत्रस्त्वमसि जबाला तु नामाहमस्मि सत्यकामो नाम त्वमसि स सत्यकाम एव जाबालो ब्रुवीथा इति॥

She said unto him, "I know not, child, of what gotra you are. During my youth when I got thee I was engaged in attending on many [guestes who frequented the house of my husband and had no opportunity of making any inquiry on the subject], I know not of what gotra you are, Jabālā is my name and Satyakāma thine; say, therefore, of thyself, Satyakāma, son of Jabālā [when any body enquireth of thee]."

3. स ह हारिद्रुमतं गौतममेत्योवाच ब्रह्मचर्यं भगवति वत्स्याम्युपेयां भगवन्तमिति॥

He repaired to Hāridrumata of the Gautama gotra and said, "approach your venerable self to abide by your worship as a Brahmacārin."

4. तꣳ होवाच किंगोत्रो नु सोम्यासीति स होवाच नाहमेतद्वेद भो यद्गोत्रोऽहमस्म्यपृच्छं मातरꣳ सा मा प्रत्यब्रवीद्बह्वहं चरन्ती परिचारिणी यौवने त्वामलभे साहमेतन्न वेद यद्गोत्रस्त्वमसि जबाला तु नामाहमस्मि सत्यकामो नाम त्वमसीति सोऽहꣳ सत्यकामो जाबालोऽस्मि भो इति॥

Of him enquired he [the tutor] : "Of what gotra are you, my good boy ?" He replied : "I know not of what gotra I am. I enquired about it of my mother and she said, 'In my youth when I got thee I was engaged in attending on many, and know not of what gotra you are; Jabālā is my name and Satyakāma thine' : I am that Satyakāma son of Jabālā."

5. तꣳ होवाच नैतदब्राह्मणो विवक्तुमर्हति समिधꣳ सोम्याहरोपत्वा नेष्ये न सत्यादगा इति तमुपनीय कृशानामबलानां चतुःशता गा निराकृत्योवाचेमाः सोम्यानुसंव्रजेति ता अभिप्रस्थापयन्नुवाच नासहस्रेणावर्तयेति स ह वर्षगणं प्रोवास ता यदा सहस्रꣳ संपेदुः॥

Unto him said the other, "None but a Brāhman can say so. You have not departed from the truth, and I shall invest you [with the brāhmanical rites]. Do you collect, child, the necessary sacrificial wood ?" Having ordained him, he selected four hundred head of lean and weakly cows and said, "Do you, child, attend to these." While leading the cows, he [the neophyte] said, "I shall not return until these become a thousand." Thus he passed many years, until the cattle had multiplied to a thousand.

SECTION V

1. अथ हैनमृषभोऽभ्युवाद सत्यकाम ३ इति भगव इति ह प्रतिशुश्राव प्राप्ताः सोम्य सहस्रꣳ स्मः प्रापय न आचार्यकुलम्॥

A Bull said unto him, "O Satyakāma !" He replied "Sir," the Bull said, "We have now come to thousand, do you take us back to your tutor.

2. ब्रह्मणश्च ते पादं ब्रवाणीति ब्रवीतु मे भगवानिति तस्मै होवाच प्राची दिक्कला प्रतीची दिक्कला दक्षिणा दिक्कलोदीची दिक्कलैष वे सोम्य चतुष्कलः पादो ब्रह्मणः प्रकाशवान्नाम॥

"I will relate to you,[6] something regarding Brahman." "Relate it to me, Sir [if you please]." It said unto him, "the eastern quarter is a portion, the western quarter is a portion, the southern quarter is a portion, the northern quarter is a portion ; these are the four portions, of a fourth food of Brahman. It is called *Prakāśavān* [renowned].

3. स य एतमेवं विद्वाꣳश्चतुष्कलं पादं ब्रह्मणः प्रकाशवानित्यु–पास्ते प्रकाशवानस्मिँल्लोके भवति प्रकाशवतो ह लोकाञ्जयति य एतमेवं विद्वाꣳश्चतुष्कलं पादं ब्रह्मणः प्रकाशवानित्यपास्ते॥

"He becomes renowned in this world, who knowing thus adoreth the four membered foot of Brahman as the renowned. He overcomes all renowned regions, who knowing thus adoreth the four membered foot of Brahman as the renowned.

SECTION VI

1. अग्निष्टे पादं वक्तेति स ह श्वोभूते गा अभिप्रस्थापयांचकार ता यत्राभि सायं बभूवुस्तत्राग्निमुपसमाधाय गा उपरुध्य समिधमाधाय पश्चादग्नेः प्राङुपोपविवेश॥

"Agni will explain to you [the nature of] the next foot of

Brahman." On the morrow he [the cow-herd] turned towards his tutor with the cattle. When night arrived he lighted a fire, folded the cattle, placed fuel on the fire, and sat behind it facing the east.[7]

2. तमग्निरभ्युवाद सत्काम ३ इति भगव इति ह प्रतिशुश्राव।।

Unto him said Agni, "O Satyakāma !" "Lord," responded the other.

3. ब्रह्मणः सोम्य ते पादं ब्रवाणीति ब्रवीतु मे भगवानिति तस्मै होवाच पृथिवी कलान्तरिक्षं कला द्यौः कला समुद्रः कलैष वै सोम्य चतुष्कलः पादो ब्रह्मणोऽनन्तवान्नाम।।

"Child, I will explain to you a foot of Brahman." "Explain it, Sir, if you please." Unto him said the other, "the earth is a part, the sky is a part, the heaven is a part, the ocean is a part;—these four parts, O child, constitute the foot of Brahman called the endless [Anantavān].

4. स य एतमेवं वद्वाँश्चतुष्कलं पादं ब्रह्मणोऽनन्तवानित्युपास्तेऽनन्तवानस्मिँल्लोके भवत्यनन्तवतो ह लोकाञ्जयति य एतमेवं विद्वाँश्चतुष्कलं पादं ब्रह्मणोऽनन्तवानित्यु- पास्ते।।

"He becomes endless[8] even in this world, who knowing this adores the four membered foot of Brahman as the endless; he conquers the regions of the immortals, who knowing this adores the four-membered foot of Brahman as the endless.

SECTION VII

1. हंस्ते पादं वक्तेति स ह श्वोभूते गा अभिप्रस्थापयांचकार ता यत्राभिसायं बभूवुस्तत्राग्निमुपसमाधाय गा उपरुध्य समिधमाधाय पश्चादग्नेः प्राङुपोपविवेश।।

"The sun will explain to you the nature of the next foot of Brahman." On the morrow he started again towards the house of his tutor, and when night approached he lighted a fire, folded the cattle, placed fuel on the fire and sat behind it facing the east.

2. तं हंस उप निपत्याभ्युवाद सत्यकाम ३ इति भगव इति ह प्रतिशुश्राव।।

The sun approaching him said, "O Satyakāma ! "Lord," responded the other.

3. ब्रह्मणः सोम्य ते पादं ब्रवाणीति ब्रवीतु मे भगवानिति तस्मै होवाचाग्निः कला सूर्यः कला चन्द्रः कला विद्युत्कलैष वै सोम्य चतुष्कलः पादो ब्रह्मणो ज्योतिष्मान्नाम।।

"I will relate to thee a foot of Brahman," said he. "Relate, O Lord," said the second. [Unto him, said the first], "the fire [Agni] is a part, the sun [Śūrya] is a part, the moon [Candra] is a part, the lightning is a part;—these four parts, O child, constitute the foot of Brahman as the radiant.

4. स य एतमेवं विद्वांश्चतुष्कलं पादं ब्रह्मणो ज्योतिष्मानित्युपास्ते ज्योतिष्मानस्मिँल्लोके भवति ज्योतिष्मतो ह लोकाञ्जयति य एतमेवं विद्वांश्चतुष्कलं पादं बह्मणो ज्योतिष्मानित्युपास्ते।।

"He becomes radiant in this world, who knowing this adores the four membered foot of Brahman as the radiant,—he overcomes the region of the radiant,[9] who knowing this adores the four membered foot of Brahman as the radiant."

Section VIII

1. मद्गुष्टे पादं वक्तेति स ह श्वोभूते गा अभिप्रस्थापयांचकार ता यत्राभिसायं बभूवुस्तत्राग्निमुपसमाधाय गा उपरुध्य समिधमाधाय पश्चादग्नेः प्राङुपोपविवेश।।

"The Madgu [wind] will explain to you the nature of the next foot of Brahman." On the morrow he started again towards the house of his tutor, and when night approached, he lighted a fire, folded the cattle, placed fuel on the fire and sat behind it, facing the east.

2. तं मद्गुरुपनिपत्याभ्युवाद सत्यकाम ३ इति भगव इति
तं प्रतिशुश्राव ।।

The wind approaching hims said, "O Satyakāma !" "Lord," responded the other.

3. ब्रह्मणः सोम्य ते पादं ब्रवाणीति ब्रवीतु मे भगवानिति
तस्मै होवाच प्राणः कला चक्षुः कला श्रोत्रं कला मनः
कलैष वै सोम्य चतुष्कलः पादो ब्रह्मण आयतनवान्नाम ।।

"I will explain to thee, O child, a foot of Brahman," said the first. "Relate, O lord," returned he. Unto him said the first : "Life is a part, the eyes are a part, the ears are a part, the mind is a part;—these four parts constitute the foot of Brahman called the Spacious [ĀYATANAVĀN].

4. स य एतमेवं विद्वांश्चतुष्कलं पादं ब्रह्मण आयतनवानित्युपास्त
आयतनवानस्मिँल्लोके भवत्यायतनवतो ह लोकाञ्जयति य
एतमेवं विद्वांश्चतुष्कलं पादं ब्रह्मण आयतनवानित्युपास्ते ।।

"He becomes the receptacle of many, in this world, who, knowing this, adores the four-membered foot of Brahman as the Spacious; he attains to the region of the Spacious who, knowing this, adores the four-membered foot of Brahman as the Spacious."

SECTION IX

1. प्राप हाचार्यकुलं तमाचार्योऽभ्युवाद सत्यकाम ३ इति
भगव इति ह प्रतिशुश्राव ।।

He reached the house of his tutor. Unto him said the tutor. "O Satyakāma" "Lord," responded he.

2. ब्रह्मविदिव वै सोम्य भासि को नु त्वानुशशासेत्यन्ये
मनुष्येभ्य इति ह प्रतिजज्ञे भगवांस्त्वेव मे कामं ब्रूयात् ।।

"Child ! you speak as if you knew Brahman; who has given

thee instruction ?" "Other than man," said he, and added. "Instruct me as I wish to hear of it from you."

3. श्रुतꣳ ह्येव मे भगवद्दृशेभ्य आयार्चाद्ध्येव विद्या विदिता साधिष्ठं प्रापतीति तस्मै हैतदेवोवाचात्र ह न किंचन वीयायेति वीयायेति।।

"I have heard from sages like unto yourself that knowledge got from tutors is most excellent," Accordingly he related every thing [as narrated above] omitting,—verily omitting nothing.

SECTION X

1. उपकोसलो ह वै कामलायनः सत्यकामे जाबाले ब्रह्मचर्यमुवास तस्य ह द्वादशवर्षाण्यग्नीन्परिचचार स ह स्मान्यानन्तेवासिनः समावर्तयꣳ स्तꣳ ह स्मैव न समावर्तयति।।

Of a truth Upakosala, son of Kamala, (Kāmalāyana) abided by Satyakāma, son of Jabālā, as a Brahmacārin, and for twelve years carefully attended his household fires. The tutor granted leave to his other pupils to return home, but refused that indulgence to him.

2. तं जायोवाच तप्तो ब्रह्मचारी कुशलमग्नीन्परिचचारीन्मा त्वाग्नयः परिप्रवोचन्प्रब्रूह्यस्मा इति तस्मै हाप्रोच्यैव प्रवासांचक्रे।।

To the tutor said his wife. "This exhausted Brahmacārin has successfully attended the household fires; let not the fires upbraid thee; explain to him [what he wants]." He [the tutor], without [condescending to grant the] explanation, went out on his pilgrimage.

3. स ह व्याधिनानशितुं दध्रे तमाचार्यजायोवाच ब्रह्मचारिन्नशान किंनु नाश्नासीति स होवाच बहव इमेऽस्मिन्पुरुषे कामा नानात्यया व्याधिभिः प्रतिपूर्णोऽस्मि नाशिष्यामीति।।

The disciple fell ill and abstained from food. Unto him said the wife of the tutor; "Brahmacārin, take food ; why abstain from sustenance ?" He replied : "Many and variously disposed are my desires; I am full of diseases and shall take no food."

4. अथ हाग्रयः समूदिरे तप्तो ब्रह्मचारी कुशलं नः पर्यचारीद्धन्तास्मै प्रब्रवामेति तस्मै होचुः।।

Next, verily, the fires said : "This exhausted Brahmacārin has carefully attended us, we will explain unto him [what he wants]," and then continued :

5. प्राणो ब्रह्म कं ब्रह्म खं ब्रह्मेति स होवाच विजानाम्यहं यत्प्राणो ब्रह्म कं च तु खं च न विजानामीति ते होचुर्यद्वाव कं तदेव खं यदेव खं तदेव कमिति प्राणं च हास्मै तदाकाशं चोचुः।।

"Life [prāṇa] is Brahman, Ka is Brahman and Kha is Brahman." He replied : "I know the Prāṇa to be Brahman, but know not Ka nor Kha." They said : "Verily, that which is Ka is Kha, and that which is Kha is Ka." They spoke, of a truth, of life and the sky.

. . . That [happiness] which has been indicated by ka is likewise kha, the sky. As the epithet bluish added to red alters the original signification of the latter term, so ka (happiness) qualified as above becomes distinct from that which proceeds from the attainment of sensual objects by the organs of sense. The sky to which we allude by the term kha is the happiness indicated by the term ka. Thus the kha [sky] qualified by happiness becomes distinct from the elemental inanimate object indicated by kha, on the logic of the aforesaid bluish-red. The meaning is "a happiness depending on the sky, and not a worldly one; and a sky which is the receptacle of happiness, but not the element so called". But if you wish to qualify sky by happiness and make the latter the adjective [allowing the clause of stand thus] : "That which is happiness [ka] is the sky," you make the rest of the passage redundant, or if you take the latter clause : "That which is the sky [kha] is happiness," the first becomes unnecessary ? Why this argument, when I have already explained that the object is to exclude both terrestrial happiness and the material sky ? By qualifying the sky by happiness, are not both the primitive objects excluded by virtue of their meaning ? True. But by qualifying the sky by happiness only the former—and not also the happiness qualified by the epithet sky—becomes the object of meditation; as the effect of an adjective relating to its substantive ceaseth with qualifying the same.

Hence it is necessary to qualify the happiness by the sky to indicate that likewise is an object of meditation.

SECTION XI

1. अथ हैनं गार्हपत्योऽनुशशास पृथिव्यग्निरन्नमादित्य इति य एष आदित्ये पुरुषो दृश्यते सोऽहमस्मि स एवाहमस्मीति।।

Next, Gārhapatya (the household fire) instructed him, [saying] : "Earth, fire, aliment and the sun [constitute my body]. Thereof the being who is seen in the sun, is I,—verily I am he.

2. स य एतमेवं विद्वानुपास्तेऽपहते पापकृत्यां लोकीभवति सर्वमायुरेति ज्योग्जीवति नास्यावरपुरुषाः क्षीयन्त उप वयं तं भुञ्जामोऽस्मिंश्च लोकेऽमुष्मिंश्च य एतमेवं विद्वानुपास्ते।।

"He destroyed sin who, knowing this, adoreth him; he attaineth the region [of Agni], enjoyeth the full limit of existence, passeth his life in glory, and his race waste not. We support him in this and other regions who, knowing this, adoreth him [the household fire]."

SECTION XII

1. अथ हैनमन्वाहार्यपचनोऽनुशशासापो दिशो नक्षत्राणि चन्द्रमा इति य एष चन्द्रमसि पुरुषो दृश्यते सोऽहमस्मि स एवाहमस्मीति।।

Next, Anvāhāryapacana [fire] instructed him [saying] : "Water, the quarters of the globe, the stars and the moon [constitute my body]. Thereof the being who is seen in the moon is I,—verily I am he.

2. स य एतमेवं विद्वानुपास्तेऽपहते पापकृत्यां लोकीभवति सर्वमायुरेति ज्योग्जीवति नास्यावरपुरुषाः क्षीयन्त उप वयं तं भुञ्जामोऽस्मिंश्च लोकेऽमुष्मिंश्च य एतमेवं विद्वानुपास्ते।।

"He destroyeth sin who, knowing this adoreth him; he attaineth the region [of that fire], enjoyeth the full limit of existence, passeth his life in glory, and his race waste not. We support him in this and other regions who, knowing this, adoreth him [the Anvātrārya-pacana fire]."

SECTION XIII

1. अथ हैनमाहवनीयोऽनुशशास प्राण आकाशो द्यौर्विद्युदिति य एष विद्युति पुरुषो दृश्यते सोऽहमस्मि स एवाहमस्मीति ।।

Next Āhavanīya [fire] instructed him [saying] : "The life, the sky, the heaven and lightning [constitute my body]. Thereof the being who is seen in lightning is I,—verily I am he.

2. स य एतमेवं विद्वानुपास्तेऽपहते पापकृत्यां लोकीभवति सर्वमायुरेति ज्योग्जीवति नास्यावरपुरुषाः क्षीयन्त उप वयं तं भुञ्जामोऽस्मिꣳश्च लोकेऽमुष्मिꣳश्च य एतमेवं विद्वानुपास्ते ।।

"He destroyeth sin who, knowing this, adoreth him; he attaineth the region [of that Agni], enjoyeth the full limit of existence, passeth his life in glory, and his race waste not. We support him in this and other regions who, knowing this, adoreth him [the Āhavanīya fire]."

SECTION XIV

1. ते होचुरुपकोसलैषा सोम्य तेऽस्मद्विद्यात्मविद्या चाचार्यस्तु ते गतिं वक्तेत्याजगाम हास्याचार्यस्तमाचार्योऽभ्युवादो-पकोसल ३ इति ।।

They [the different fires together] said : "Child Upakosala, [we have now explained] to you the knowledge relating to ourselves and to the soul. Your tutor will explain to you the fruit of that knowledge." [At this time] the tutor returned [from his pilgrimage] and addressed his pupil [saying] : "O Upakosals !"

2. भगव इति ह प्रतिशुश्राव ब्रह्मविद इव सोम्य ते मुखं भाति को नु त्वानुशशासेति को नु मानुशिष्याद्भो इतीहापेव निह्नुत इमे नूनमीदृशा अन्यादृशा इतीहाग्नीनभ्यूदे किं नु सोम्य किल तेऽवोचन्निति।।

"Sir," returned he. "Child, your appearance shines like that of the knowers of Brahman : who has given thee instruction ?" He replied : [as if to make a secret] "Who will instruct me, Sir ?" And then pointing to the fires said [of them] : "These verily that are thus, were otherwise." "Did they, child, speak unto you ?" inquired the tutor.

3. इदमिति ह प्रतिजज्ञे लोकान्वाव किल सोम्य तेऽवोचन्नहं तु वे तद्वक्ष्यामि यथा पुष्करपलाश आपो न श्लिष्यन्त एवमेवंविदि पापं कर्म न श्लिष्यत इति ब्रवीतु मे भगवानिति तस्मै होवाच।।

"Even so," responded the pupil. [The tutor said] : "Child, they have spoken to you abot regions, I too will speak to you about them; as water attacheth not unto the leaf of the lotus, so doth sin attach not unto him who understands them." "Relate it then unto me, Sir," [the pupil] unto him.

Section XV

1. य एषोऽक्षिणि पुरुषो दृश्यत एष आत्मेति होवाचैतदमृतम–भयमेतद्ब्रह्मेति तद्यद्यप्यस्मिन्सर्पिर्वोदकं वा सिञ्चति वर्त्मनी एव गच्छति।।

"That being who is seen within the eyes, is verily the soul," said [the tutor] : "He is deathless and fearless; he is Brahman ; should any ghee or water drop on him, that passeth away.

2. एतꣳ संयद्वाम इत्याचक्षत एतꣳ हि सर्वाणि वामान्यभिसंयन्ति सर्वाण्येनं वामान्यभिसंयन्ति य एवं वेद।।

"He is called Saṁyadvāma ; all adorable objects [vāma] merge into him; all adorable objects merge into him who knoweth this.

3. एष उ एव वामनीरेष हि सर्वाणि वामानि नयति सर्वाणि
वामानि नयति य एवं वेद॥

"Oh ! he is verily the great Receptacle, for all adorable objects merge into him; all adorable objects merge into him who knoweth this.

4. एष उ एव भामनीरेष हि सर्वेषु लोकेषु भाति सर्वेषु
लोकेषु भाति य एवं वेद॥

"It is verily Refulgent [Bhāmanī], for it shines everywhere.[10] He becomes refulgent everywhere who knoweth this.

5. अथ यदु चैवास्मिञ्छव्यं कुर्वन्ति यदि च नार्चिषमेवाभि-
संभवन्त्यर्चिषोऽहरह्न आपूर्यमाणपक्षमापूर्यमाणपक्षा-
द्यान्षडुदङ्ङेति मासाꣳस्तान्मासेभ्य संवत्सरꣳ संवत्सरादा-
दित्यमादित्याच्चन्द्रमसं चन्द्रमसो विद्युतं तत्पुरुषोऽमानवः॥

"Now, whether any funeral service be performed with reference to him [the knower of the Refulgent] or not, still after death he obaineth the regents of the sun-beams [Arciḥ]; thence he passeth to the regents of day [Ahaḥ], thence to the regents of the light fortnight, thence to those of the six months during which the sun moves to the north of the equator, thence to those of the year, thence to the sun, thence to the moon, and thence to the regents of lightning; whence an unearthly being.

6. स एनान्ब्रह्म गमयत्येष देवपथो ब्रह्मपथ एतेन प्रतिपद्यमाना
इमं मानवमावर्तं नावर्तन्ते नावर्तन्ते॥

"Takes such knowers to [the region of] Brahman. This is the way to gods [Deva patha];—this the way to Brahman [Brahma-patha]. Those who betake to this path return not—verily return not—to this mortal sphere."[11]

... "He takes away such knowers to Brahman" in the Satyaloka [the region of truth], as is evident from the allusion to the goer, the place to go, and the conductor, in the attainment of the true Brahman, such expressions would be inapplicable; in that case, "becoming Brahman he attained Brahman," would be the most appropriate expression.[12]

Section XVI

1. एष ह वै यज्ञो योयं पवत एष ह यान्नदः सर्वं पुनाति यदेष यन्निदः सर्वं पुनाति तस्मादेष एव यज्ञस्तस्य मनश्च वाक्च वर्तनी ।।

Verily that which bloweth, is sacrifice [Yajña,] for blowing it purifieth all this. Because blowing it purifieth, hence is it Yajña, of which mind and speech are the two paths.

2. तयोरन्यतरां मनसा सꣳस्करोति ब्रह्मा वाचा होताध्वर्युरुद्गातान्यतराꣳ स यत्रोपाकृते प्रातरनुवाके पुरा परिधानीयाया ब्रह्मा व्यववदति ।।

Of the two paths the first is purified by Brahmā[13] through his mind. The second is purified by the Hotā, the Adhvaryu and the Udgātā through speech. In such cases a Brahmā after commencing the morning ritual, but before the recitation of the closing verses of the Ṛk, speaketh.

3. अन्यतरामेव वर्तनीꣳ सꣳस्करोति हीयतेऽन्यतरा स यथैकपाद्व्रजन्रथो वैकेन चक्रेण वर्तमानो रिष्यत्येवमस्य यज्ञो रिष्यति यज्ञꣳ रिष्यन्तं यजमानोऽनुरिष्यति स इष्ट्वा पापीयान्भवति ।।

The last of the two paths may be purified, but the former is defiled, and the sacrifice goes wrong as the man of one leg or a one-wheeled car goeth astray. On the failure of the sacrifice, the institutor faileth, and by the performance of that ceremony becomes sinful.

4. अथ यत्रोपाकृते प्रातरनुवाके न पुरा परिधानीयाया ब्रह्मा व्यववदत्युभे एव वर्तनी सꣳस्कुर्वन्ति न हीयतेऽन्यतरा ।।

Next, where, after the commencement of the morning ritural, but before the recitation of the closing Ṛk Verses, the Brahmā speaketh not, [the performers of the ceremony] purify both the paths, and none is defiled :

5. स यथोभयपाद्व्रजन्नथो वोभाभ्यां चक्राभ्यां वर्तमानः प्रतितिष्ठत्येवमस्य यज्ञः प्रतितिष्ठति यज्ञं प्रतितिष्ठन्तं यजमानोऽनु प्रतितिष्ठति स इष्ट्वा श्रेयान्भवति॥

And as a man walking on two legs or a car mounted on two wheels standeth firm, so doth such sacrifice stand firm; in the confirmation of the sacrifice, the institutor standeth firm, and the performers of the ceremony become great.

SECTION XVII

1. प्रजापतिर्लोकानभ्यतपत्तेषां तप्यमानानाꣳ रसान्प्रावृहदग्निं पृथिव्या वायुमन्तरिक्षादादित्यं दिवः॥

Prajāpati reflected on regions, and from the reflected, extracted their essences, *viz.*, Fire from the earth, Air from the sky, and the Sun from heaven.

2. स एतास्तिस्रो देवता अभ्यतपत्तासां तप्यमानानाꣳ रसान्प्रावृहदग्नेर्ऋचो वायोर्यजूꣳषि सामान्यादित्यात्॥

He reflected on the three gods, Fire, Air and the Sun, and from the reflected extracted their essences, *viz.*, the Ṛk from Agni, the Yajus from Vāyu [air], and the Sāma from the Sun.

3. स एतां त्रयीं विद्यामभ्यतपत्तस्यास्तप्यमानाया रसान् प्रावृहद्भूरित्यृग्भ्यो भुवरिति यजुर्भ्यः स्वरिति सामभ्यः॥

He reflected on the three-fold knowledge and from the reflected extracted its essences, *viz.*, Bhūḥ [the word] from the Ṛk, Bhuvaḥ [the word] from the Yajus, and Svaḥ [the word] from the Sāma.

4. तद्यद्यृक्तो रिष्येद्भूः स्वाहेति गार्हपत्ये जुहुयादृचामेव तद्रसेनर्चां वीर्येणर्चां यज्ञस्य विरिष्टꣳसंदधाति॥

[In the performance of a ceremony] should any Ṛk hymn happen to be misused [the performer of that sacrifice] should offer an oblation to the Gārhapatya [household] fire, [saying] : "May this prove acceptable to Bhu !" [Bhūḥ Svāhā.] [The Ṛk in that case] by its essence and majesty corrects all the improprieties of the Yajña, as far as they relate to the Ṛk hymns.

5. अथ यदि यजुष्टो रिष्येद्भुवः स्वाहेति दक्षिणाग्नौ जुहुयाद्यजुषामेव तद्रसेन यजुषां वीर्येण यजुषां यज्ञस्य विरिष्टꣳसंदधाति ।।

Now should any Yajus hymn happen to be misused [he] should offer an oblation to the Dakṣinā [Southern] fire, [saying] : "May this prove acceptable to Bhuva !" [Bhuvaḥ Svāhā.] [The Yajus in that case] by its essence and majesty corrects all the improprieties of the Yajña, as far as they relate to the Yajur hymns.

6. अथ यदि सामतो रिष्येत्स्वः स्वाहेत्याहवनीये जुहुयात्साम्नामेव तद्रसेन साम्नां वीर्येण साम्नां यज्ञस्य विरिष्टꣳसंदधाति ।।

Now, should any Sāma hymn happen to be misused, he should offer an oblation to the Ahavanīya fire [saying]. "May this prove acceptable to Sva." [Svaḥ Svāhā.] [The Sāma in that case] by its essence and majesty corrects all the improprieties of the Yajña, as far as they relate to the Sāma hymns.

7. तद्यथा लवणेन सुवर्णꣳ संदध्यात्सुवर्णेन रजतꣳ रजतेन त्रपु त्रपुणा सीसꣳ सीसेन लोहं लोहेन दारु दारु चर्मणा ।।

As gold is corrected by borax, and silver by gold, and tin by silver, and lead by tin, and iron by lead, and wood by iron or leather.

8. एवमेषां लोकानामासां देवतानामस्यास्त्रय्या विद्याया वीर्येण यज्ञस्य विरिष्टꣳ संदधाति भेषजकृतो ह वा एष यज्ञो यत्रैवंविद्ब्रह्मा भवति ।।

So doth the majesty of these regions, of these gods and of these three systems of knowledge, correct the improprieties of the sacrifice. That sacrifice becomes efficacious of which the Brahmā is conscient of all this.

9. एष ह वा उदक्प्रवणो यज्ञो यत्रैवंविद्ब्रह्मा भवत्येवंविदꣳ ह वा एषा ब्रह्माणमनुगाथा यतो यत आवर्तते तत्तद्गच्छति ।।

That sacrifice slopeth to the north[14] of which the Brahmā knoweth all this. With reference to the Brahmā who knoweth all this there is this verse [extant] : "Whenever any flaw happeneth in a ceremony [this knowledge of the Brahmā] setteth everything to right."

10. मानवो ब्रह्मैवैक ऋत्विक्कुरूनश्वाभिरक्षत्येवंविद्ध वै ब्रह्मा यज्ञं यजमानꣳ सर्वांश्चर्त्विजोऽभिरक्षति तस्मादेवंविदमेव ब्रह्माणं कुर्वीत नानेवंविदं नानेवंविदम् ॥

Such a willing Brahmā is verily the chief priest. Like as warriors are defended by their mares,[15] so doth such a knowing Brahmā preserve the sacrifice, its institutor, and all the officiating priests. Therefore, of a truth, such knowing Brahmās should perform ceremonies and not those who know not—not those who know not [their duty].

Foot Notes

1. Haṁsa. This word in common acceptation means a goose, but the vehicle of Brahma likewise called a Haṁsa, is generally represented of the form of a flamingo. According to the Purāṇas, the Mānasasarovara (lake) is a favourite resort of Haṁsas which in modern Tibetan or rather in the language of the people of the Hun desa is the specific name of the flamingo. We may add that while geese are very scarce, flamingoes are seen in large flocks, in the vicinity of Mānasasarovara (lake).
2. In lovely places near rivers and pools in mountains and groves.—Śaṅkara.
3. In order to see what may follow, adds Śaṅkara.
4. Agni [fire], Sūrya [sun], Candra [moon], and Āpaḥ [water].
5. This verse may be translated interrogatively and begin with; "who is he who swalloweth," etc.
6. Lit. a fourth—पाद.
7. And reflecting on the advice of the bull, adds the Commentator.
8. *i.e.,* His race never becomes extinct—Ānandagiri.
9. Gods.
10. Lit., in all regions.
11. Lit., Region of the descendants of Manu.

12. The drift of the argument is that in the attainment of the allpervading truthful Brahman, no translation to a higher sphere or the reliance on any particular guide or path is necessary, the attainment being immediate and independent of all secondary means.
13. Sacrifices with the juice of the moon plant are performed by four officiating priests; of these the first is called Brahmā and his office is to superintend the performance and to instruct the other priests in their respective duties. The second, Hotā, pours the oblations on the fire; the third, Adhvaryu, repeats the Yajur Vedic mantras, and the fourth, Udgātā, singeth the Sāma hymns.
14. *i.e.,* it prepareth the way to the attainment of knowledge. The way of the jñāni is called *Uttaramārga,* or the "northern passage," and that which slopes towards it necessarily makes that passage easy of acquisition.
15. It is a common notion with Oriental warriors that in speed, bottom and courage, mares are superior to horses, and that in the battlefield the former exert their utmost often at the risk of their own lives, for the preservation of their riders. It is on this account that the Mahratha cavalry is invariably supplied with mares.

FIFTH CHAPTER

Section I

1. ॐ। यो ह वै ज्येष्ठं च श्रेष्ठं च वेद ज्येष्ठश्च ह वै श्रेष्ठश्च भवति प्राणो वाव ज्येष्ठश्च श्रेष्ठश्च।।

Om ! Verily he becomes the eldest and greatest who knows the Eldest and Greatest (jyeṣṭha-sreṣṭha). Life is verily the Eldest and Greatest.

2. यो ह वै वसिष्ठं वेद वसिष्ठो ह स्वानां भवति वाग्वाव वसिष्ठः।।

He who knows that which is the Envelope [of the world; Vasiṣṭha] becomes the protector of his people. Speech his verily the Envelope.

"Vasiṣṭha," the envelope or cover of this world, from Vāsa;—or wealthy, from *Vasu* wealth. Speech is described as the Envelope, because it comprehends all; or Wealthy because wealth may be earned by it.

3. यो ह वै प्रतिष्ठां वेद प्रति ह तिष्ठत्यस्मिꣳश्च लोकोऽमुष्मिꣳश्च चक्षुर्वाव प्रतिष्ठा।।

Verily, he becomes firmly placed in this and the next world who knows the Steady [pratiṣṭhā]. Verily vision is the Steady.

Vision is the chief agent through which the nature of high and low grounds are ascertained, and therefore it is described as the Steady.

4. यो ह वै संपदं वेद सꣳहास्मै कामाः पद्यन्ते दैवाश्च मानुषाश्च श्रोत्रं वाव संपत्।।

He who knows the Sampat [fortune], obtains whatever is the desirable in this or the other world. Audition is verily the Sampat.

Through the ears the Vedas are heard, and through the knowledge thereby acquired, men attain to prosperity, hence is audition called the Sampat.

5. यो ह वा आयतनं वेदायतनꣳह स्वानां भवति मनो ह वा आयतमम्।।

He who knows the Receptacle [Āyatana] verily becomes the receptacle of his people. The mind is verily the Receptacle.

The mind being the receptacle of all our knowledge.

6. अथ ह प्राणा अहꣳश्रेयसि व्यूदिरेऽहꣳश्रेयानस्म्यहꣳश्रेयानस्मीति।।

Now, these organs of sense quarrelled about their [respective] superiority, each proclaiming : "I am the chief; I am the chief."

7. ते ह प्राणाः प्रजापतिं पितरमेत्योचुर्भगवन्को नः श्रेष्ठ इति तान्होवाच यस्मिन्व उत्क्रान्ते शरीरं पापिष्ठतरमिव दृश्येत स वः श्रेष्ठ इति।।

They, the organs, repaired to the Patriarch Prajāpati and enquired; "Lord, which of us is the chief ?" Unto them said he : "Of you, he, whose departure makes the body to appear as whorthless, is the chief."

8. सा ह वागुच्चक्राम सा संवत्सरं प्रोष्य पर्येत्योवाच कथमशकततेर्ते मज्जीवितुमिति यथाऽकला अवदन्तः प्राणन्तः प्राणेन पश्यन्तश्चक्षुषा शृणवन्तः श्रोत्रेण ध्यायन्तो मनसैवमिति प्रविवेश ह वाक्।।

Of a truth, Speech departed [from the body]; it returned after a year's absence and said [to the other organs] : "How did ye survive my separation ?" "In the same way," replied they, "in which the dumb, without speaking, breathes through [the agency of] his life, seeth by his eyes, heareth by his ears, and reflecteth in his mind." Speech resumed his place.

9. चक्षुर्होच्चक्राम तत्संवत्सरं प्रोष्य पर्येत्योवाच कथमशकतर्ते मज्जीवितुमिति यथान्धा अपश्यन्तः प्राणन्तः प्राणेन वदन्तो वाचा शृण्वन्तः श्रोत्रेण ध्यायन्तो मनसैवमिति प्रविवेश ह चक्षुः।।

Verily, Vision departed [from the body]; it returned after a year's absence and enquired [of the other organs] : "How did ye survive my separation ?" "In the same way," replied they, "in which the blind, without seeing, breathes through [the agency of] his life, speaketh through the organs of speech, heareth by his ears, and reflecteth in his mind." Vision resumed his place.

10. श्रोत्रꣳ होच्चक्राम तत्संवत्सरं प्रोष्य पर्येत्योवाच कथमशकततें मज्जीवितुमिति यथा बधिरा अशृण्वन्तः प्राणन्तः प्राणेन वदन्तो वाचा पश्यन्तश्चक्षुषा ध्यायन्तो मनसैवमिति प्रविवेश ह श्रोत्रम्॥

Of a truth, Audition departed [from the body]; it returned after a year's absence and enquired [of the other organs] : "How did ye survive my separation ?" "In the same way," replied they, "in which the deaf, without hearing, breathes through [the agency of] his life, speaketh through the organs of speech, seeth by his eyes, and reflecteth in his mind." Audition resumed his place.

11. मनो होच्चक्राम तत्संवत्सरं प्रोष्य पर्येत्योवाच कथमशकततें मज्जीवितुमिति यथा बाला अमनसः प्राणन्तः प्राणेन वदन्तो वाचा पश्यन्तश्चक्षुषा शृण्वन्तः श्रोत्रेणैवमिति प्रविवेश ह मनः॥

Of a truth, Mind departed [from the body]; it returned after a year's absence and enquired [of the other organs] : "How did ye survive my separation ?" "In the same way," replied they, in which an infant without possessing the power of reflection, breathes through [the agency] of his life, speaketh through the organ of speech, seeth by his eyes, and heareth by his ears." Mind resumed his place.

12. अथ ह प्राण उत्त्चिक्रमिषन्स यथा सुहयः पड्वीशशङ्कून्संखिदेदेवमितरान्प्राणान्समखिदत्तꣳ हाभिसमेत्योचुर्भगवन्नेधि त्वं नः श्रेष्ठोऽसि मोत्क्रमीरिति॥

Next verily did Life attempt to depart; and in the very attempt, as a mighty charger, when whipped, plucks out from their places all the pegs to which is feet may be tied, did it dislodge all the organs of sense. They approached it and said : "Lord, remain in thy place; thou art the greatest of us all; pray, depart not."

13. अथ हैनं वागुवाच यदहं वसिष्ठोऽस्मि त्वं तद्वसिष्ठोऽसीत्यथ हैनं चक्षुरुवाच यदहं प्रतिष्ठास्मि त्वं तत्प्रतिष्ठासीति।।

Next of a truth, Speech said unto it [Life] : "The quality of enveloping all, which belongeth to me, is due to thee." Then did Vision say unto it : "The quality of steadiness, which belongeth to me, is due to thee."

14. अथ हैनं श्रोत्रमुवाच यदहꣳ संपदस्मि त्वं तत्संपदसीत्यथ हैनं मन उवाच यदहमायतनमस्मि त्वं तदायतनमसीति।।

Then did Audition say unto it; "The quality of being fortunate, which belongeth to me, is due to thee." Then did Mind say unto it: "The quality of containing all, which belongeth to me, is due to thee."

15. न वै वाचो न चक्षूꣳषि न श्रोत्राणि न मनाꣳसीत्याचक्षते प्राण इत्येवाचक्षते प्राणो ह्येवैतानि सर्वाणि भवन्ति।।

Verily neither speech, nor vision, nor audition, nor mind is worth of its name. Those functions all belong to life; from life proceedeth all.[1]

SECTION II

1. स होवाच किं मेऽन्नं भविष्यतीति यत्किंचिदिदमाश्वभ्य आ शकुनिभ्य इति होचुस्तद्वा एतदनस्यान्नमनो ह वै नाम प्रत्यक्षं न ह वा एवंविदि किंचनानन्नं भवतीति।।

Of a truth it [life] enquired : "What should be my food ?" They replied : "Whatever is food for beasts and birds[2] is meet food for thee." Therefore, verily all that is eatable belongeth to life; hence ana [exertion] is its self-evident name. For him who knoweth this, verily there is nothing that is not appropriate food.

2. स होवाच किं मे वासो भविष्यतीत्याप इति होचुस्तस्माद्वा एतदशिष्यन्तः पुरस्ताच्चोपरिष्टाच्चाद्भिः परिदधति लम्भुको ह वासो भवत्यनग्नो ह भवति ।।

Of a truth it enquired : "What shall be my raiment ?" "Water" : replied they. Hence people at their meals begin and end with water.[3] It [always] obtains its raiment; it never remains naked.[4]

3. तद्धैतत्सत्यकामो जाबालो गोश्रुतये वैयाघ्रपद्यायोक्त्वोवाच यद्यप्येनच्छुष्काय स्थाणवे ब्रूयाज्जायेरन्नेवास्मिञ्छाखाः प्ररोहेयुः पलाशानीति ।।

Satyakāma, son of Jabālā, having explained the above to Gośrutī, son of Vyāghrapāda, said : "Were you to explain this to the withered stump of a tree, it would shoot forth new leaves and branches."

4. अथ यदि महज्जिगमिषेदमावास्यायां दीक्षित्वा पौर्णमास्यां रात्रौ सर्वौषधस्य मन्थं दधिमधुनोरुपमथ्य ज्येष्ठाय श्रेष्ठाय स्वाहेत्यग्रावाज्यस्य हुत्वा मन्थे संपातमवनयेत् ।।

Now, should anybody wish for greatness, having observed the usual restrictions on the day of the new moon, he should, on the night of the full moon, husk [the seeds of] all [such] annuals [as are available in or about a town] : beat the same with curds and honey, then pour [a spoonful of] the mixture into the fire in lieu of clarified butter, saying : "May this prove acceptable to the eldest and greatest (Jyeṣṭhāya Śreṣṭhāya svāhā)" ; and preserve in the mixing pot whatever might remain in the oblation spoon.

5. वसिष्ठाय स्वाहेत्यग्रावाज्यस्य हुत्वा मन्थे संपातमव-नयेत्प्रतिष्ठायै स्वाहेत्यग्रावाज्यस्य हुत्वा मन्थे संपातमवनयेत्संपदे स्वाहेत्यग्रावाज्यस्य हुत्वा मन्थे संपातमवनयेदायतनाय स्वाहेत्यग्रावाज्यस्य हुत्वा मन्थे संपातमवनयेत् ।।

Then offering an oblating to the fire with the mixture in lieu of clarified butter, saying : "May this prove acceptable to Vasiṣtha" (Vasiṣṭhāya svāhā), he should preserve in the mixing pot whatever might remain in the oblation spoon. Then offering an oblation to the fire with it in lieu of clarified butter, saying : "May this prove acceptable to Pratiṣṭhā," (Prastiṣṭhāyai svāhā), he should preserve in the mixing pot whatever might remain in the oblation spoon. Then offering an oblation to the fire with it in lieu of clarified butter, saying : "May this prove acceptable to Sampat," (Sampade svāhā) he should preserve in the mixing pot whatever might remain in the oblation spoon. Then offering an oblation to the fire with it in lieu of clarified butter, saying : "May this prove acceptable to Ayatana," (Āyatanāya svāhā,) he should preserve in the mixing pot whatever might remain in the oblation spoon.

6. अथ प्रतिसृप्याञ्जलौ मन्थमाधाय जपत्यमो नामास्यमा हि ते सर्वमिदꣳ स हि ज्येष्ठः श्रेष्ठो राजाधिपतिः स मा ज्यैष्ठ्यꣳ श्रैष्ठ्यꣳ राज्यमाधिपत्यं गमयत्वहमेवेदꣳ सर्वमसानीति।।

Next, approaching the fire and taking [the remains of the] mixture in his joined hands, he should slowly repeat : "Thy name is ama ! All this abide by him ! He is the eldest, the greatest, the king of all, the lord of all ! May he make me the eldest, and greatest and bestow on me kingdoms and empires ! I shall become everything !"

7. अथ खल्वेतयर्चा पच्छ आचामति तत्सवितुर्वृणीमह इत्याचामति वयं देवस्य भोजनमित्याचामति श्रेष्ठꣳ सर्वधातममित्याचामति तुरं भगस्य धीमहीति सर्वं पिबति।।

Then while repeating the verse : "We long for the best and all-sustaining food for that god, [who is] the prime cause of all, [that we may] quickly meditate on [the soul of] that adorable [being],"[5] he should take a mouthful at the end of every foot [of the verse] and drink the residue at the end.

8. निर्णिज्य कꣳसं चमसं वा पश्चादग्नेः संविशति चर्मणि वा स्थण्डिले वा वाचंयमोऽप्रसाहः स यदि स्त्रियं पश्येत्समृद्धं कर्मेति विद्यात्।।

Then washing the vessel in which the offering was kept which is shaped like a kaṁsa (a musical instrument) or a camasa (spoon), he should lie down on a deer skin, or on the ground behind the fire, without speaking and careful so as to avoid dreaming. Should he in such a state dream of women, he may know that his sacrifice has proved fruitful.

9. तदेष श्लेकः। यदा कर्मसु काम्येषु स्त्रियःस्वप्नेषु पश्यति।
समृद्धिं तत्र जानीयात्तस्मिन्स्वप्ननिदर्शने तस्मिन्स्वप्ननिदर्शने।।

Hence is the verse : "Whenever in course of the performance of a ceremony the performer, with some worldly object in view, dreameth of women he should rest assured from the dream—verily from that dream—that the ceremony has proved fruitful."

SECTION III

1. श्वेतकेतुर्हारुणेयः पञ्चालानाः समितिमेयाय तःह प्रवाहणा जैवलिरुवाच कुमारानु त्वाशिषत्पितेत्यनु हि भगव इति।।

Of a truth, Śvetaketu Āruṇeya[6] repaired to the court [of the king] of Pañcāla. Unto him said Pravāhaṇa Jaivali :[7] "Boy, has thy father given thee instruction ?" "Yes, Sir, he has," replied he.

2. वेत्थ यदितोऽधि प्रजाः प्रयन्तीति न भगव इति वेत्थ यथा पुनरावर्तन्त ३ इति न भगव इति वेत्थ पथोर्देवयानस्य पितृयाणस्य च व्यावर्तना ३ इति न भगव इति।।

[Jaivali enquired] : "Knoweth ye where men rise to from this earth ?" "No, Sir" [replied he]. "Know ye how they return ?" "No, Sir," [replied he]. "Know ye where the Deva Yāna, and the Pitṛ Yāna divide ?" "No, Sir" [replied he].

3. वेत्थ यथासौ लोको न संपूर्यत ३ इति न भगव इति वेत्थ यथा पञ्चम्यामाहुतावापः पुरुषवचसो भवन्तीति नैव भगव इति।।

"Know ye why yonder region [where men rise to after death,] does not fill up ?" "No Sir" [replies he]. "Know ye why the fluids of the fifth oblation are called Puruṣa ?" "No, Sir," [I know not, replied he].

4. अथानु किमनुशिष्टोऽवोचथा यो हीमानि न विद्यात्क-
थꣳसोऽनुशिष्टो ब्रुवीतेति स हायस्तः पितुरर्धमेयाय तꣳ
होवाचाऽननुशिष्य वाव किल मा भगवानब्रवीदनु त्वाशिषमिति।।

"How came you then to say that you have got instruction ? How can you say he is instructed who knoweth not [what I have enquired] ?" He [the boy] returned sorrowfully to his parent and said : "Verily, without giving me instructions, lord, you said that you have.

5. पञ्च मा राजन्यबन्धुः प्रश्नानप्राक्षीत्तेषां नैकंचनाशकं
विवक्तुमिति स होवाच यथा मा त्वं तदैतानवदो यथाहमेषां
नैकंचन वेद यद्यहमिमानवेदिष्यं कथं ते नावक्ष्यमिति।।

"That wretched king asked me five questions, and I could not answer even one of them." He [the father] said, "I know not the reply to even one of the questions you have put to me; had I known them why should I have refused thee ?"

6. स ह गौतमो राज्ञोऽर्धमेयाय तस्मै ह प्राप्तयार्हांचकार स
ह प्रातः सभाग उदेयाय तꣳहोवाच मानुषस्य भगवन्गौतम
वित्तस्य वरं वृणीथा इति स होवाच तवैव राजन्मानुषं
वित्तं यामेव कुमारस्यान्ते वाचमभाषथास्तामेव मे ब्रहीति।।

He [the father] of the Gautama gotra repaired to the house of the king. On his arrival, the king performed the duties of hospitality. In the morning he [of the Gautama gotra] appeared in the king's court. Unto him said [the king] : "O Gautama, ask for what you think to be the best of all worldly objects." He replied : "Let those warldly objects remain with thee [I seek them not] : O king, explain unto me what you ask of my son."

7. स ह कृच्छ्रीबभूव तꣳह चिरं वसेत्याज्ञापयांचकार तꣳ होवाच यथा मा त्वं गौतमावदो यथेयं न प्राक् त्वत्तः पुरा विद्या ब्राह्मणान्गच्छति तस्मादु सर्वेषु लोकेषु क्षत्रियस्यैव प्रशासनमभूदिति तस्मै होवाच।।

"He [the king] was afflicted : he ordered him saying : "Remain with me for a time." He [also] said : "Since you have thus enquired, and inasmuch as no Brāhmana ever knew it before, hence of all people in the world, the Kṣatriyas alone have the right of imparting instruction on this subject." He further continued :[8]

"He," the king, "was afflicited" by the idea how he could impart the sacred knowledge to the Brāmaṇa. But knowing that they should not be refused a favour and that he should instruct the applicant in due course, he ordered him to remain by him, and he ordered to ask pardon for the cause of his refusal and delay in explaining his object, said to him. Although all learning belongs to Brāhmaṇas, since you have acknowledged your want of information, by the interrogatory, "Relate unto me" the nature of that knoweledge; listen to what I have to say. It is a well-known fact the theretofore Brāhmaṇas knew nothing of this subject, nor were they guided by this knowledge; the Kṣatriya race alone, in this world, are its professors; hitherto it has been preserved among them from generation to generation. I shall relate it now unto you, and henceforward it will remain with the Brāhmaṇas.

SECTION IV[9]

1. असौ वाव लोको गौतमाग्निस्तस्यादित्य एव समिद्रश्मयो धूमोऽहरर्चिश्चन्द्रमा अङ्गारा नक्षत्राणि विस्फुलिङ्गाः।।

"Verily, O Gautama, yonder region is fire; of that fire the sun is the fuel, the light of the sun is its smoke, the days are its flame, the moon is its charcoal, and the stars are its scintillations.

2. तस्मिन्नेतस्मिन्नग्नौ देवाः श्रद्धां जुह्वति तस्या आहुतेः सोमो राजा संभवति।।

"On that fire the Devas offer their faith in oblation; therefrom proceedeth the Soma rājā.[10]

Section V

1. पर्जन्यो वाव गौतमाग्निस्तस्य वायुरेव समिदभ्रं धूमो विद्युदर्चिरशनिरङ्गारा ह्रादनयो विस्फुलिङ्गाः।।

"O Gautama, Parjñaya[11] is verily fire, the wind is its fuel, the cloud is its smoke, the lightning its flame, the thunderbolt its charcoal, and the rolling of clouds its scintillations.

2. तस्मिन्नेतस्मिन्नग्नौ देवाः सोमꣳराजानं जुह्वति तस्या आहुतेर्वर्षꣳ संभवति।।

"On that fire the Devas offer the Soma rājā in oblation, and therefrom proceedeth rain.

Section VI

1. पृथिवी वाव गौतमाग्निस्तस्याः संवत्सर एव समिदाकाशो धूमो रात्रिरर्चिर्दिशोऽङ्गारा अवान्तरदिशो विस्फुलिङ्गा।।

" O Gautama, the earth is verily fire, the years are its fuel, the sky its smoke, the night its flame, the quarters are its charcoal, and the intermediate quarters its scintillations.

2. तस्मिन्नेतस्मिन्नग्नौ देवा वर्षं जुह्वति तस्या आहुतेरन्नꣳ संभवति।।

"On that fire, the Devas offer the rain in oblations, thence proceedeth aliment.

Section VII

1. पुरुषो वाव गौतमाग्निस्तस्य वागेव समित्प्राणो धूमो जिह्वार्चिश्चक्षुरङ्गाराः श्रोत्रं विस्फुलिङ्गाः।।

"O Gautama, man is verily fire; of that fire speech is the fuel, breath is the smoke, the tongue is the flame, the eyes are charcoal and the ears scintillations.

2. तस्मिन्नेतस्मिन्नग्नौ देवा अन्नं जुह्वति तस्या आहुते रेतः संभवति॥

"On that fire, the Devas offer the aliment in oblation, whence proceedeth productive power.

SECTION VIII

1. योषा वाव गौतमाग्निस्तस्या उपस्थ एव समिद्यदुपमन्त्रयते स धूमो योनिरर्चिर्यदन्तः करोति तेऽङ्गारा अभिनन्दा विस्फुलिङ्गाः॥

"O Gautama, woman is verily fire. In this case the sexual organ is the fuel; when one invites, the smoke; the vulva the flame; when one inserts, the coals; the sexual pleasure the sparks.

2. तस्मिन्नेतस्मिन्नग्नौ देवा रेतो जुह्वति तस्या आहुतेर्गर्भः संभवति॥

"On that fire the Devas offer their productive power in oblation, thence followeth conception.

SECTION IX

1. इति तु पञ्चम्यामाहुतावापः पुरुषवचसो भवन्तीति स उल्बावृतो गर्भो दश वा नव वा मासानन्तः शयित्वा यावद्वाथ जायते॥

"This [is the reply] to [your query] 'Why is the water of the fifth oblation called Puruṣa.' The being [thus originated] after lying in the amnion for about ten months takes his birth.

2. स जातो यावदायुषं जीवति तं प्रेतं दिष्टमितोऽग्नय एव हरन्ति यत एवेतो यतः संभूतो भवति॥

"After birth he lives to the end of the alloted period of his life.[12] On his death and transition to a hereafter,[13] his sons carry his corpse away for consignment to the fire, whence he had come and taken his birth.[14]

Section X

1. तद्य इत्थं विदुर्येचेमेऽरण्ये श्रद्धा तप इत्युपासते तेऽर्चिषम-
भिसंभवन्त्यर्चिषोऽहरह्न आपूर्यमाणपक्षमापूर्यमाणपक्षा-
द्यान्षड्उदङ्ङेति मासाः स्तान॥

"Of them [men so created] those who know this [origin of the Puruṣa] and those who worship God with faith and penance in a desert, repair after death to [the region of] light [Arcil]; thence to [that of] the day [Ahaḥ], thence to [that of the light half of the moon], thence to [that of] the six months during which the sun has a northern declination [Uttarāyaṇa]

To the query; "Know ye where man rises to from this earth?" an answer is now accorded. "Of them," *i.e.,* of the men inhabiting this region; *i.e.,* householders having the right to study this subject; "those who know this", *i.e.,* know the relation of the five fires; their birth successively from the several fires, such as the sky, etc., and that they are the type of the fire, and that the five fires constitute their souls. "How do you deduce from the expression : 'Those who know this,' that the parties should be householders and none else ?" Because it is [immediately after] said, that those householders who know this not, and are devoted exclusively to sacrifices, dedications of thanks, etc., and charity, go to the region of the moon by a darksome path, etc., and that those who live in deserts, such as sages and hermits, who discharge their religious duties by faith and penance, like unto those who know this, go by the path of light, etc. (Arci) ; the only remaining class in the [conscient] householders, and consequently it is to him that the verse alludes.

* * * * *

The means of transition and the kind of immortality assigned to the householder conscient of *his relation to the fire, etc.,* and to the dwellers of the forest have been declared to be the same. It follows therefore that knowledge with reference to the latter is redundant, and yet the Śruti is opposed [to such a deduction, for we hear] : "Neither the performers of sacrifice nor the ingnorant hermit attain to that [immortaility]." (The passage) : "He [the Deity] supports not in immortality those who know him not," would also be against it. No, such would not be the case, the object of the expression "immortality" (अमृतत्त्व) [in such phrases] being a temporary existence *lasting only* to the period of the destruction of the earth. Thus says the expounders of the Purāṇas : "Immortality means, the period to the destruction of the earth." The passages—"The performers of ceremony attain not to that"; "He supports not in immortality those who know him not" ; apply to extreme or final immortality (आत्यन्तिकममृतत्त्वम्); therefore there is no inconsistency. You cannot say that the passages—"They come not here again"; "They pass not again through this mundane transmigration" : would be opposed to such a deduction; because of the terms, "this mundane," and "to this" [which at once indicate the true meaning]. If there were no return at all, the terms, "This mundane" and "to this," would be useless. Nor can you say that those terms are mere expletives, for the expression "no return" (अनावृत्ति) implies an absolute negation of returns and to apprehend from it any chance of return is absurd; while for the sake of the words "this" and "to this" (इमम्, इह) a return somewhere must be assumed.

It is not to be believed that those who rely on the truth of the maxims : "(God is) truth" : "[He is] one without a second" : have any transition by the meridional path (the path of light aforesaid); since there are a hundred passages (to the effect that such people) "becoming Brahman, obtain Brahman" "therefore they are become everythng"; "Their animal powers (प्राणाः) never depart"; "Even here they merge into the Deity." Why not suppose that the meaning of such passages is that at the time of transition from this earth the animal powers (प्राणाः) depart not from the soul, but go together with it ? No; You cannot. Because that would be opposed to the text : "Even here they merge into the Deity." The departure of the soul being evident from the passage : "All the vital airs follow [the soul]," it is not to be suspected that they ever depart from it. May it not be that because the course of the liberated (मोक्ष) is different from that of other people, and it may be doubted whether in his case, the vital airs depart with the soul or not, this passage [definitively] settles [the point by the words] "Therefore they depart not ?" We say in reply, that in that case the text : "even here they merge into the Deity" becomes absurd; for taken apart from the vital airs, the soul cannot be said to have any motion or even individuality,[15] the soul being formless and allpervading. Its association with those airs causes its individuality like sparks from a fire (which owe their individuality to inflammable particles and not to any inherent individuality of their own); consequently you cannot assign to it any individuality or motion when apart from them. Thereof the Śruti itself affords sufficient proof.

You cannot assume that a particle of the Universal Soul (lit. *sat* or truth) breaking off from it, becomes the individual soul, and that it again penetrates through that Universal Soul. Hence the passage, "thereby [by the meridional path or an imaginary foramen on the crown of the head] coming above, he obtains immortality," implies that the transition of those who adore the Brahman as possessed of attributes, takes place through the artery (नाड़ि) called Suṣumnā, and that their immortality is only comparative and not absoulte, "In that (region) there is a city unassailable by all others" : "There is an exhilarating racy lake"—and such like passages being the adjectives to their Brahmaloka (region of Brahma of the Brahmacāris). From these arguments it is evident that those householders who know the five fires, the inhabitants of forests such as Vānaprastha, (ascetics) and the Parivrājakas (mendicants) including those Brahmacāris who observe the rules of their order all life through—men who fulfil their religious oblations, by reliance on the dictates of the Śāstra and by penance—as also those who, according to another Śruti, adore the truthful Brahma Hiraṇyagarbha, are the people who "attain to Arci" (light), that is, the presiding deity of Arci, and the other regions described in the text, and not the adorer of Brahman without attributes [whose reward is immediate emancipation].

2. मासेभ्यः संवत्सरꣳ संवत्सरादादित्यमादित्याच्चन्द्रमसं चन्द्रमसो विद्युतं तत्पुरुषोऽमानवः स एनान्ब्रह्म गमयत्येष देवयानः पन्था इति॥

Thence to [that of] the year; thence to [that of] the sun; thence to [that of] the moon; and thence to [that of] the lightning; thence an inhuman being takes them to [the region of] Brahman. This is the way to the gods [*Deva Yāna*].

3. अथ य इमे ग्राम इष्टापूर्ते दत्तमित्युपासते ते धूममभिसंभवन्ति धूमाद्रात्रिं रात्रेरपरपक्षमपरपक्षाद्यान्षड्दक्षिणैति मासाꣳस्तान्नैते संवत्सरमभिप्राप्नुवन्ति॥

Now those villagers who accomplish their religious duties by the performance of sacrifice (iṣṭa), by the dedication of tanks, wells, halting-places, etc. (pūrta), and by charity beyond the boundary of the altar (datta), are borne, after death, to [the region of darkness] [dhūma]. From [the region of] darkness [they proceed] to [that of] the night; from [that of] the night to [that of] the dark fortnight; from the dark fortnight to [that of] the six months during which the sun has a southern declination; from the six months of the winter solstice they attain not the year;

4. मासेभ्यः पितृलोकं पितृलोकादाकाशमाकाशाच्चन्द्रमसमेष सोमो राजा तद्देवानामन्नं तं देवा भक्षयन्ति।।

["But] thence [they go] to [the region of] the Pitṛs, from [the region of] the Pitṛs [they go] to the sky, and from the sky to the moon. That moon is the king Soma. They are the food of the gods. The gods do eat them.

Since the lunar sphere [lit. moon] itself is the food of the Devas, those who attain to that region, becoming a part thereof, must likewise be their food. If then by the performance of ceremony men become the food of gods, such ceremonies are sources of mischief ? No, there is no mischief in that. The object of the expression is to indicate that they become dependant, for the gods eat not by putting things in their mouth. They only become the dependants of the gods, such as are wives, servants and domestic animals. We see the word (anna) food used to express dependants; thus *striyo annam* [the wife is a dependant]; *"paśavaḥ annam"* [domestic animals are dependant]"; *"viśaḥ annam rājñām"* [the vaiśya is a dependant of the king]. And inasmuch as wives, servants, and domestic animals, notwithstanding their being intended for the enjoyment of others, are not without enjoyment of their own, so the performers of ceremonies, notwithstanding their destination for the gratification of the gods, have some enjoyment for themselves.

5. तस्मिन्यावत्संपातमुषित्वाथैतमेवाध्वानं पुनर्निवर्तन्ते यथेतमाकाशमाकाशाद्वायुं वायुर्भूत्वा धूमो भवति धूमो भूत्वाभ्रं भवति।।

"After remaining there for such time as the effects of their actions last, they return by the road to be prescribed, *i.e.*, thence to the sky, and from the sky to the wind; after becoming wind they become smoke, and from the smoke the scattered cloud is formed.

6. अभ्रं भूत्वा मेघो भवति मेघो भूत्वा प्रवर्षति त इह व्रीहियवा ओषधिवनस्पतयस्तिलमाषा इति जायन्तेऽतो वै खलु दुर्निष्प्रपतरं यो यो ह्यन्नमत्ति यो रेतः सिञ्चति तद्भूय एव भवति॥

"From the scattered clouds proceed condensed or raining clouds, which rain. From that proceed rice, corn, annuals, trees, sesamum, lentils and the like. Now, verily it is difficult to descend therefrom.[17] Those who eat rice and procreate, become manifold.

7. तद्य इह रमणीयचरणा अभ्याशो ह यत्ते रमणीयां योनिमापद्येरन्ब्राह्मणयोनिं वा क्षत्रिययोनिं वा वैश्ययोनिं वाथ य इह कपूयचरणा अभ्याशो ह यत्ते कपूयां योनिमापद्येरन् श्वयोनिं वा सूकरयोनिं वा चाण्डालयोनिं वा॥

"Therefore he, whose conduct is good, quickly attains to some good existence, such as that of a Brāhmaṇa, a Kṣatriya or a Vaiśya. Next, he who is viciously disposed, soon assumes the form of some inferior creature; such as that of a dog, a hog, or a Caṇḍāla.

8. अथैतयोः पथोर्न कतरेण चन तानीमानि क्षुद्राण्यसकृदावर्तीनि भूतानि भवन्ति जायस्व म्रियस्वेत्येतत्तृतीयꣳ स्थानं तेनासौ लोको न संपूर्यते तस्माज्जुगुप्सेत तदेष श्लोकः॥

"Now, those who have not come to either of these two ways—become small creatures of repeated birth. They are born and they die. This is the third place or 'receptacle'. This is the reason why the place [where men go to after death] filleth not. This is the reason why [this career] should be detested : thereof is the verse :

9. स्तेनो हिरण्यस्य सुरां पिबꣳश्च गुरोस्तल्पमावसन्ब्रह्महा च। एते पतन्ति चत्वारः पञ्चमश्चाचरꣳस्तैरिति॥

"The robber of gold, the drunkard who drinks spirit, the defiler of his master's bed, and the murderer of a Brāhmaṇa, are debased and filthy, and fifthly, so is he who associates with these four."

10. अथ ह य एतानेवं पञ्चाग्नीन्वेद न स ह तैरप्याचरन्पाप्मना लिप्यते शुद्धः पूतः पुण्यलोको भवति य एवं वेद य एवं वेद॥

Now, he, who thus knoweth the five fires, never becomes affected by sin, even if he associate with these vicious people. He remaineth pure and holy and of virtuous region, who knoweth—verily who knoweth—this.

Section XI

1. प्राचीनशाल औपमन्यवः सत्ययज्ञः पौलुषिरिन्द्रद्युम्नो भाल्लवेयो जनः शार्कराक्ष्यो बुडिल आश्वतराश्विस्ते हैते महाशाला महाश्रोत्रियाः समेत्य मीमाꣳ सांचक्रुः को नु आत्मा किं ब्रह्मेति॥

Prācīnaśala, son of Upamanyu, Satyayajña, son of Puluṣa, Indradyumna, son of Bhallava, Jana, son of Śarkarākṣa, and Buḍila, son of Aśvatarāśva, were great householders and knowers of the Veda. They met together and discussed "which is our soul and which is Brahman" ?

2. ते ह संपादयांचक्रुरुद्दालको वै भगवन्तोऽयमारुणिः संप्रतीममात्मानं वैश्वानरमध्येति तꣳहन्ताभ्यागच्छामेति तꣳहाभ्याजग्मुः॥

[Being unable to come to conclusion] : They decided, "Let us go to Uddālaka, son of Aruṇa, who has lately learned of the soul Vaiśvānara." They repaired to him.

3. स ह संपादयांचकार प्रक्ष्यन्ति मामिमे महाशाला महाश्रोत्रियास्तेभ्यो न सर्वमिव प्रतिपत्स्ये हन्ताहमन्यमभ्यनुशासानीति॥

Of a truth he [Uddālaka] resolved [in his mind] : "These great householders and knowers of the Veda will question me, but I shall not be able to explain all their queries, I should therefore point out to them some other tutor."

4. तान्होवाचाश्वपतिर्वै भगवन्तोयं कैकयः संप्रतीममात्मानं वैश्वानरमध्येति तꣳ हन्ताभ्यागच्छामेति तꣳ हाभ्याजग्मुः।।

He said to them : "Sirs, Let us go to Aśvapati, son of Kekaya, who hath lately learned of the soul Vaiśvānara." Of a truth they went to him.

5. तेभ्यो ह प्राप्तेभ्यः पृथगर्हाणि कारयांचकार स ह प्रातः संजिहान उवाच न मे स्तेनो जनपदे न कदर्यो न मद्यपो नानाहिताग्निर्नाविद्वान स्वैरी स्वैरिणी कुतो यक्ष्यमाणो वै भगवन्तोऽहमस्मि यावदेकैकस्मा ऋत्विजे धनं दास्यामि तावद्भगवद्भ्यो दास्यामि वसन्तु भगवन्त इति।।

He [Aśvapati] caused [his dependants] to receive them with due respect. On the morrow, appearing before them, [and offering some wealth] he [asked them to accept thereof, but being refused and thinking that he had committed some fault] said : "There is no thief in my kingdom, nor misers, nor drunkards, nor neglecters of the household fire, nor ignorant people, nor adulterers much less adulteresses," and [on being told that they sought not wealth, thinking that they refused, because his offering was insufficient,] continued. "Venerable Sirs, I wish to perform a sacrifice and at that sacrifice the allowance of an officiating priest shall be offered to each of you. Remain with me, Sirs [for a time]."

6. ते होचुर्येन हैवार्थेन पुरुषश्चरेत्तꣳहैव वदेदात्मानमेवेमं वैश्वानरꣳ संप्रत्यध्येषि तमेव नो ब्रूहीति।।

They replied : "Give that to your guests what they seek; you know of the soul Vaiśvānara, explain that unto us."

7. तान्होवाच प्रातर्वः प्रतिवक्तास्मीति ते ह समित्पाणयः पूर्वाह्णे प्रतिचक्रमिरे तान्हानुपनीयैवैतदुवाच।।

He answered them : "I shall tell you [about it] tomorrow morning." On the morrow they came to him, bringing the usual sacrificial woods with them. Without investing them with the Brāhmanical thread, he said.

SECTION XII

1. औपमन्यव कं त्वमात्मानमुपास्स इति दिवमेव भगवो राजन्निति होवाचैष वै सुतेजा आत्मा वैश्वानरो यं त्वमात्मानमुपास्से तस्मात्तव सुतं प्रसुतमासुतं कुले दृश्यते॥

"Aupamanyava, to which soul do you offer your adorations ?"[18] "To the heaven [diva], O king, O Lord" : [replied he]. "The soul", returned the first, "whom you adore is verily the glory [Sutejāḥ] of the Universal Soul (Vaiśvānara); hence it is that the juice of the moon plant is seen to be well and fully[19] expressed in your family.

2. अत्स्यन्नं पश्यसि प्रियमत्त्यन्नं पश्यति प्रियं भवत्यस्य ब्रह्मवर्चसं कुले य एतमेवमात्मानं वैश्वानरमुपास्ते मूर्धा त्वेष आत्मन इति होवाच मूर्धा ते व्यपतिष्यद्यन्मां नागमिष्य इति॥

And you consume food [with good appetite] and behold dear objects,[20] [for] he consumeth food [with good appetite] and beholdeth dear objects, and his race becomes possessed of Vedic glory, who thus adoreth the soul Vaiśvānara, [The heaven] is verily the head of that Soul. Your head would [however] have fallen off [thy neck] had you not come unto me."[21]

SECTION XIII

1. अथ होवाच सत्ययज्ञं पौलुषिं प्राचीनयोग्य कं त्वमात्मानमुपास्स इत्यादित्यमेव भगवो राजन्निति होवाचैष वै विश्वरूप आत्मा वैश्वानरो यं त्वमात्मानमुपास्से तस्मात्तव बहु विश्वरूपं कुले दृश्यते॥

He next addressed Satyayajña, son of Puluṣa, saying : "O chief,[22] to which soul do you offer your adorations ?" "To the sun,

O Lord, O king" : [replied he, Aśvapati] said : "The soul, whom you adore, is the all-pervading form [Viśvarūpa] on the Universal Soul; hence many forms (conveniences) are seen in your family";

2. प्रवृतोऽश्वतरीरथो दासीनिष्कोऽत्स्यन्नं पश्यसि प्रियमत्त्यन्नं पश्यति प्रियं भवत्यस्य ब्रह्मवर्चसं कुले य एतमेवमात्मानं वैश्वानरमुपास्ते चक्षुष्टेतदात्मन इति होवाचान्धोऽभविष्य-द्यन्मां नागमिष्य इति।।

"Mules yoked to carts, follow you; [even] your maids are adorned with necklace; you consume food [with good appetite] and behold objects; (for) he consumeth [well this] food, and beholdeth dear objects, and his race becomes possessed of Vedic glory, who thus adoreth the Universal Soul. The sun is the eye of that Soul. You would have [however] become blind had you not come unto me."

SECTION XIV

1. अथ होवाचेन्द्रद्युम्नं भाल्लवेयं वैयाघ्रपद्य कं त्वमात्मानमुपास्स इति वायुमेव भगवो राजन्निति होवाचैष वै पृथग्वर्त्मात्मा वैश्वानरो यं त्वमात्मानमुपास्से तस्मात्त्वां पृथग्बलय आयन्ति पृथग्रथश्रेणयोऽनुयन्ति।।

He then said to Indradyumna Bhāllaveys : "O descendant of Vyāghrapāda ! to which soul do you offer your adorations ?" "To the winds, O Lord, O king" : [replied he. Aśvapati] said : "The soul whom you adore is [one of] the various courses [pṛthakvartmā] of the Universal Soul; hence various armies submit to you and varied trains of chariots follow you.

2. अत्स्यन्नं पश्यसि प्रियमत्त्यन्नं पश्यति प्रियं भवत्यस्य ब्रह्मवर्चसं कुले य एतमेवमात्मानं वैश्वानरमुपास्ते प्राणस्त्वेष आत्मन इति होवाच प्राणस्त उदक्रमिष्यद्यन्मा नागमिष्य इति।।

And you consume food [with good appetite] and behold dear

objects; [for] he consumeth [well his] food and beholdeth dear objects, and his race becomes possessed of Vedic glory, who thus adoreth the Universal Soul. The wind is the breath of that Soul. Your breath would have [however] passed from you, had you not come unto me."

SECTION XV

1. अथ होवाच जनᳬ शार्कराक्ष्य कं त्वमात्मानमुपास्स इत्याकाशमेव भगवो राजन्निति होवाचैष वै बहुल आत्मा वैश्वानरो यं त्वमात्मानमुपास्से तस्मात्त्वं बहुलोऽसि प्रजया च धनेन च।।

He then said to Jana, "O Śārkarākṣya, to which soul do you offer your adorations ?" "To the sky, O Lord, O king" : [replied he. Aśvapati] said : "The soul, whom you adore is the multiform manifestation [Bahula] of the Universal Soul, hence are you full of wealth and tenants;

2. अत्स्यन्नं पश्यसि प्रियमत्त्यन्नं पश्यति प्रियं भवत्यस्य ब्रह्मवर्चसं कुले य एतमेवमात्मानं वैश्वानरमुपास्ते संदेहस्त्वेष आत्मन इति होवाच संदेहस्ते व्यशीर्यद्यन्मां नागमिष्य इति।।

And hence do you consume food [with good appetite] and behold dear objects; [for] he consumeth [well his] food and beholdeth dear objects, and his race becomes possessed of Vedic glory, who thus adoreth the Universal Soul. The sky is the trunk of that Soul. Had you not [however] come unto me, thy trunk would have dried up."

SECTION XVI

1. अथ होवाच बुडिलमाश्वतराश्विं वैयाघ्रपद्य कं त्वमात्मानमुपास्स इत्यप एव भगवो राजन्निति होवाचैष वै रयिरात्मा वैश्वानरो यं त्वमात्मानमुपास्से तस्मात्त्वᳬ रयिमान्पुष्टिमानसि।।

He then said to Buḍila Āśvatarāśvi, "O Vaiyāghrapadya, to which soul do you offer your adorations ?" "To water, O Lord, O king" [replied he. Aśvapati] said : "The soul whom you adore is the wealth [rayi] of the Universal Soul; hence are you wealthy and healthy;

2. अत्स्यन्नं पश्यसि प्रियमत्त्यन्नं पश्यति प्रियं भवत्यस्य ब्रह्मवर्चसं कुले य एतमेवमात्मानं वैश्वानरमुपास्ते बस्तिस्त्वेष आत्मन इति होवाच बस्तिस्ते व्यभेत्स्यद्यन्मां नागमिष्य इति।।

And hence do you consume food [with good appetite] and behold dear objects; [for] he consumeth [well his] food and beholdeth dear objects, and his race becomes possessed of Vedic glory, who thus adoreth the Universal Soul. The water is the pelvic region of that Soul. Had you not [however] come to me, your pelvic region would have been severed from your body."

Section XVII

1. अथ होवाचोद्दालकमारुणिं गौतम कं त्वमात्मानमुपास्स इति पृथिवीमेव भगवो राजन्निति होवाचैष वै प्रतिष्ठात्मा वैश्वानरो यं त्वमात्मानमुपास्से तस्मात्त्वं प्रतिष्ठितोऽसि प्रजया पशुभिश्च।।

He then said to Uddālaka Āruṇi, "O Gautama, to which soul do you offer your adorations ?" "To the earth, O King, O Lord": [replied he. Aśvapati] said : "The soul whom you adore is the feet of the Universal Soul, hence are you well established in descendants and cattle.

2. अत्स्यन्नं पश्यसि प्रियमत्त्यन्नं पश्यति प्रियं भवत्यस्य ब्रह्मवर्चसं कुले य एतमेवमात्मानं वैश्वानरमुपास्ते पादौ त्वेतावात्मन इति होवाच पादौ ते व्यम्लास्येतां यन्मां नागमिष्य इति।।

"And hence do you consume food [with good appetite] and behold dear objects; [for] he consumeth [well his] food and beholdeth dear objects, and his race becomes possessed of Vedic glory, who thus adoreth the Universal Soul. The earth is the feet of that Soul. Had you not [however] come to me your feet would have lost their energy.

SECTION XVIII

1. तान्होवाचैते वै खलु यूयं पृथगिवेममात्मानं वैश्वानरं विद्वाꣳसोऽन्नमात्थ यस्त्वेतमेवं प्रादेशमात्रमभिविमानमात्मानं वैश्वानरमुपास्ते स सर्वेषु लोकेषु सर्वेषु भूतेषु सर्वेष्वात्म-स्वन्नमत्ति।।

Next, addressing them all, he said : "You consume food," knowing the Universal Soul to be many; but he, who adoreth that Universal Soul[23] which pervadeth the heaven and the earth,[24] and is the *principal* object indicated by [the pronoun] I, consumeth food everywhere and in all regions, in every form and in every faculty.

2. तस्य ह वा एतस्यात्मनो वैश्वानरस्य मूर्धैव सुतेजाश्चक्षुर्विश्व-रूपः प्राणः पृथग्वर्त्मात्मा संदेहो बहुलो बस्तिरेव रयिः पृथिव्येव पादावुर एव वेदिर्लोमानि बर्हिर्हृदयं गार्हपत्यो मनोऽन्वाहार्यपचन आस्यमाहवनीयः।।

"Verily of that All-pervading Soul, the heaven is the head, the sun is the eye, the wind is the breath, the sky is the trunk, the moon is the fundament, and the earth is the feet. The altar is His breast, the sacrificial grass constitutes the hair of His body, the household or Gārhapatya fire forms His heart, the Anvāhārya-pacana fire forms His mind, and the Āhavanīya fire His face.[25]

SECTION XIX

1. तद्यद्भक्तं प्रथममागच्छेत्तद्धोमीयꣳस यां प्रथमामाहुतिं जुहुयात्तां जुहुयात्प्राणाय स्वाहेति प्राणस्तृप्यति।।

"Therein, whatever food is first brought, that forms the first oblation. He (the wise) who knows it, the first mouthful, to be the first oblation, should offer it with the words, 'I offer it to Prāṇa' [Prāṇāya svāhā]. Life (prāṇa) is thereby satisfied.

2. प्राणे तृप्यति चक्षुस्तृप्यति चक्षुषि तृप्यत्यादित्यस्तृप्यत्यादित्ये तृप्यति द्यौस्तृप्यति दिवि तृप्यन्त्यां यत्किंच द्यौश्चादित्य-श्चाधितिष्ठतस्तत्तृप्यति तस्यानुतृप्तिं तृप्यति प्रजया पशुभिरन्नाद्येन तेजसा ब्रह्मवर्चसेनेति ।।

By the satisfaction of Prāṇa vision is satisfied; by the satisfaction of vision the sun is satisfied; by the satisfaction of the sun the heaven is satisfied; by the satisfaction of the heaven whatever depends upon the sun and the heaven is satisfied; through its satisfaction [the performer of the sacrifice] is satisfied with [the possession of] descendants, cattle, food, splendour and Vedic glory.

SECTION XX

1. अथ यां द्वितीयां जुहुयात्तां जुहुयाद्व्यानाय स्वाहेति व्यानस्तृप्यति ।।

"Now, that which is the second oblation should be offered with [the words] 'I offer this to Vyāna' [Vyānāya svāhā]. Thereby is Vyāna satisfied.

2. व्याने तृप्यति श्रोत्रं तृप्यति श्रोत्रे तृप्यति चन्द्रमास्तृप्यति चन्द्रमसि तृप्यति दिशस्तृप्यन्ति दिक्षु तृप्यन्तीषु यत्किंच दिशश्च चन्द्रमाश्चाधितिष्ठन्ति तत्तृप्यति तस्यानुतृप्ति तृप्यति प्रजया पशुभिरन्नाद्येन तेजसा ब्रह्मवर्चसेनेति ।।

"By the satisfaction of Vyāna audition is satisfied, by the satisfaction of audition the moon is satisfied; by the satisfaction of the moon the quarters are satisfied; by the satisfaction of the quarters whatever depends upon the moon and the quarters is satisfied; through its satisfaction [the performer of the sacrifice] is satisfied with [the possession of] descendants, cattle, food, splendour and Vedic glory.

Section XXI

1. अथ यां तृतीयां जुहुयात्तां जुहुयादपानाय स्वाहेत्यपानस्तृप्यति ।।

"Now that which is the third oblation should be offered with [the words] 'I offer this to Apāna' [Apānāya svāhā]. Thereby is Apāna satisfied."

2. अपाने तृप्यति वाक्तृप्यति वाचि तृप्यन्त्यामग्निस्तृप्यत्यग्नौ तृप्यति पृथिवी तृप्यति पृथिव्यां तृप्यन्त्यां यत्किंच पृथिवी चाग्निश्चाधितिष्ठतस्तत्तृप्यति तस्यानुतृप्तिं तृप्यति प्रजया पशुभिरन्नाद्येन तेजसा ब्रह्मवर्चसेनेति ।।

"By the satisfaction of Apāna speech is satisfied; by the satisfaction of speech Agni is satisfied; by the satisfaction of Agni the earth is satisfied; by the satisfaction of the earth whatever depends upon the earth and Agni is satisfied; through its satisfaction [the performer of the sacrifice] is satisfied with [the possession of] descendants, cattle, food, splendour, and Vedic glory."

Section XXII

1. अथ यां चतुर्थीं जुहुयात्तां जुहुयात्समानाय स्वाहेति समानस्तृप्यति ।।

"Now that which is the fourth oblation should be offered with [the words] 'I offer this to Samāna,' [Samānāya svāhā]. Thereby is Samāna satisfied."

2. समाने तृप्यति मनस्तृप्यति मनसि तृप्यति पर्जन्यस्तृप्यति पर्जन्ये तृप्यति विद्युत्तृप्यति विद्युति तृप्यन्त्यां यत्किंच विद्युच्च पर्जन्यश्चाधितिष्ठतस्तत्तृप्यति तस्यानुतृप्तिं तृप्यति प्रजया पशुभिरन्नाद्येन तेजसा ब्रह्मवर्चसेनेति ।।

"By the satisfaction of Samāna the mind is satisfied; by the satisfaction of the mind the cloud is satisfied; by the satisfaction of the cloud the lightning is satisfied; by the satisfaction of the lightning whatever depends upon the lightning and the cloud is satisfied; through its satisfaction [the performer of the sacrifice] is satisfied with [the possession of] descendants, cattle, food, splendour and Vedic glory."

Section XXIII

1. अथ यां पञ्चमीं जुहुयात्तां जुहुयादुदानाथ स्वाहेत्युदानस्तृप्यति।।

"Now, that which is the fifth oblation should be offered with [the words] 'I offer this to Udāna' [Udānāya svāhā]. Thereby is Udāna satisfied."

2. उदाने तृप्यति त्वक् तृप्यति त्वचि तृप्यन्त्यां वायुस्तृप्यति वायौ तृप्यत्याकाशस्तृप्यत्याकाशे तृप्यति यत्किंच वायुश्चाकाशश्चाधितिष्ठतस्तत्तृप्यति तस्यानुतृप्तिं तृप्यति प्रजया पशुभिरन्नाद्येन तेजसा ब्रह्मवर्चसेनेति।।

"By the satisfaction of Udāna the wind [Vāyu] is satisfied; by the satisfaction of the wind the sky is satisfied; by the satisfaction of the sky whatever depends upon the sky and the wind is satisfied; through its satisfaction, [the performer of the sacrifice] is satisfied with [the possession of] descendants, cattle, food, splendour and Vedic glory."

Section XXIV

1. स य इदमविद्वानग्निहोत्रं जुहोति यथाङ्गारानपोह्य भस्मनि जुहुयात्तादृक्तत्स्यात्।।

"He who, without knowing this, performs a fire sacrifice, [has the same reward as he] who, forsaking burning coals, pours his oblations upon ashes."

2. अथ य एतदेवं विद्वानग्निहोत्रं जुहोति तस्य सर्वेषु लोकेषु सर्वेषु भूतेषु सर्वेष्वात्मसु हुतं भवति।।

"Next, with regard to him who knowing this, performs a fire-sacrifice, the sacrifice is complete everywhere and in every region, in every form and in every faculty [of the body]."

3. तद्यथेषीकातूलमग्नौ प्रोतं प्रदूयेतैवꣳहास्य सर्वे पाप्मानः प्रदूयन्ते य एतदेवं विद्वानग्निहोत्रं जुहोति॥

"As reed-tops when cast on fire [readily] burn to ashes so do the sins of him who, knowing all this, performs a fire sacrifice."

4. तस्मादु हैवंविद्यद्यपि चण्डालायोच्छिष्टं प्रयच्छेदात्मनि हैवास्य तद्वैश्वानरे हुतꣳ स्यादिति तदेष श्लोकः॥

"Therefore verily, were he, who knows this to offer the remnant of his food [even] to a Caṇḍāla, he would effect an offering to the All-pervading Soul : therefore is the verse :

5. यथेह क्षुधिता बाला मातरं पर्युपासते। एवꣳ सर्वाणि भूतान्यग्निहोत्रमुपासत इत्याग्निहोत्रमुपासत इति॥

"As in common life hungry children look up to their mothers, so do all creatures look up to the fire-sacrifice *(Agnihotra)*—verily they look up to the fire-sacrifice."

Foot Notes

1. Śaṅkara takes great pains to explain to his readers that the parable of the life and the organs of sense, is intended to illustrate the superiority of life over the other organs, and that in reality there never was any departure of dispute of the kind. We think, he might have spared himself the trouble, without the danger of any body being led astray. The similarity of the tale of the story of the belly and the members need scarcely be noted.
2. Literally, dogs and vultures.
3. This refers to the formal washing of the mouth at the beginning and at the end of meals prescribed by the Smṛtis (Ācamana) and does not enjoy and especial drinking or washing, says Śaṅkara.
4. Freely translated.
5. The following are the words of the verse arranged in feet : "Of that prime cause of all, the sun, [सवितुः] we long" (a mouthful).

"We the god's food" (ditto).
"Best and all-sustaining" (ditto).
"Quickly we meditate on the adorable" (the remainder of the mixture).

6. Āruṇeya, grandson of Aruṇa.
7. The king, son of Jīvala, a Kṣatriya.
8. Considering that the Brāhmanas have been the sole repositories of the sacred writings of the Hindus for more than three thousand years, the existence of this verse, so prejudicial to the interest and dignity of the priestly caste, speaks volumes in favour of the authenticity of the Chāndogya-Upaniṣad. If any liberty had been taken, it is hard to suppose, that the Brāhmanas would have spared a verse which ascribes the origin of the most important element of the Vedic theology, its dispensation of a future state, to their rivals the Kṣatriyas. It would seem from it that the religion of the Brāhmanas once included only the ceremonials and sacrifices of the Veda and omitted its metaphysics; accordingly we hear in the *Mantra Varṇa*. "The Brāhmanas represent the One as many, Agni, Yama, Matariśvā, etc."

   एकं सत् विप्रा बहुधा वदन्ति अग्निं यमं मातरिश्वानमाहुः।

   The subject is of great importance and deserves further enquiry.
9. This and the next six sections allegorically describe the concatenation of natural causes which, according to the expounder, produces the creation.
10. Śaṅkara explains the Devas to mean the human organs of vision, audition, etc., and the Somarājā the form which performers and institutors of sacrifices assume after death.
11. Parjanya is described by Śaṅkara, as the presiding deity of rain and the Purāṇas identify him with Indra.
12. *Yāvadāyuṣam.* The period he is destined to live through the effect of his actions in a former life.
13. *i.e.,* the place of his reward and punishment.
14. His birth having proceeded from the aforesaid oblations to the several fires.
15. *Jivatva,* nature of being; the soul as possessed of motion and sensation.
16. For according to the Śruti : "It is without parts; It is without action; It is all tranquil, etc."—*Ānandagiri.*

17. It is not distinct whether the descent is to be from the cloud or from the rice, etc.
18. Lit., What soul do you adore.
19. *Prasuta,* from *pra* "well," and *suta,* the moon plant, and *Āsuta,* from *ā* "full," "complete" and *suta.* The first term is applied to the expression of the juice for an occasional, the latter for the daily, sacrifice.
20. *i.e.,* Your descendants don't die before you.
21. The heaven being only a part, should not be adored as the Universal Soul itself; those who adore it as such are liable to the punishment aforesaidl; so on in the following sections.—*Ānandagiri.*
22. Lit., Worthy of being reckoned as the first.
23. In Sanskrit वेश्वानर, which, according to Śaṅkara, may mean, he who ordains, (nayati) the rewards and punishments due to the virtue and vice of all mankind (viśvān), or he who is the soul of creation *viśva* and *nara,* or he whom all mankind reckon as their soul. The lexicographical meaning of the word is fire, that, however, is not the object alluded to in the text.
24. He whose extension प्रदेश is the span between the heaven and the earth whom the Śāstra describes (देशयति) in detail प्र as extending from the heaven to the earth.
25. The soul is assumed to be the sum total of five vital airs, which support the body; the *pneuma (*πνευμα) of Greek philosophers, they are Prāṇa or breath, Vyāna or the air diffused all over the body, Apāna the flatus in the lower intestines, Samāna or the air essential to digestion, and Udāna or that which rises up the throat and passes into the head.

SIXTH CHAPTER

SECTION I

हरिः ॐ

1. श्वेतकेतुर्हारुणेय आस तꣳ ह पितोवाच श्वेतकेतो वस ब्रह्मचर्यं न वै सोम्यास्मत्कुलीनोऽननूच्य ब्रह्मबन्धुरिव भवतीति ।।

Hari ! Om ! Of a truth there lived Śvetaketu grandson of Aruṇa. Unto him said the father : "O Śvetaketu, [go and] abide as a Brahmacāri [in the house of a tutor], for verily, child, none of our race has neglected the Vedas[1] and thereby brought disgrace on himself."[2]

2. स ह द्वादशवर्ष उपेत्य चतुर्विꣳ शतिवर्षः सर्वान्वेदानधीत्य महामना अनूचानमानी स्तब्ध एयाय तꣳह पितोवाच श्वेतकेतो यन्नु सोम्येदं महामना अनूचानमानी स्तब्धोऽस्युत तमादेशमप्राक्ष्यः ।।

3. येनाश्रुतꣳ श्रुतं भवत्यमतं मतमविज्ञातं विज्ञातमिति कथं नु भगवः स आदेशो भवतीति ।।

Of a truth he having repaired to a tutor, on his twelfth year, and studied all the Vedas to the twenty-fourth year of his age, returned home a vain-minded [youth], confident of his knowledge of the Vedas, and proud. Unto him said his father : "O Śvetaketu, since you are, child, so vain-minded, so confident of your knowledge of the Vedas, and so proud, have you enquired of your tutor about that subject which makes the unheard of heard, the unconsidered considered, and the unsettled settled ?" "What is that subject, O Lord ?"

The object of this chapter is to show that a knowledge of the whole of the Vedas proves worthless, unless accompanied by a knowledge of the Deity.

4. यथा सौम्यैकेन मृत्पिण्डेन सर्वं मृन्मयं विज्ञातः
स्याद्वाचारम्भणं विकारो नामधेयं मृत्तिकेत्येव सत्यम्।।

"Verily, child, as the knowledge of [the nature of] a single clod of earth makes manifest [the nature of] all earthen objects, [and shows] that the various [fictile] fabrications indicated by different words and names are of truth only earth—

5. यथा सोम्यैकेन लोहमणिना सर्वं लोहमयं विज्ञातः
स्याद्वाचारम्भणं विकारो नामधेयं लोहमित्येव सत्यम्।।

"Child, as the knowledge of [the nature of] a single [lump of] gold shows that all articles of gold indicated by different words and names, are mere variations of forms, but in truth gold alone—

6. यथा सोम्यैकेन नखनिकृन्तनेन सर्वं कार्ष्णायसं विज्ञातः
स्याद्वाचारम्भणं विकारो नामधेयं कृष्णायसमित्येव
सत्यमेवः सोम्य स आदेशो भवतीति।।

"Child, as by a knowledge of the nail-cutter, all iron instruments are known to be modifications of that substance, differing only in name and words, but of a truth iron alone, so is the subject [I allude to]."

7. न वै नूनं भगवन्तस्य एतदवेदिषुर्यद्ध्येतदवेदिष्यन् कथं
मे नावक्ष्यन्निति भगवाः स्त्वेवमेतद्ब्रवीत्विति तथा सोम्येति
होवाच।।

"Verily my learned tutors [said Śvetaketu] know it not. Had they known it, why should they have omitted to impart it to me ? Lord, do you relate that unto me ?" "Be it so, child," said the father.

It is improper to speak ill of one's tutors, but the dread of being sent back to his tutors, makes Śvetaketu surmise that they knew not the subject mooted.

Section II

1. सदेव सोम्येदमग्र आसीदेकमेवाद्वितीयं तद्धैक आहुरसदेवेदमग्र आसीदेकमेवाद्वितीयं तस्मादसतः सज्जायत ।।

"Before, O child, this was a mere state of being[3] (sat), one only, without a second. Thereof verily others say : 'Before this was non-being, one alone, without a second; from that non-being proceeds the state of being."

Sat is that substance which is mere being or existence; it is invisible, indistinct, all-pervading, one only, without defect, without members, knowledge itself, and that which is indicated by all the Vedāntas. The word *eva*, 'mere,' is used to make the declaration positive. But what does it make positive ? We say in reply that this world, which we see with its name and form, full of actions and mutations, was [at one time in a state of] mere being, and this *assertion* is made positive by the connection of *eva* with the word "it was," *āsīt*. When was the world so ? It is replied, "before," *i.e.*, anterior to the time of the creation of this world. Then is the world not in existence now, which you describe was in a state of being before ? No, not so. Why then the qualifications "beforc" ? Even now it is in a state of being, and has become the object of our senses by its name, form and other qualification, and is indicated by the word "this"; while "before," *i.e.*, anterior to the time of its creation, it could be indicated only by the word *sat* "being," and understood only by the idea of being, and therefore it is said, "before this was mere being."

No substance can be declared before its creation to be *this*, of such a name and such a form, and yet its existence can easily be conceived, just as on waking from a deep sleep, one feels that during his sleep he was merely in existence [but bereft of all actions] so was the world in existence or in a state of being before its creation. Again, in this world when one observes, in the morning, a potter intent on making wares with his clay, and having passed the day in another village on his return in the evening, sees a variety of pots, pans and other wares, he says these pots and pans were in the morning mere clay; so is it said [with reference to the world], "this was in a state of mere being before."

"On alone," that is, one unconnected with every thing that might relate to it.

"Without a second" : in the case of a pitcher or other earthen vessel, there is beside the clay, the potter, etc., who gives it shape, but in the case of the being in question the epithet "without a second" precludes all coadjutors or co-efficients. "Without a second" (consequently means), that nothing else existed along with it.

But do not the Vaiśeṣikas include every thing in the word *sat*, being ? By them both substances and their qualities are indicated by the same word *sat*, and we accordingly see such expressions as "substance is being" [sat dravyam], quality is being" [sat guṇaḥ] "action is being" [sat karma].

It may be so at present; but the Vaiśeṣikas do not recognize that an object before its creation is in a state of being; on the contrary they maintain the unreality[4] [asatwa] of objects before their creation, and do not with to uphold (the doctrine) that "the being one alone without a second" existed before. Hence it is evident that the being here indicated is other than what is indicated by the Vaiśeṣikas, particularly from the instance quoted of the clay, potter, etc.

"Therefore," *i.e.*, in this discussion about the being before creation, some Vaināsikās, after defining what is substance, maintain, that before the creation of this world only a non-being or a total absence of every thing, alone without a second existed. The Bauddhas imagine a total absence of substance before creation, but do not advocate for any thing antagonistic to being like unto the Naiyāyikas, who maintain all substance to be (double) being or reality and its opposite.

But if the Vaināśikās maintain "only the absence of being before creation, how do they say that before creation a non-being alone without a second existed," indicating thereby its relation to time, number, and individuality ?

Well, it is inconsistent in those who maintain the absence of substance [before its creation]; the belief on non-being itself is inconsistent, for that implies the inconsistency of the non-being of those who maintain such non-existence.

But we admit its existence now, and deny it only before creation.

That won't hold good, for if there be no proof extant of the existence of a being before creation, the same will apply to that of a non-being at the same time. It may be argued that the meaning of a word being the image it conveys to the mind, how can you have a meaning in the word "a non-being alone existed without a second," and if there be no meaning in the words they become absurd. But there is no harm in this expression, the object being only the exclusion of being, for being implies the image of existence, and the expression "one alone without a second" and "existed" are its epithets, and by the addition of a negation to the word *being* all that was indicated by it is excluded.

Would it thence follow that whatever we see is false, as the impression of snake produced by a rope ? No. Truth alone being conceived in different forms, we assert that such a substance as falsehood never and nowhere exists.

2. कुतस्तु खलु सोम्यैवꣳस्यादिति होवाच कथमसतः सज्जायेतेति सत्त्वेव सोम्येदमग्र आसीदेकमेवाद्वितीयम्॥

He continued : "but of a truth. O child, how can this be ? How can being proceed from non-being ? Before, O child, this was only being, one only, without a second.

3. तदैक्षत बहु स्यां प्रजायेयेति तत्तेजोऽसृजत तत्तेज ऐक्षत बहु स्यां प्रजायेयेति तदपोऽसृजत। तस्माद्यत्र क्वच शोचति स्वेदते वा पुरुषस्तेजस एव तदध्यापो जायन्ते॥

"It willed[5] 'I shall multiply and be born.' It created heat[6] That heat willed 'I shall multiply and be born.' It created water.[7]

"Therefore wherever and whenever any body is heated or perspires, it is from heat that water is produced.

4. ता आप ऐक्षन्त बह्व्यः स्याम प्रजायेमहीति ता अन्नमसृजन्त तस्माद्यत्र क्वच वर्षति तदेव भूयिष्ठमन्नं भवत्यद्भ्य एव तदध्यन्नाद्यं जायते॥

"The water willed, 'I shall multiply and be born.' It created aliment. Therefore wherever and whenever rain falls, much aliment is produced; verily it is from water that aliment is produced.

SECTION III

1. तेषां खल्वेषां भूतानां त्रीण्येव बीजानि भवन्त्याण्डजं जीवजमुद्भिज्जमिति॥

"Verily of all these living objects there are three sources, *viz.*, oviparous, viviparous, and sprouting objects.[8]

2. सेयं देवतैक्षत हन्ताहमिमास्तिस्रो देवता अनेन जीवेनात्मनानु- प्रविश्य नामरूपे व्याकरवाणीति॥

"That Deity willed : entering these three objects *(devatās)* in the form of life[9] (jīvātmā) I shall be manifest in various names and forms.

(It may be said that) it would not appear consistent for a divine omniscient deity intelligently to wish to enter a created body, the receptacle of innumerable evils, and undergo the fruits thereof. (Nor is it consistent that), being independent, (he should cease to be so) by amalgamation with a subordinate. (In reply) I admit that it would not be consistent if the Deity were to enter (a body) and undergo the sufferings individually, without any transformation. But such is not the case. How so ? Because of the words "In the form of life (Jīvātmā)". Jīva (life) is but the reflection of the Supreme Deity. It is produced by its relation to intelligence (Buddhi) and other subtle elements, like the image of the sun in water or of a man in a looking-glass. The relation to Buddhi of that Deity of inscrutable and endless power and the reflection of his intelligence have for their instrumental cause the ignorance of his true nature; and from them proceed the feelings of "I am happy," "I am suffering," "I am ignorant," etc. Entering into mundance objects in the form of a reflection that Deity in his own self is not involved in any corporeal pleasure or pain. As a human being or the sun entering a mirror or water in the form of a reflection, does not acquire the defects of the reflecting surface, so is the case with the Deity. Thus in the Kaṭha-Upaniṣad, "as the sun, although the eye of the whole world, yet is not affected by the defects of the (observing) eye or of external causes, so the Soul as the inner Soul of all being is not affected by mundane causes, because it is beyond them. " Chap. V, verse 11. "Like unto space it pervades all and is eternal." Again in the Vājasaneya-Upaniṣad: "He seems as if reflecting as if moving."[10]

(It may be argued that) if life *(jīva)* is nothing but a word, it is then false, and what has it to do with this or a future world ? But there is no harm in that : truth being its essence, it is taken as truth. All objects in their varied names and forms are true when associated with the Truthful Soul, and false when separated therefrom. All transformations owe their origin to words, they are nominal, and the maxim is perfectly true in the case of life. The saying is "as is the Deity so is the offering" (*i.e.,* the life itself being but a mere reflection, its relation to the fruits of action cannot be more substantial). Hence in maintaining the reality of all actions and mutations in relation to the Soul and their unreality when dissociated therefrom the Tārkikas cannot attribute any fault.

3. तासां त्रिवृतं त्रिवृतमेकैकां करवाणीति सेयं देवतेमास्तिस्रो
देवता अनेनैव जीवेनात्मनानुप्रविश्य नामरूपे व्याकरोत्।।

"It shall convert each of these three sources into a trinary form."[11] That Deity entering the three elements (devatās) in the form of life manifested them with (due) names and forms.

4. तासां त्रिवृतं त्रिवृतमेकैकामकरोद्यथा नु खलु सोम्येमास्तिस्रो देवता स्त्रिवृत्त्रिवृदेकैका भवति तन्मे विजानीहीति ।।

"Them did he convert into trinary forms. Learn from me, my child, how these three elements each became a trinary form.

Section IV

1. यदग्ने रोहितः रूपं तेजसस्तद्रूपं यच्छुक्लं तदपां यत्कृष्णं तदन्नस्यापागादग्नेरग्नित्वं वाचारम्भयणं विकारो नामधेयं त्रीणी रूपाणीत्येव सत्यम् ।।

The redness of Agni is due to heat, its whiteness to water, and its darkness to earth; hence Agni ceases to be Agni.[12] It is nothing but a word; it is an effect and is nominal. Its three forms are alone true.

2. यदादित्यस्य रोहितः रूपं तेजसस्तद्रूपं यच्छुक्लं तदपां यत्कृष्णं तदन्नस्यापागादादित्यादादित्यत्वं वाचारम्भणं विकारो नामधेयं त्रीणि रूपाणीत्येव सत्यम् ।।

"The redness of the sun is due to heat, its whiteness to water, and its darkness to earth. Hence the sun ceases to be sun. It is nothing but a word; it is an effect and is nominal. Its three forms are alone true."

3. यच्चन्द्रमसो रोहितः रूपं तेजसस्तद्रूपं यच्छुक्लं तदपां यत्कृष्णं तदन्नस्यापागाच्चन्द्राच्चन्द्रत्वं वाचारम्भणं विकारो नामधेयं त्रीणि रूपाणीत्येव सत्यम् ।।

"The redness of the moon is due to heat, its whiteness to water, and its darkness to earth. Hence the moon ceases to be the moon. It is nothing but a word; it is an effect and is nominal. Its three forms are alone true."

4. यद्विद्युतो रोहितः रूपं तेजसस्तद्रूपं यच्छुक्लं तदपां यत्कृष्णं तदन्नस्यापागाद्विद्युतो विद्युत्वं वाचारम्भणं विकारो नामधेयं त्रीणि रूपाणीत्येव सत्यम् ।।

"The redness of lightning is due to heat, its whiteness to water, and its darkness to earth. Hence the lightning ceases to be lightning. It is nothing but a word; it is an effect and is nominal. Its three forms are alone true."

5. एतद्ध स्म वै तद्विद्वाꣳस आहुः पूर्वे महाशाला महाश्रोत्रिया न नोऽद्य कश्चनाश्रुतममतमविज्ञातमुदाहरिष्यतीति ह्येभ्यो विदांचक्रुः।।

"Verily, knowing this the great house-holders and knowers of the Vedas (śrotrias) of yore said, 'From this day none of us shall talk of anything of which he has not heard, nor considered, nor known; for of a truth, hence he has learn (every thing).

6. यदु रोहितमिवाभूदिति तेजसस्तद्रूपमिति तद्विदांचक्रुर्यदु शुक्लमिवाभूदित्यपाꣳ रूपमिति तद्विदांचक्रुर्यदुकृष्णमि-वाभूदित्यन्नस्य रूपमिति तद्विदांचक्रुः।।

"Whatever appeared to them red, they knew to be due to heat; whatever appeared to them white, they knew to be the form of water; and whatever appeared dark, they attributed to the earth.

7. यद्वविज्ञातमिवाभूदित्येतासामेव देवतानाꣳ समास इति तद्विदांचक्रुर्यथ नु खलु सोम्येमास्तिस्रो देवताः पुरुषं प्राप्य त्रिवृत्त्रिवृदेकैका भवति तन्मे विजानीहीति।।

"Verily whatever appeared to be inscrutable they took to be a union of these three elements (devatās). Now of a truth learn from me, my child, how every object (devatā) becomes threefold in living beings."

SECTION V

1. अन्नमशितं त्रेधा विधीयते तस्य यः स्थविष्ठो धातुस्तत्पुरीषं भवति यो मध्यमस्तन्माꣳसं योऽणिष्ठस्तन्मनः।।

"Aliment when consumed becomes threefold : the gross particles become excrement, the middling ones flesh, and the fine ones the mind.

2. आपः पीतास्त्रेधा विधीयन्ते तासां यः स्थविष्ठो धातुस्तन्मूत्रं भवति यो मध्यमस्तल्लोहितं योऽणिष्ठः स प्राणः।।

"Water when drunk becomes threefold : the gross particles become urine, the middling ones blood, and the fine ones respiration (prāṇa).

3. तेजोऽशितं त्रेधा विधीयते तस्य यः स्थविष्ठो धातुस्तदस्थि भवति यो मध्यमः स मज्जा योऽणिष्ठः सा वाक्।।

"Heat, when consumed,[13] becomes threefold : the gross particles become bones, the middling ones marrow, and the fine ones speech.

4. अन्नमयꣳहि सोम्य मन आपोमयः प्राणस्तेजोमयी वागिति भूय एव मा भगवान्विज्ञापयत्विति तथा सोम्येति होवाच।।

"The mind, my child, is (the result of) aliment, the prāṇa is (that of) water, and speech (is that of) heat." "Will it please my Lord to explain this again unto me." "Be it so, my child."

Section VI

1. दध्नः सोम्य मथ्यमानस्य योऽणिमा स ऊर्ध्वः समुदीषति तत्सर्पिर्भवति।।

"My child, when curd is churned, its fine particles which rise upwards, form butter.

2. एवमेव खलु सोम्यान्नस्याश्यमानस्य योऽणिमा स ऊर्ध्वः समुदीषति तन्मनो भवति।।

"Thus, my child, when food is consumed, the fine particles, which rise upwards, form the mind.

3. उपाꣳसोम्य पीयमानानां योऽणिमा स ऊर्ध्वः समुदीषति स प्राणो भवति।।

"Again, my child, when the water is drunk, the fine particles which ascend upwards, form the prāṇa.

4. तेजसः सोम्याश्यमानस्य योऽणिमा स ऊर्ध्वः समुदीषति सा वाग्भवति।।

"My child, when heat is consumed, the fine particles, which rise upwards, form speech.

5. अन्नमयꣳहि सोम्य मन आपोमयः प्राणस्तेजोमयी वागिति भूय एव मा भगवान्विज्ञापयत्विति तथा सोम्येति होवाच।।

"(Hence) verily the mind is aliment, the prāṇa water, and the speech heat." "Will it please my Lord to explain this again unto me ?" "Be it so, my child."

SECTION VII

1. षोडशकलः सोम्य पुरुष पञ्चदशाहानि माशीः काममपः पिबापोमयः प्राणो न पिबतो विच्छेत्स्यत इति।।

"Man, my child, is sixteen-fold.[14] Let him not eat for fifteen days, but let him drink according to his desire, for life is formed of water, and if it be sustained thereby it will not leave him."

2. स ह पञ्चदशाहानि नाशाथ हैनमुपससाद किं ब्रवीमि भो इत्यृचः सोम्य यजूꣳषि सामानीति स होवाच न वै मा प्रतिभान्ति भो इति।।

Verily he (Śvetaketu) did not eat for fifteen days. Then did he repair to the tutor and enquire, "Sir, what shall I repeat now ?" (The father said) "Do you, my child, repeat the Ṛk, Yajus and Sāma hymns." He replied, "Sir, of a truth none of them occurs (now) to my memory."

3. तꣳ होवाच यथा सोम्य महतोऽभ्याहितस्यैकोऽङ्गार खद्योतमात्रः परिशिष्टः स्यात्तेन ततोऽपि न बहु दहेदेवꣳ सोम्य ते षोडशानां कलानामेका कलातिशिष्टा स्यात्तयैतर्हि वेदान्नानुभवस्यशानाथ मे विज्ञास्यसीति।।

Unto him said the tutor, "My child, when a large fire leaves a small remnant, insignificant as (the spark of) the fire-fly, it cannot consume much (fuel, if the same be at once heaped over it); so of your sixteen parts only one now remains, and therefore you remember not the Vedas. Do you go and eat (first) what is meet. And then will you learn from me."

4. स हाशाथ हैनमुपससाद तꣳ ह यत्किंच पप्रच्छ सर्वꣳ ह प्रतिपेदे ।।

Verily, he ate, and then repaired to his tutor. Whatever he asked him he knew it all.

5. तꣳ होवाच यथा सोम्य महतोऽभ्याहतस्यैकङ्गारं खद्योतमात्रं परिशिष्टं तं तृणैरुपसमाधाय प्राज्वलयेत्तेन ततोऽपि बहु दहेत् ।।

He said to him "O my child, as a small remnant, insignificant as (the spark of) the fire-fly, of a large fire invigorated with little bits of hay or straw becomes powerful and able to consume much,

6. एवꣳ सोम्य ते षोडशानां कलानामेका कलातिशिष्टा-भूत्साऽन्नेनोपसमाहिता प्राज्वालीत्तयैतर्हि वेदाननुभवस्यन्न-मयꣳहि सोम्य मन आपोमयः प्राणस्तेजोमयी वागिति तद्धास्य विजज्ञाविति विजज्ञाविति ।।

"Even so when the last single remnant of thy sixteen parts is invigorated with food, you are enabled to understand the Vedas. Verily, the mind, my child, is made of food, the prāṇa of water, and the speech of heat." Of a truth he understood—verily he understood this.

SECTION VIII

1. उद्दालको हारुणिः श्वेतकेतुं पुत्रमुवाच स्वप्नान्तं मे सोम्य विजानीहीति यत्रैतत्पुरुषः स्वपिति नाम सता सोम्य तदा संपन्नो भवति स्वमपीतो भवति तस्मादेनꣳ स्वपितीत्याचक्षते स्वꣳ ह्यपीतो भवति ।।

Uddālaka, son of Aruṇa, unto his son Śvetaketu said, "Learn from me, my child, the nature of sleep. When man assumes the epithet 'sleeping' he identifies himself with the Universal Soul *(sat,* truth) he attains his self (sva), therefore he is said to be svapiti ('sleeping'); for then he attains his self.[15]

2. **स यथा शकुनिः सूत्रेण प्रबद्धो दिशं दिशं पतित्वान्यत्रायतनमलब्ध्वा बन्धनमेवोपश्रयत एवमेव खलु सोम्य तन्मनो दिशं दिशं पतित्वान्यत्रायतनमलब्ध्वा प्राणमेवोपश्रयते प्राणबन्धनꣳ हि सोम्य मन इति।।**

"A bird tied to a string after flying towards the sides and finding no place of rest, at last has recourse to the spot to which it is tied. Even so the mind, my child, after roaming towards all sides and failing to obtain a resting-place, at last takes the shelter of the Soul (prāṇa). Verily the mind has the Soul of its tie-rope.

3. **अशनापिपासे मे सोम्य विजानीहीति यत्रैतत्पुरुषोऽशिशिषति नामाप एव तदशितं नयन्ते तद्यथा गोनायोऽश्वनायः पूरुषनाय इत्येवं तदप आचक्षतेऽशनायेति तत्रैतच्छुङ्गमुत्पतितꣳ सोम्य विजानीहि नेदममूलं भविष्यतीति।।**

"Learn from me, my child, the nature of hunger and thirst. When man assumes the epithet 'hungry' (Aśiśiṣati) verily water then carries down the food, (through his gullet). Those who lead cattle are called *gonāya,* those who lead horses are called *aśvanāya,* those who lead men are *puruṣanāya;* accordingly water (which leads down food) is called *aśanāya.* Thereof this (body) is a product. Think not, O child, that it has proceeded without a cause."

4. **तस्य क्व मूलꣳ स्यादन्यत्रान्नादेवमेव खलु सोम्यान्नेन शुङ्गेनापोमूलमन्विच्छाद्भिः सोम्य शुङ्गेन तेजोमूलमन्विच्छ तेजसा सोम्य शुङ्गेन सन्मूलमन्विच्छ सन्मूलाः सोम्येमाः सर्वाः प्रजाः सदायतनाः सत्प्रतिष्ठाः।।**

(What is its cause, enquired Śvetaketu). "Where can be its cause (answered his father) except in aliment ? Thus, my child, you should know water to be the cause of the product aliment. Thus again heat is the cause of the product water; and of that product heat Truth is the cause. Hence verily, my child, all the varied objects of the universe have the Truth for their origin.

5. अथ यत्रैतत्पुरुषः पिपासति नाम तेज एव तत्पीतं नयते तद्यथा गोनायोऽश्वनायः पुरुषनाय इत्येवं तत्तेज आचष्ट उदन्येति तत्रैतदेव शुङ्गमुत्पतितꣳ सोम्य विजानीहि नेदममूलं भविष्यतीति।।

"When man assumes the epithet 'thirsty,' it is heat that carries down the drink through his gullet. Those who lead cattle are called *gonāya,* those who lead horses are called *aśvanāya,* those who lead men are called *puruṣanāyā*; and accordingly heat is called *undanya* (carrier of water); thereof this (body) is the product. Think not, my child, that it has proceeded, without a cause."

6. तस्य क्व मूलꣳ स्यादन्यत्राद्भ्योऽद्भिः सोम्य शुङ्गेन तेजोमूलमन्विच्छ तेजसा सोम्य शुङ्गेन सन्मूलमन्विच्छ सन्मूलाः सोम्येमाः सर्वाः प्रजाः सदायतनाः सत्प्रतिष्ठा यथा तु खलु सोम्येमास्तिस्रो देवताः पुरुषं प्राप्य त्रिवृत्त्रिवृदेकैका भवति तदुक्तं पुरस्तादेव भवत्यस्य सोम्य पुरुषस्य प्रयतो वाङ्मनसि संपद्यते मनः प्राणे प्राणस्तेजसि तेजः परस्यां देवतायाम्।।

"What is its cause ?" (enquired Śvetaketu). "What can be its cause but water ?" (replied his father). "Thus, my child, you should know heat to be the cause of the product water, and of that heat know Truth to be the cause. Hence Verily, my child, all these varied objects of the universe have the Truth for their origin, sustenance and end. How each of these three objects becomes threefold in man has been already described. When man departs (this life) his speech merges into the mind; the mind merges into life; the life into heat, and the heat into the Supreme Deity. This is its abstract form.

7. स य एषोऽणिमैतदात्म्यमिदꣳ सर्वं तत्सत्यꣳ स आत्मा तत्त्वमसि श्वेतकेतो इति भूय एव मा भगवान् विज्ञापयत्विति तथा सोम्येति होवाच॥

"All this universe has the (Supreme) Deity for its life. That Deity is Truth. He is the Universal Soul. Thou art He, O Śvetaketu."

"Will it please my Lord to explain this farther unto me ?" "Be it so, my child" : replied the tutor.

SECTION IX

1. यथा सोम्य मधु मधुकृतो निस्तिष्ठन्ति नानात्ययानां वृक्षाणाꣳरसान्समवहारमेकताꣳ रसं गमयन्ति॥

"As the bees, my child, intent upon making honey, collect the essence of various trees from different quarters and reduce them to one uniform fluid.

2. ते यथा तत्र न विवेकं लभन्तेऽमुष्याहं वृक्षस्य रसोऽस्म्यमुष्याहं वृक्षस्य रसोऽस्मीत्येवमेव खलु सोम्येमाः सर्वाः प्रजाः सति संपद्य न विदुः सति संपद्यामह इति॥

"Which no longer retains the idea of its having belonged to different trees; so, my child, created beings, when dead, know not they have attained the Truth.[16]

3. त इह व्याघ्रो व सिꣳहो वा वृको वा वराहो वा कीटो वा पतङ्गो व दꣳशो वा मशको वा यद्यद्भवन्ति तदाभवन्ति॥

"They are born again in the form in which they lived before, whether that be of a tiger, a lion, a wolf, a bear, a worm, an insect, a gnat, or a mosquito.

4. स य एषोऽणिमैतदात्म्यमिदꣳ सर्वं तत्सत्यꣳ स आत्मा तत्त्वमसि श्वेतकेतो इति भूय एव मा भगवान् विज्ञापयत्विति तथा सोम्येति होवाच॥

"That particle which is the Soul of all this is Truth : it is the universal Soul. O Śvetaketu, thou art That." "Will it please, my Lord, to explain it again unto me ?" "Be it so, my child," replied he.

Men having slept in their homes repair to a distant village and there remember that they have come away from their houses; but created beings do not remember that they have come away from the Truth; Why so : this is the question which the father is to explain.

SECTION X

1. इमाः सोम्य नद्यः पुरस्तात्प्राच्यः स्यन्दन्ते पश्चात्प्रतीच्यस्ताः समुद्रात्समुद्रमेवापियन्ति स समुद्र एव भवति ता यथा तत्र न विदुरियमहमस्मीति॥

"These rivers, my child, proceed from the East towards the West, thence from the ocean (they rise in the form of vapour and dropping again they flow towards the South and) merge into the ocean. Here as they do not remember what they were;[17]

2. एवमेव खलु सोम्येमाः सर्वाः प्रजाः सत आगत्य न विदुः सत आगच्छामह इति त इह व्याघ्रो वा सिꣳहो वा वृको वा वराहो वा कीटो वा पतङ्गो वा दꣳशो वा मशको वा यद्यद्भवन्ति तदा भवन्ति॥

"Even so all these created beings having proceeded from the Truth, know not that they have issued therefrom. They therefore become of the form they had before, whether that be of a tiger, a lion, a wolf, a bear, a worm, an insect, a gnat, or a mosquito.

3. स य एषोऽणिमैतदात्म्यमिदꣳ सर्वं तत्सत्यꣳ स आत्मा तत्त्वमसि श्वेतकेतो इति भूय एव मा भगवान् विज्ञापयत्विति तथा सोम्येति होवाच॥

"That particle which is the Soul of all this is Truth; it is the Universal Soul. O Śvetaketu, thou art That ." "Will it please my Lord to explain it (once) again unto me (how beings, after attaining, during sleep and after death, the one Universal Soul, do not lose their identity) ?" "Be it so, my child," replied he.

Section XI

1. अस्य सोम्य महतो वृक्षस्य यो मूलेऽभ्याहन्याज्जीवन्स्रवेद्यो मध्येऽभ्याहन्याज्जीवन्स्रवेद्योऽग्रेऽभ्याहन्याज्जीवन्स्रवेत्स एष जीवेनात्मनानुप्रभूतः पेपीयमानो मोदमानस्तिष्ठति॥

"My child, were one to strike once on the root of yonder wide-spreading tree, it would discharge (a little of its) sap : struck over on the middle the tree would (still) discharge its sap, and so would it if it were struck once on the top. Pervaded by life it would continue to draw the humours (of the earth) and thrive.

2. अस्य यदेकाꣳ शाखां जीवो जहात्यथ सा शुष्यति द्वितीयां जहात्यथ सा शुष्यति तृतीयां जहात्यथ सा शुष्यति सर्वं जहाति सर्वः शुष्यत्येवमेव खलु सोम्य विद्धीति होवाच॥

"(But) thereof when life forsakes one of the branches, it dries up. When a second is forsaken, it dries up. When a third is forsaken, it too dries up; and when the entire tree is forsaken by life, the whole dries up. Verily, know my pupil," continued he.

3. जीवापेतं वाव किलेदं म्रियते न जीवो म्रियत इति स य एषोऽणिमैतदात्म्यमिदꣳ सर्वं तत्सत्यꣳ स आत्मा तत्त्वमसि श्वेतकेतो इति भूय एव मा भगवान् विज्ञापयत्विति तथा सोम्येति होवाच॥

"When this (body) is forsaken by life it dies, but the life dies not. That particle which is the soul of this (body) is Truth; it is the Universal Soul. O Śvetaketu. Thou art That." "Will it please my Lord to explain it once again unto me" (how the creation proceedeth from the invisible Truth which has neither name nor form and is mere existence)?" "Be it so, my child," said the father.

Section XII

1. न्यग्रोधफलमत आहरेतीदं भगव इति भिन्धीति भिन्नं भगव इति किमत्र पश्यसीत्यण्व्य इवेमा धाना भगव इत्यासामङ्गैकां भिन्धीति भिन्ना भगव इति किमत्र पश्यसीति न किंचन भगव इति॥

"Bring me a fruit of the Nyagrodha[18] tree." "Here it is, my Lord," said the pupil. "Break it." "It is broken, my Lord." "What do you perceive in it ?" "Some very small seeds, my Lord." "Will you, dear , break one of them ?" "Here, I have broken it, my Lord." "What do you perceive in it ?" "Nothing, my Lord."

2. तꣳ होवाच यं वै सोम्यैतमणिमानं न निभालयस एतस्य वै सोम्यैषोऽणिम्न एवं महान्नयग्रोधस्तिष्ठति।।

Unto him said the father, "Where, my child, you perceive nothing, there dwells invisibly a mighty Nyagrodha.

3. श्रद्धत्स्व सोम्येति स य एषोऽणिमैतदात्म्यमिदꣳ सर्वं तत्सत्यꣳ स आत्मा तत्त्वमसि श्वेतकेतो इति भूय एव मा भगवान् विज्ञापयत्विति तथा सोम्येति होवाच।।

"Mind it, my child, that particle which is the soul of all, that is Truth—it is the Universal Soul. O Śvetaketu, thou art That." "Will it please my Lord to explain to once again (how, since the creation proceeds from the Truth, it does not attain permanence—truthfulness ?)" "Be it so, my child," said the father.

SECTION XIII

1. लवणमेतदुदकेऽवधायाथ मा प्रातरुपसीदथा इति स ह तथा चकार तꣳ होवाच यद्दोषा लवणमुदकेऽवाधा अङ्ग तदाहरेति तद्धावमृश्य न विवेद।।

"Dissolve this salt in that water, and appear before me to-morrow morning." He did so, unto him said (the father), "My child, find out the salt that you put in that water last night." The salt, having been dissolved, could not be made out. (Unto Śvetaketu said his father,) "Child."

2. यथा विलीनमेवाङ्गास्यान्तादाचामेति कथमिति लवणमिति मध्यादाचामेति कथमिति लवणमित्यन्तादाचामेति कथमिति लवणमित्यभिप्राश्यैनदथ मोपसीदथा इति तद्ध तथा चकार तच्छश्वत्संवर्तते तꣳहोवाचात्र वाव किल सत्सोम्य न निभालयसेऽत्रैव किलेति।।

"Do you taste a little from the top of that water." The child did so. (After a while the father enquired) "How tastes it ?" "It is saltish" (said Śvetaketu). "Try a little from the middle." (He did so The father then enquired) "How is it ?" "It is saltish" (replied the son). "Taste a little from the bottom," (ordered he. The son did so). (The father then enquired) "How is it ?" "It is saltish." "If so (throwing it away) wash your mouth and grieve not," verily he did so, (and said to his father), "The salt that I put in the water exists for ever; (through I perceive it not by my eyes, it is felt by my tongue) " (Unto him) said (his father), "Verily such is the case with the Truth, my child. Though you perceive it not, it nevertheless pervades this (body).

3. स य एषोऽणिमैतदात्म्यमिदꣳ सर्वं तत्सत्यꣳ स आत्मा तत्त्वमसि श्वेतकेतो इति भूय एव मा भगवान् विज्ञापयत्विति तथा सोम्येति होवाच॥

"That particle which is the soul of all this is Truth; it is the Universal Soul. O Śvetaketu, thou art That." "Will it please my Lord to explain farther (how, like the salt, which though invisible is still perceptible by the tongue, can the Soul, the cause of the world, unperceivable by the organs of perception, be grasped by the mind—the Soul by not attaining which, I am unblest, and by attaining which I am blest; and what means exist for its attainment ?)" "Be it so, my child," replied (the father).

SECTION XIV

1. यथा सोम्य पुरुषं गन्धारेभ्योऽभिनद्धाक्षमानीय तं ततोऽतिजने विसृजेत्स यथा तत्र प्राङ्वोदङ्वाधराङ्वा प्रत्यङ्वा प्रध्मायीताभिनद्धाक्ष आनीतोऽभिनद्धाक्षो विसृष्टः॥

"O my child, in the world when a man with blind-folded eyes, is carried away from Gandhāra[19] and left in a lonely place, he makes the East and the North and the West resound by crying, 'I have been brought here blind-folded. I am here left blind-folded.'

2. तस्य यथाभिनहनं प्रमुच्य प्रब्रूयादेतां दिशं गन्धारा एतां दिशं व्रजेति स ग्रामाद्ग्रामं पृच्छन् पण्डितो मेधावी गन्धारानेवोपसंपद्येतैवमेवेहाचार्यवान् पुरुषो वेद तस्य तावदेव चिरं यावन्न विमोक्ष्येऽथ संपत्स्य इति।।

"Thereupon (some kind-hearted man) unties the fold on his eyes and says, 'This is the way to Gandhāra' proceed thou by this way.' The sensible man proceeds from village to village, enquiring the way, and reaches at last the (province) of Gandhāra. Even thus a man who has a duly qualified teacher learns (his way) and thus remains liberated (from all wordly ties) till he attains (the Truth—Mokṣa).

3. स य एषोऽणिमैतदात्म्यमिदꣳ सर्वं तत्सत्यꣳस आत्मा तत्त्वमसि श्वेतकेतो इति भूय एव मा भगवान्विज्ञापयत्विति तथा सोम्येति होवाच।।

"That particle which is the soul of all this is Truth—it is the Universal Soul. O Śvetaketu, thou art That."

"Will it please my Lord to explain farther (by example, how one attains the Truth) ?" "Be it so my child," replied (the father).

Section XV

1. पुरुषꣳ सोम्योतोपतापिनं ज्ञातयः पर्युपासते जानासि मां जानासि मामिति तस्य यावन्न वाङ्मनसि संपद्यते मनः प्राणे प्राणस्तेजसि तेजः परस्यां देवतायां तावज्जानाति।।

"My child, when a man is laid up with a mortal illness, his relations, surround him to render him service and enquire 'Do you recognise me, do your recognise me ?' He recognises them until his speech merges into his mind, his mind merges into his life, his life merges into heat, and the heat into the Supreme Deity.

2. अथ यदास्य वाङ्मनसि संपद्यते मनः प्राणे प्राणस्तेजसि तेजः परस्यां देवतायामथ न जानाति।।

"When his speech is merged into his mind, and his mind is

merged into his life, his life is merged into heat, and heat into the Supreme Deity, he recognises them not.

3. स य एषोऽणिमैतदात्म्यमिदꣳ सर्वं तत्सत्यꣳ स आत्मा तत्त्वमसि श्वेतकेतो इति भूय एव मा भगवान् विज्ञापयत्विति तथा सोम्येति होवाच॥

"That particle which is the soul of all this is Truth—it is the Universal Soul. O Śvetaketu, thou art That." "Will it please my Lord to explain farther (by an example, why the ignorant, after death should return to this world, while the liberated does not, although the dead and the liberated seem equally to attain the truth)?" "Be it so, my child," replied (the father).

SECTION XVI

1. पुरुषꣳ सोम्योत हस्तगृहीतमानयन्त्यपहार्षीत्स्तेयमकार्षीत्परशुमस्मै तपतेति स यदि तस्य कर्ता भवति तत एवानृतमात्मानं कुरुते सोऽनृताभिसन्धोऽनृतेनात्मानमन्तर्धाय परशुं तप्तं प्रतिगृह्णाति स दह्यतेऽथ हन्यते॥

"O my child, when a man (suspected of theft) is brought with his hands tied up and told, 'Thou hast stolen.' (He denies. The magistrate thereupon orders), 'Let the hatchet be heated for him.'[20] If he should happen to be the author of the theft, and seek to protect himself in untruth, he, the upholder of untruth, enveloping his soul in an untruth, grasps the heated blade and is burnt as well as punished.

2. अथ यदि तस्याकर्ता भवति तत एव सत्यमात्मानं कुरुते स सत्याभिसन्धः सत्येनात्मानमन्तर्धाय परशुं तप्तं प्रतिगृह्णाति स न दह्यतेऽथ मुच्यते॥

"While, if he happened not to be the author of the theft and be desirous of making himself truthful, he, the upholder of truth, enveloping his soul in truth, grasps the heated blade which burns him not, and liberates himself (from his fetters).

3. स यथा तत्र नादाह्येतैतदात्म्यमिदꣳ सर्वं तत्सत्यꣳ स आत्मा तत्त्वमसि श्वेतकेतो इति तद्धास्य विजज्ञाविति विजज्ञाविति ।।

"Even as he, (by the intervention of truth,) escapes from the heated blade, so all this has truth for its soul; it is the Truth : it is the Universal Soul. O Śvetaketu, thou art That.

Thus verily was he instructed—thus was he instructed.

Foot Notes

1. Lit., not reading अननूच्य.
2. Lit., Has become *Brahmabandhu* or a friend or relation of a *Brāhmaṇa* but not himself a Brāhmaṇa.

   The commentator supposes that after this injunction Āruṇi must have proceeded on a pilgrimage, or else, being a learned man, he would have himself taught his son instead of sending him to a foreign tutor.

3. The use of the word *existence* would have perhaps obviated the necessity of the periphrasis—"a state of being"; but existence *(ex sistere),* according to the accidental metaphysicians, is the actuality of essence; it is the act by which the essences of things are actually in *rerum natura*—beyond their causes; whereas—the object here is to imply a state when things are in the objective power of their causes, *i.e.,* before they are produced by their causes. This state is best indicated by the *To ov* "that which is" of the ancients; and we have therefore used its English equivalent "being," and its periphrasis—or the nearest, though not the most elegant, version of the Sanskrit *sat.* The Upaniṣad here enters upon the most important ontological question—a belief in To öv as opposed to To övTa—in one and not in many fundamental principles of things, and a correct appreciation of the term, therefore, is of the utmost consequence.
4. 'That which did not exist before is-substance,' says the author of the *Tarkasangraha* कार्यं प्रागभावप्रतियोगी।
5. *Lit.,* He saw. The expression *aikṣata,* 'seeing' in the case of inanimate heat and water is metaphorical, says Śaṅkara.
6. That which burns, digests, gives light and is red. According to Śaṇkara, it is presumed that the Intelligence first created space, then wind and then heat, as described in the Taittirīya-upaniṣad.

7. The word *ap* in Sanskrit is always used in the plural, but for the sake of consistency we have here retained the singular form.

8. The commentator explains why the oviparous and other creations are made the sources instead of eggs, wombs and seeds, by observing that the eggs, etc., cannot come to existence unless they proceed from their parents, and hence the true sources are the parents and not their issue.

9. The form he had conceived.—Śaṅkara.

10. This verse does not occur in the Vājasaneya-Upaniṣad.

11. *i.e.,* each to be divided into two parts and one of them to be subdivided into two parts, which art to be mixed with the halves of the other two, so that each trinary form will include half of one and a quarter of each of the two other elements.—Śaṅkara.

12. The commenator explains this by a very appropriate illustration. He says cloth is an aggregate of threads; remove them, and the cloth ceases to be. So Agni is an aggregate of its three qualities, which taken away it is no longer existent.

13. The commentator observes that by 'heat-producing,' articles such as oil and butter are meant.

14. The commentator does not explain what is meant by the epithet sixteen-fold. The text of the Praśna, however, leaves no doubt as to what is here alluded to.

15. A play on the word *Sva* "self" and *svap* "to sleep." Analogues like unto this occur very frequently in the Upaniṣads. Sleep and death are here taken as synonymous.

16. *Sati sampadya,* "merging in truth."

17. Lit., that I am this, I am this.

18. Here the *Ficus indica* is evidently meant, although the word is also applied to the *Mimosa albida,* and the *Solviniaicarculta.*

19. This word is used in the plural in the Sanskrit text.

20. Adverting to the ordeal by fire.

SEVENTH CHAPTER

Section I

1. ॐ । अधीहि भगव इति होपससाद सनत्कुमारं नारदस्तꣳ होवाच यद्वेत्थ तेन मोपसीद ततस्त ऊर्ध्वं वक्ष्यामीति ।।

OM ! Of a truth Nārada repaired to Sanatkumāra. He said, "Deign to give me instruction, O Lord." Unto him said the other, "Relate unto me what you know, I shall then teach you what is beyond."

2. स होवाचर्ग्वेदं भगवोऽध्येमि यजुर्वेदꣳ सामवेदमाथर्वणं चतुर्थमितिहासपुराणं पञ्चमं वेदानां वेदं पित्र्यꣳ राशिं दैवं निधिं वाकोवाक्यमेकायनं देवविद्यां ब्रह्मविद्यां भूतविद्यां क्षत्रविद्यां नक्षत्रविद्याꣳ सर्पदेवजनविद्यामेतद्भगवोऽध्येमि ।।

He replied "O Lord, I have read the Ṛg-Veda, the Yajur-Veda, the Sāma-Veda, fourth, the Atharva-Veda, fifth, the Itihāsa and Purāṇa,[1] grammar, [2] rituals, the science of number,[3] physics,[4] chronology,[5] logic, polity,[6] technology,[7] the sciences cognate to the Vedas,[8] the science of spirits,[9] archery,[10] astronomy, the science of antidotes,[11] and the fine arts.[12] All these have I read, O Lord.

3. सोऽहं भगवो मन्त्रविदेवास्मि नात्मविच्छ्रुतꣳ ह्येव मे भगवद्दृशेभ्यस्तरति शोकमात्मविदिति सोऽहं भगवः शोचामि तं मा भगवाञ्छोकस्य पारं तारयत्विति तꣳ होवाच यद्वै किंचैतदध्यगीष्ठा नामैवैतत् ।।

"Thus do I know, Sir, the Mantras or words only, and not the spirit (thereof). I have heard that the wordly-afflicited can find relief through men like unto your lordship. Even I am, O Lord, in grief. Pray relieve me from my afflicition." Unto him said Sanatkumāra, "All that you have learnt is nominal.

4. नाम वा ऋग्वेदो यजुर्वेदः सामवेद आथर्वणश्चतुर्थ इतिहास-पुराणः पञ्चमो वेदानां वेदः पित्र्यो राशिर्दैवो निधिर्वाकोवाक्य- मेकायनं देवविद्या ब्रह्मविद्या भूतविद्या क्षत्रविद्या नक्षत्रविद्या सर्वदेवजनविद्या नामैवेतन्नामोपास्वेति।।

"The names only of Ṛg-Veda, the Yajur-Veda, the Sāma-Veda, fourth, the Atharva-Veda, fifth the Itihāsa and Purāṇa, grammar, rituals, the science of numbers, physics, chronology, logic, polity, technology, the sciences cognate to the Vedas, the science of spirits, archery, astronomy, the science of antidotes, and the fine arts,—these are names only that you have adored.

5. स यो नाम ब्रह्मेत्युपास्ते यावन्नाम्नो गतं तत्रास्य यथाकामचारो भवति यो नाम ब्रह्मेत्युपास्तेऽस्ति भगवो नाम्नो भूय इति नाम्नो वाव भूयोऽस्तीति तन्मे भगवान्ब्रवीत्विति।।

"(Hear from me what is the reward of him) who adores the name (itself) as Brahman. He who believes the name itself to be Brahman the moment he acquires that name becomes able to perform whatever he desires." "Is there anything, O Lord, greater than a name ?" "There is something greater than a name." "Will it please my Lord to explain that unto me ?"

Section II

1. वाग्वाव नाम्नो भूयसी वाग्वा ऋग्वेदं विज्ञापयति यजुर्वेदः सामवेदमाथर्वणं चतुर्थमितिहासपुराणं पञ्चमं वेदानां वेदं पित्र्यः राशिं दैवं निधिं वाकोवाक्यमेकायनं देवविद्यां ब्रह्मविद्यां भूतविद्यां क्षत्रविद्यां नक्षत्रविद्याः सर्पदेवजनविद्यां दिवं च पृथिवीं च वायुं चाकाशं चापश्च तेजश्च देवाःश्च मनुष्याःश्च पशुःश्च वयाः सि च तृणवनस्पतीञ्छ्वाप-दान्याकीटपतङ्गपिपीलकं धर्मं चाधर्मं च सत्यं चानृतं च साधु च साधु च हृदयज्ञं चाहृदयज्ञं च यद्वै वाङ्नाभविष्यन्न

धर्मो नाधर्मो व्यज्ञापयिष्यन्न सत्यं नानृतं न साधु नासाधु न हृदयज्ञो नाहृदयज्ञो वागेवैतत्सर्वं विज्ञापयति वाचमुपास्स्वेति।।

"Verily Speech is greater than a name. Speech points out the Ṛg-Veda, so does it indicate the Yajur-Veda, the Sāma -Veda, fourth the Atharva-Veda, fifth the Itihāsa and Purāṇa, grammar, ritual, the sciences of numbers, physics, chronology, logic, polity, technology, the sciences cognate to the Vedas, the science of spirits, archery, astronomy, the science of antidotes, the fine arts, the heaven, the earth, the air, the sky, light, gods, men, beasts, birds, grasses, trees, carnivorous animals, worms, insects, ants, virtue, vice, truth, untruth, propriety, impropriety, gratefulness, and ungratefulness; Speech indicates all these. Do you therefore adore Speech ?

2. स यो वाचं ब्रह्मेत्युपास्ते यावद्वाचो गतं तत्रास्य यथाकामचारो भवति यो वाचं ब्रह्मेत्युपास्तेऽस्ति भगवो भूय इति वाचो वाव भूयोऽस्तीति तन्मे भगवान्ब्रवीत्विति।।

"(Hear from me what is the reward of him) who adores Speech as Brahman. He who adores Speech as Brahman, the moment he attains the regions[13] of Speech, he becomes able to perform whatever he desires." "Is there anything, O Lord, greater than Speech ?" "There is something even greater than Speech." "Will it please my Lord to explain that unto me ?"

SECTION III

1. मनो वाच वाचो भूयो यथा वै द्वे वामलके द्वे वा कोले द्वौ वाक्षौ मुष्टिरनुभवत्येवं वाचं च नाम च मनोऽनुभवति स यदा मनसा मनस्यति मन्त्रानधीयीयेत्यथाधीते कर्माणि कुर्वीतेत्यथ कुरुते पुत्रांश्च पशूंश्चेच्छेयेत्यथेच्छत इमं च लोकममुं चेच्छेयेत्यथेच्छते मनो ह्यात्मा मनो हि लोको मनो हि ब्रह्म मन उपास्स्वेति।।

"Verily Mind is greater than Speech. When two myrobalans[14] or two plums, or two *harītaki*[15] fruits are held in the closed fist, they are therein inclosed, so are Name and Speech included in the mind. When one wishes in his mind to study the mantras he does it; when he wishes to perform works he does them; when he wishes for children or cattle he has them; when he wishes for this region or that, he has it; the Mind is life, the Mind is regions, the Mind is Brahman. Do ye adore the mind.

2. स यो मनो ब्रह्मेत्युपास्ते तावन्मनसो गतं यत्रास्य यथाकामचारो भवति यो मनो ब्रह्मेत्युपास्तेऽस्ति भगवो मनसो भूय इति मनसो वाव भूयोऽस्तीति तन्मे भगवान्ब्रवीत्विति॥

"(Hear from me what is the reward of him) who adores the Mind as Brahman. He who adores the Mind as Brahman, the moment he attains the regions of the Mind becomes able to perform whatever he desires." "Is there anything, O Lord, greater than the Mind ?" "There is something even greater than the Mind." "Will it please My Lord to explain that unto me ?"

SECTION IV

1. संकल्पो वाव मनसो भूयान्यदा वै संकल्पयतेऽथ मनस्यत्यथ वाचमीरयति तामु नाम्नीरयति नाम्नि मन्त्रा एकं भवन्ति मन्त्रेषु कर्माणि॥

"Verily Will[16] is even greater than the Mind. When one wills he desires; next he articulates speech in a name; in that name mantras identify themselves; and in the mantras abide all ritual works.

2. तानि ह वा एतानि संकल्पैकायनानि संकल्पात्मकानि संकल्पे प्रतिष्ठितानि समक्लृपतां द्यावापृथिवी समकल्पेतां वायुश्चाकाशं च समकल्पन्तामापश्च तेजश्च तेषां संक्लृप्त्यै वर्षं संकल्पते वर्षस्य संक्लृप्त्या अन्नं संकल्पतेऽन्नस्य संक्लृप्त्यै प्राणाः संकल्पन्ते प्राणानां संक्लृप्त्यै मन्त्राः

संकल्पन्ते मन्त्राणाः संक्लृप्त्यै कर्माणि संकल्पन्ते कर्मणाः संक्लृप्त्यै लोकः संकल्पते लोकस्य संक्लृप्त्यै सर्वः संकल्पते स एष संकल्पः संकल्पमुपास्स्वेति।।

"Of a truth those (works) have an only support in Will; they have the Will for their soul; they abide in the Will. The heaven and the earth are united (as by will);[17] the air and the sky are united (as by will); water and heat are united (as by will). By their union the year is formed. By the formation (saṅkḷptyai) of the year, aliment is produced (saṅkalpate). By the production (Saṅkḷptyai) of aliment, animated creatures are produced (saṅkalpante). By the production (saṅkḷptyai) of mantras ritual works are produced (saṅkalpante). By the production (saṅkḷptyai) of ritual works (their) fruition *is* produced (saṅkalpate). By the production (saṅkḷptyai) of fruition the earth is produced (saṅkalpate). Even thus is Will (saṅkalpa). Do thou adore Will.

3. स यः संकल्पं ब्रह्मेत्युपास्ते क्लृप्तान्वै स लोकान् ध्रुवान् ध्रुवः प्रतिष्ठितान् प्रतिष्ठितोऽव्यथमानानव्यथमानोऽ-भिसिध्यति यावत् संकल्पस्य गतं तत्रास्य यथाकामचारो भवति यः संकल्पं ब्रह्मेत्युपास्तेऽस्ति भगवः संकल्पाद्भूय इति संकल्पाद्वाव भूयोऽस्तीति तन्मे भगवान्ब्रवीत्विति।।

"He who adores the Will as Brahman abides permanently and without pain, in the permanent, renowned and painless regions of Will. He who adores Will as Brahman, the moment he obtains the regions of Will, becomes able to perform whatever he desires," "Is there, O Lord, anything greater than Will ?" There is something even greater than Will. "Will it please my Lord to explain that unto me ?"

SECTION V

1. चित्तं वाव संकल्पाद्भूयो यदा वै चेतयतेऽथ संकल्पयतेऽथ मनस्यत्यथ वाचमीरयति तामु नाम्नीरयति नाम्नि मन्त्रा एकं भवन्ति मन्त्रेषु कर्माणि।।

Verily Sensitivity is[18] even greater than Will. When one feels, he wills, next he desires, he then articulates speech, which merges into a name, in that name the mantras identify themselves, and in the mantras abide all ritual works.

2. तानि ह वा एतानि चित्तैकायनानि चित्तात्मानि चित्ते प्रतिष्ठितानि तस्माद्यद्यपि बहुविदचित्तो भवति नायमस्ती-त्येवैनमाहुर्यदयं वेद यद्वा अयं विद्वान्नेत्थमचित्तः स्यादित्यथ यद्यल्पविच्चित्तवान्भवति तस्मा एवोत शुश्रूषन्ते चित्तꣳह्येवैषामेकायनं चित्तमात्मा चित्तं प्रतिष्ठा चित्तमुपास्स्वेति।।

"Of a truth those works have an only support in Sensitivity; they have Sensitivity for their soul; they abide in Sensitivity. Therefore were one will versed in many Śāstras to be without Sensitivity, people would say with reference to him, 'Whatever he knows is nothing, for he knows not (what is) Sensitivity, while all wish to hear him who with a little knowledge (of the Śāstras) possesses Sensitivity. Verily Sensitivity is the one source of all these; Sensitivity is the soul; Sensitivity is the stand-point (*pratiṣṭhā).* Do thou adore Sensitivity.

3. स यश्चित्तं ब्रह्मेत्युपास्ते चित्तान्वै स लोकान् ध्रुवान् ध्रुवः प्रतिष्ठितान् प्रतिष्ठितोऽव्यथमानानव्यथमानोऽभिसिद्ध्यति यावच्चित्तस्य गतं तत्रास्य यथाकामचारो भवति यश्चित्तं ब्रह्मेत्युपास्तेऽस्ति भगवाश्चित्ताद्भूय इति चित्ताद्वाव भूयोऽस्तीति तन्मे भगवान्ब्रवीत्विति।।

"He who adores Sensitivity as Brahman, abides permanently with renown and painlessness in permanent, painless and renowned regions. He who adores Sensitivity as Brahman, the moment he obtains the regions of Sensitivity, becomes able to perform whatever he desires." "Is there, O Lord, anything greater than Sensitivity ?" "There is something even greater than Sensitivity." Will it please my Lord to explain that unto me?"

SECTION VI

1. ध्यानं वाव चित्ताद्भूयो ध्यायतीव पृथिवी ध्यायतीवान्तरिक्षं ध्यायतीव द्यौर्ध्यायन्तीवापो ध्यायन्तीव पर्वता ध्यायन्तीव देवमनुष्यास्तस्माद्य इह मनुष्याणां महत्तां प्राप्नुवन्ति ध्यानापादाꣳशा इवैव ते भवन्त्यथ येऽल्पाः कलहिनः पिशुना उपवादिनस्तेऽथ ये प्रभवो ध्यानापादाꣳशा इवैव ते भवन्ति ध्यानमुपास्स्वेति॥

"Verily Relflection is even greater than Sensitivity. The earth abides as if in Reflection;[19] the sky abides as if in Reflection; the heaven abides as if in Reflectinon; the water abides as if in Reflection; the mountains abide as if in Reflections, even gods and men abide as if in Reflection. Therefore those who attain greatness among men become as it were partakers of Reflection. So do those who are unmindful, quarrelsome, cruel and slanderous, become as it were partakers of Reflection. Do thou adore Reflection.

2. स यो ध्यानं ब्रह्मेत्युपास्ते यावद्ध्यानस्य गतं तत्रास्य यथाकामचारो भवति यो ध्यानं ब्रह्मेत्युपास्तेऽस्ति भगवो ध्यानाद्भूय इति ध्यानाद्वाव भूयोऽस्तीति तन्मे भगवान्ब्रवीत्विति॥

"*Listen what is the reward of him* who adores Reflection as Brahman. He who adores Reflection as Brahman, the moment he attains the Regions of Reflection, becomes able to perform whatever he desires ?" "Is there, O Lord, anything greater than this Reflection ?" "There is something even greater than this Reflection." "Will it please my Lord to explain that unto me ?"

SECTION VII

1. विज्ञानं वाव ध्यानाद्भूयो विज्ञानेन वा ऋग्वेदं विजानाति यजुर्वेदꣳ सामवेदमाथर्वणं चतुर्थमितिहासपुराणं पञ्चमं

वेदानां वेदं पित्र्यꣳराशिं दैवं निधिं वाकोवाक्यमेकायनं देवविद्यां ब्रह्मविद्यां भूतविद्यां क्षत्रविद्यां नक्षत्रविद्याꣳ सर्पदेवजनविद्यां दिवं च पृथिवीं च वायुं चाकाशं चापश्च तेजश्च देवाꣳश्च मनुष्याꣳश्च पशूꣳश्च वयाꣳसि च तृणवनस्पतीञ्छ्वापदान्याकीटपतङ्गपिपीलकं धर्मं चाधर्मं च सत्यं चानृतं च साधु चासाधु च हृदयज्ञं चाहृदयज्ञं चान्नं च रसं चेमं च लोकममुं च विज्ञानेनैव विजानाति विज्ञानमुपास्स्वेति।।

"Verily Knowledge[20] is even greater than Reflection. From Knowledge men know the Ṛg-Veda, the Yajur-Veda, the Sāma-Veda, fourth the Ātharva, fifth the Itihāsa and Purāṇa, grammar, rituals, the science of numbers, physics, chronology, logic, polity, technology, the sciences congnate to the Vedas, the science of spirits, archery, astronomy, the science of antidotes, the fine arts,[21] the heaven, the earth, the air, the sky, the water, light, the gods, men, birds, grasses and trees, wild beasts, as also worms, insects, and ants, virtue, vice, truth, untruth, the honest and the dishonest, him who knoweth the heart as well as him who knoweth it not, aliment, humours, and this region and that : all these are known through Knowledge. Do thou adore Knowledge.

2. स यो विज्ञानं ब्रह्मेत्युपास्ते विज्ञानवतो वै स लोकाञ्ज्ञानवतोऽभिसिद्ध्यति यावद्विज्ञानस्य गतं तत्रास्य यथाकामचारो भवति यो विज्ञानं ब्रह्मेत्युपास्तेऽस्ति भगवो विज्ञानाद्भूय इति विज्ञानाद्वाव भूयोऽस्तीति तन्मे भगवान्ब्रवीत्विति।।

"He who adores Knowledge as Brahman, abides in wisdom in the region of Knowledge.[22] He who adores Knowledge as Brahman, the moment he attains the regions of Knowledge, becomes able to achieve whatever he desires." "Is there, O Lord, anything greater than Knowledge ?" "There is something yet greater than Knowledge." "Will it please my Lord to explain that unto me?"

SECTION VIII

1. बलं वाव विज्ञानाद्भूयोऽपि ह शतं विज्ञानवतामेको बलवानाकम्पयते स यदा बली भवत्यथोत्थाता भवत्युत्तिष्ठन्परिचरिता भवति परिचरन्नुपसत्ता भवत्युपसीदन्द्रष्टा भवति श्रोता भवति मन्ता भवति बोद्धा भवति कर्ता भवति विज्ञाता भवति बलेन वै पृथिवी तिष्ठति बलेनान्तरिक्षं बलेन द्यौर्बलेन पर्वता बलेन देवमनुष्या बलेन पशवश्च वयाꣳसि च तृणवनस्पतयः श्वापदान्याकीटपतङ्गपिपीलकं बलेन लोकस्तिष्ठति बलमुपास्स्वेति ॥

"Verily Power is even greater than Knowledge. Even a single powerful man can make a hundred men of Knowledge tremble. When one becomes powerful he rises; rising he becomes subservient (to his tutors);[23] subserving he becomes their favourite companion.[24] From being a favourite companion he becomes well taught, well informed, docile, intelligent, able to act, and full of knowledge. Of a truth the earth is supported by power; the ethereal space, the heaven, mountains, men and gods, beasts and birds, grasses and trees, wild animals, as also worms, insects, ants and even the world, are supported[25] by power. Do thou adore Power.

2. स यो बलं ब्रह्मेत्युपास्ते यावद्बलस्य गतं तत्रास्य यथाकामचारो भवति यो बलं ब्रह्मेत्युपास्तेऽस्ति भगवो बलाद्भूय इति बलाद्वाव भूयोऽस्तीति तन्मे भगवान्ब्रवीत्विति ॥

"*Listen what is the reward of him* who adores Power as Brahman. He who adores Power as Brahman, the moment he attains the regions of Power, becomes able to perform whatever he desires." "Is there anything, O Lord, superior to Power ?" "There is something yet greater than Power." "Will it please my Lord to explain that unto me ?"

SECTION IX

1. अन्नं वाव बलाद्भूयस्तस्माद्यद्यपि दशरात्रीर्नाश्नीयाद्यद्युह जीवेदथवाद्रष्टाश्रोतामन्ताबोद्धाकर्ताविज्ञाता भवत्यथान्नस्यायै द्रष्टा भवति श्रोता भवति मन्ता भवति बोद्धा भवति कर्ता भवति विज्ञाता भवत्यन्नमुपास्स्वेति।।

"Verily Aliment is even greater than Power; for were one to fast for ten nights he would be unable to see, unable to hear, unable to think, unable to consider, unable to act and unable to acquire knowledge. While by consuming Aliment he is enabled to see, to hear, to think, to consider, to act and to acquire knowledge. Do thou adore Aliment.

2. स योऽन्नं ब्रह्मेत्युपास्तेऽन्नवतो वै स लोकान्पानवतोऽभिसिद्ध्यति यावदन्नस्य गतं तत्रास्य यथाकामचारो भवति योऽन्नं ब्रह्मेत्युपास्तेऽस्ति भगवोऽन्नाद्भूय इत्यन्नाद्वाव भूयोऽस्तीति तन्मे भगवान्ब्रवीत्विति।।

"He who adores Aliment as Brahman, acquires regions replete with food and drink. He who adores Aliment as Brahman, the moment he attains the regions of Aliment, becomes able to achieve whatever he desires." "Is there anything, O Lord, greater than Aliment ?" "Yes, there is something yet greater than Aliment ?" "Will it please my Lord to explain that unto me ?"

SECTION X

1. आपो वावान्नाद्भूयस्यस्तस्माद्यदा सुवृष्टिर्न भवति व्याधीयन्ते प्राणा अन्नं कनीयो भविष्यतीत्यथ यदा सुवृष्टिर्भवत्यानन्दिनः प्राणा भवन्त्यन्नं बहु भविष्यतीत्याप एवेमा मूर्ता येयं पृथिवी यदन्तरिक्षं यद् द्यौर्यत्पर्वता यद्देवमनुष्या यत्पशवश्च वयाꣳसि च तृणवनस्पतयः श्वापदान्याकीटपतङ्गपिपीलकमाप एवेमा मूर्ता उप उपास्स्वेति।।

"Verily Water is even greater than Aliment; for were seasonable rain not to fall, all animals would become wretched from a dread of Aliment being scantly produced; while the fall of seasonable rain cheers up all living beings of offering the prospect of food in plenty. Water is the first form of all these; even of this earth, of the sky, of the heaven, of mountains, men and beasts, of birds, grasses and trees, of wild animals, worms, insects, and ants, Water is first form (archetype). Do thou adore water.

2. स योऽपो ब्रह्मेत्युपास्त आप्नोति सर्वान्कामांस्तृप्तिमान्भवति यावदपां गतं तत्रास्य यथाकामचारो भवति योऽपो ब्रह्मेत्युपास्तेऽस्ति भगवोऽद्भ्यो भूय इत्यद्भ्यो वा भूयोऽस्तीति तन्मे भगवान्ब्रवीत्विति ॥

"He who adores Water as Brahman attains all that can be desired and in contented. He who adores water as Brahman, the moment he attains the region of water, becomes able to achieve whatever he desires." "Is there anything, O Lord, greater than water ?" "Yes, there is something yet greater than water." "Will it please my Lord to explain that unto me ?"

Section XI

1. तेजो वावाद्भ्यो भूयस्तद्वा एतद्वायुमागृह्याकाशमभितपति तदाहुर्निशोचति नितपति वर्षिष्यति वा इति तेज एव तत्पूर्वं दर्शयित्वाऽथापः सृजते तदेतदूर्ध्वाभिश्च तिरश्चीभिश्च विद्युद्भिराह्रादाश्चरन्ति तस्मादाहुर्विद्योतते स्तनयति वर्षिष्यति वा इति तेज एव तत्पूर्वं दर्शयित्वाऽथापः सृजते तेज उपास्स्वेति ॥

"Verily Heat is even greater than Water. Of a truth through the medium of the air it heats the sky, then do men say, 'it is warm, it is hot, it will rain.' Thus is Water created after the manifestation of Heat. When thunder-claps roar with the high-flying and tortuous lightning, manking proclaim, 'It flashes, it thunders, it will rain.' Thus is water created after the manifestation of Heat. Do thou adore Heat.

2. स यस्तेजो ब्रह्मेत्युपास्ते तेजस्वी वै स तेजस्वतो लोकान्भास्वतोऽपहततमस्कानभिसिद्ध्यति यावत्तेजसो गतं तत्रास्य यथाकामचारो भवति यस्तेजो ब्रह्मेत्युपास्तेऽस्ति भगवस्तेजसो भूय इति तेजसो वाव भूयोऽस्तीति तन्मे भगवान्ब्रवीत्विति ॥

"He who adores Heat as Brahman abides with splendour in regions devoid of darkness and replete with heat and light. He who adores Heat as Brahman, the moment he attains the regions of Heat, becomes able to achieve whatever he desires. "Is there anything, O Lord, greater than Heat ?" "Yes, there is something yet greater than Heat ?" Will it please my Lord to explain that unto me ?"

SECTION XII

1. आकाशो वाव तेजसो भूयानाकाशे वै सूर्याचन्द्रमसावुभौ विद्युन्नक्षत्राण्यग्निराकाशेनाह्वयत्याकाशेन शृणोत्याकाशेन प्रतिशृणोत्याकाशे रमत आकाशे न रमत आकाशे जायत आकाशमभिजायत आकाशमुपास्स्वेति ॥

"Verily space[26] is even greater than Heat. Of a truth, both the sun and the moon (exist) in space, and so do the lightning, the stars and heat. *Men* speak through Space, hear through Space, and rehear through Space; they delight in Space and delight not in Space; they are born in space and merge into space. Do you adore Space.

2. स य आकाशं ब्रह्मेत्युपास्त आकाशवतो वै स लोकान्प्रकाशवतोऽसंबाधानुरुगायवतोऽभिसिद्ध्यति यावदाकाशस्य गतं तत्रास्य यथाकामचारो भवति आकाशं ब्रह्मेत्युपास्तेऽस्ति भगव आकाशाद्भूय इत्याकाशाद्वाव भूयोऽस्तीति तन्मे भगवान्ब्रवीत्विति ॥

"He who adores the Space as Brahman abides in radiant and ethereal regions of mighty extent where exists no pain or disease.

He who adores the Space as Brahman, the moment he attains the regions of Space, becomes able to achieve whatever he desires." "Is there anything, O Lord, greater than Space ?" "yes, there is something yet greater than Space." "Will it please my Lord to explain that unto me ?"

SECTION XIII

1. स्मरो वावाकाशाद्भूयस्तस्माद्यद्यपि बहव आसीरन्नस्मरन्तो नैव ते कंचन शृणुयुर्न मन्वीरन्न विजानीरन् यदा वाव ते स्मरेयुरथ शृणुयुरथ मन्वीरन्नथ विजानीरन् स्मरेण वै पुत्रान्विजानति स्मरेण पशून् स्मरमुपास्स्वेति ।।

"Verily Memory is even greater than Space. Were there to be many (people present) and not remembered, they would not be heard, or thought of, or known. But when they are remembered they are heard, thought of and known. Through memory a father recognises his children and a master his cattle. Do ye adore Memory.

2. स यः स्मरं ब्रह्मेत्युपास्ते यावत्स्मरस्य गतं तत्रास्य यथाकामचारो भवति यः स्मरं ब्रह्मेत्युपास्तेऽस्ति भगवः स्मराद्भूय इति स्मराद्वाव भूयोऽस्तीति तन्मे भगवान्ब्रवीत्विति ।।

"Listen, what is the reward of him who adores Memory as Brahman. He who adores Memory as Brahman, the moment he attains the regions of Memory, becomes able to achieve whatever he desires." "Is there anything, O Lord, greater than Memory?" "Yes, there is something yet greater than Memory." "Will it please my Lord to explain that unto me?"

SECTION XIV

1. आशा वाव स्मराद्भूयस्याशेद्धो वै स्मरो मन्त्रानधीते कर्माणि कुरुते पुत्रांश्च पशूंश्चेच्छत इमं च लोकममुं चेच्छत आशामुपास्स्वेति ।।

"Verily Hope is even greater than Memory. Of a truth through the nourishment of Hope, Memory recites mantras, performs ceremonial works, desires children and cattle, and longs for this region and that.[27] Do you adore Hope.

2. स य आशां ब्रह्मेत्युपास्त आशयास्य सर्वे कामाः समृद्ध्यन्त्यमोघा ह्यस्याशिषो भवन्ति यावदाशाया गतं तत्रास्य यथाकामचारो भवति य आशां ब्रह्मेत्युपास्तेऽस्ति भगव आशाया भूय इत्याशाया वाव भूयोऽस्तीति तन्मे भगवान्ब्रवीत्विति ।।

"He who adores Hope as Brahman has all his desires fulfilled through Hope. His blessings become infallible who adores Hope as Brahman. The moment he attains the regions of Hope he becomes able to perform whatever he desires." "Is there anything, O Lord, greater than Hope ?" "Yes, there is something even greater than Hope." Will it please my Lord to explain that unto me ?"

SECTION XV

1. प्राणो वा आशाया भूयान्यथा वा अरा नाभौ समर्पिता एवमस्मिन् प्राणे सर्वंसमर्पितं प्राणः प्राणेन याति प्राणः प्राणं ददाति प्राणाय ददाति प्राणो ह पिता प्राणो माता प्राणो भ्राता प्राणः स्वसा प्राण आचार्यः प्राणो ब्राह्मणः ।।

"Verily Prāṇa[28] is even greater than Hope. Of a truth as the spokes of a wheel are all attached to the nave so are all things attached to Prāṇa. The Vital air moves through Prāṇa;[29] Prāṇa gives vitality, it gives animation to animals; Prāṇa is father, Prāṇa is mother, Prāṇa is brother, Prāṇa is sister, Prāṇa is tutor, Prāṇa Brāhmaṇa.

2. स यदि पितरं वा मातरं वा भ्रातरं वा स्वसारं वाचार्यं वा ब्राह्मणं वा किंचिद् भृशमिव प्रत्याह धिक्त्वाऽस्त्वित्येवैनामाहुः पितृहा वै त्वमसि मातृहा वै त्वमसि भ्रातृहा वै त्वमसि स्वसृहा वै त्वमस्याचार्यहा वै त्वमसि ब्राह्मणहा वै त्वमसीति ।।

"Were one (therefore) to say anything offensive to his father and mother, or brother, or sister, or tutor, or a Brāhmaṇa, people would turn round and say unto him, 'Shame unto thee, thou art a paricide, thou art a matricide, thou art a fratricide, thou art a sorroricide, thou art a magisterocide, thou art a Brāhmaṇacide.'

3. अथ यद्यप्येनानुत्क्रान्तप्राणान् शूलेन समासं व्यतिषंदहेन्नैवैनं ब्रूयुः पितृहासीति न मातृहासीति न भ्रातृहासीति न स्वसृहासीति नाचार्यहासीति न ब्राह्मणहासीति।।

"But when one thrusts a poker into the side of those (people) when they are dead (and placed on the funeral pyre[30]) people do not call him 'Thou art a parricide, thou art a matricide, thou art a fratricide, thou art a sorroricide, thou art a magisterocide, thou art a Brāhmaṇacide.'

4. प्राणो ह्येवैतानि सर्वाणि भवति स वा एष एवं पश्यन्नेवं मन्वान एवं विजानन्नतिवादी भवति तं चेद्ब्रूयुरतिवाद्यसीत्यतिवाद्यस्मीति ब्रूयान्नापह्नुवीत।।

"Verily Prāṇa for certain is all these. He (who knows the Prāṇa) observing, thinking and knowing them (the relations) thus (*i.e.*, to be what they are) becomes an *Ativādi.*[31] Were one to ask him, 'Art thou an ativādī ?' he replies, 'I am an ativādī,' and does not suppress the fact."

SECTION XVI

एष तु वा अतिवदति यः सत्येनातिवदति सोऽहं भगवः सत्येनातिवदानीति सत्यं त्वेव विजिज्ञासितव्यमिति सत्यं भगवो विजिज्ञास इति।।

(Nārada was satisfied by this instruction and remained silent; but Sanatkumāra, finding him to be a worthy pupil, continued,) "He is really an *ativādi* who can with true knowledge say, 'I am he.' "O Lord (said Nārada), I wish to become an *ativādi* through truth." (Sanatkumāra replied) "Truth therefore is worthy of enquiry." (Nārada returned) "Truth, O Lord, is sought by me."

Section XVII

यदा वै विजानात्यथ सत्यं वदति नाविजानन् सत्यं वदति विजानन्नेव सत्यं वदति विज्ञानं त्वेव विजिज्ञासितव्यमिति विज्ञानं भगवो विजिज्ञास इति।।

(Sanatkumāra said,) "When one knows (the truth) he speaks the truth; the ignorant does not speak the truth; the conscient alone speaks the truth; knowledge (*Vijñāna*) therefore is worthy of enquiry." "That knowledge, O Lord" (said Nārada,) "is sought by me."

Section XVIII

1. यदा वै मनुतेऽथ विजानाति नामत्वा विजानाति मत्वैव विजानाति मतिस्त्वेव विजिज्ञासितव्येति मतिं भगवो विजिज्ञास इति।।

(Sanatkumāra said) "When one has zeal[32] to learn he knoweth the truth; he who is unwilling does not know the truth; the zealous alone knoweth the truth; zeal therefore is worthy of enquiry." "That zeal, O Lord" (said Nārada), "is sought by me."

Section XIX

1. यदा वै श्रद्दधात्यथ मनुते नाश्रद्दधन्मनुते श्रद्दधदेव मनुते श्रद्धा त्वेव विजिज्ञासितव्येति श्रद्धां भगवो विजिज्ञास इति।।

"When one has faith[33] he is zealous; the faithless is not possessed of zeal; the faithful alone is zealous; faith therefore is worthy of enquiry." "That faith, O Lord" (said Nārada), "is sought by me."

Section XX

1. यदा वै निस्तिष्ठत्यथ श्रद्दधाति नानिस्तिष्ठञ्श्रद्दधाति निस्तिष्ठन्नेव श्रद्दधाति निष्ठा त्वेव विजिज्ञासितव्येति निष्ठां भगवो विजिज्ञास इति।।

"When one has reverence[34] he acquires faith; the irreverent is not possessed of faith ; the reverent alone is possessed of faith; reverence therefore is worthy of enquiry." "That reverence, O Lord" (said Nārada) "is sought by me."

Section XXI

1. यदा वै करोत्यथ निस्तिष्ठति नाकृत्वा निस्तिष्ठति कृत्वैव निस्तिष्ठति कृतिस्त्वेव विजिज्ञासितव्येति कृतिं भगवो विजिज्ञास इति।।

"When one can control his passions he possesses reverence. The man of rampant passions can never have reverence; the quiet alone can have reverence; Quietude therefore is worthy of enquiry." "That Quietude, O Lord" (said Nārada), "is sought by me."

Section XXII

1. यदा वै सुखं लभतेऽथ करोति नासुखं लब्ध्वा करोति सुखमेव लब्ध्वा करोति सुखं त्वेव विजिज्ञासितव्यमिति सुखं भगवो विजिज्ञास इति।।

"When one wishes for Felicity he acquires quietude; he who has no such wish, acquires not quietude; the anxious for Felicity alone acquires quietude; Felicity therefore is worthy of enquirty." "That Felicity, O Lord," (said Nārada) "is sought by me."

Section XXIII

1. यौ वै भूमा तत्सुखं नाल्पे सुखमस्ति भूमैव सुखं भूमा त्वेव विजिज्ञासितव्य इति भूमानं भगवो विजिज्ञास इति।।

"That which is Immensity[35] is felicity, there is no felicity in Exiguity; Immensity alone is felicity; Immensity therefore is worthy of enquiry." "That Immensity, O Lord" (said Nārada), "is sought by me."

Section XXIV

1. यत्र नान्यत्पश्यति नान्यच्छृणोति नान्यद्विजानाति स भूमाथ यत्रान्यत्पश्यत्यन्यच्छृणोत्यन्यद्विजानाति तदल्पं यो वै भूम तदमृतमथ यदल्पं तन्मर्त्यꣳस भगवः कस्मिन्प्रतिष्ठित इति स्वे महिम्नि यदि वा न महिम्नीति।।

"That, into which none can see, of which none can hear, and which none can know, is Immensity. That into which one other can see, of which another can hear, and which another can know, is Exiguity. Verily, that which is Immensity is immortal and that which is Exiguity is mortal." "Where doth that Immensity abide, my Lord ?" (enquired Nārada). "It abideth in its own glory, or (if you enquire where is that glory, I say) it doth not abide in its glory.

2. गोअश्वमिह महिमेत्याचक्षते हस्तिहिरण्यं दासभार्यं क्षेत्राण्यायतनानीति नाहमेवं ब्रवीमि ब्रवीमिति होवाचान्यो ह्यन्यस्मिन्प्रतिष्ठित इति।।

"Cattle and horses are said to be (emblems of) glory, so are elephants, gold, servants, wife and extensive fields : I allude not to them : I say," continued he, "independent objects[36] can alone abide in each other."

Section XXV

1. स एवाधस्तात्स उपरिष्ठात्स पश्चात्स पुरस्तात्स दक्षिणतः
स उत्तरतः स एवेदꣳसर्वमित्यथातोऽहङ्कारादेश एवाहमेवाध-
स्तादहमुपरिष्टादहं पश्चादहं पुरस्तादहं दक्षिणतोऽहमुत्तर-
तोऽहमेवेदꣳ सर्वमिति॥

"Verily that Immensity *extends* from below, it *extends* from above, it *extends* from behind, it *extends* from before, it *extends* from the south, it *extedns* from the north—of a truth it is all this." Next it is egoistically defined : "Verily I *extend* from below, I *extend* from above, I *extend* from behind, I *extend* from before, I *extend* from the south, I *extend* from the north—of a truth I am all this."

2. अथात आत्मादेश एवात्मैवाधस्तादात्मोपरिष्टादात्मा
पश्चादात्मा पुरस्तादात्मा दक्षिणत आत्मोत्तरत आत्मैवेदꣳ
सर्वमिति स वा एष एवं पश्यन्नेवं मन्वान एवं
विजानन्नात्मरतिरात्मक्रीड आत्ममिथुन आत्मानन्दः स
स्वराड् भवति तस्य सर्वेषु लोकेषु कामचारो भवति।
अथ येऽन्यथातो विदुरन्यराजानस्ते क्षय्यलोका भवन्ति
तेषाꣳ सर्वेषु लोकेष्वकामचारो भवति॥

Next it is psychically defined : "Verily the Soul *extends* from below, the Soul *extends* from above, the Soul *extends* from behind, the Soul *extends* from before, the Soul *extends* from the south, the Soul *extends* from the north—of a truth the Soul is all this. He, who is aware of this, seeing the Soul thus, thinking it thus, and knowing it thus, becomes (even in this life) *one* whose entire devotion is to the Soul, whose recreation is in the Soul, whose helpmate is the Soul, and wnose felicity is the Soul. (In after-life) he becomes self-resplendent. He is able to accomplish whatever he desires in all the regions of the universe. Those who believe otherwise, having others for their masters, go to perishable regions. For them nothing is accomplished in any of the regions of the universe.

SECTION XXVI

1. तस्य ह वा एवस्यैवं पश्यत एवं मन्वानस्यैवं विजानत आत्मतः प्राण आत्मत आशात्मतः स्मर आत्मत आकाश आत्मतस्तेज आत्मत आप आत्मत आविर्भावतिरोभावावा-त्मतोऽन्नमात्मतो बलमात्मतो विज्ञानमात्मतो ध्यानमात्मत-श्चित्तमात्मतः संकल्प आत्मतो मन आत्मतो वागात्मतो नामात्मतो मन्त्रा आत्मतः कर्माण्यात्मत एवेदꣳसर्वमिति॥

"For him who thus seeth, thus believeth, and thus knoweth, the vital airs proceed from the Soul; desire proceeds from the Soul; memory proceeds from the Soul; space proceeds from the Soul, heat proceeds from the Soul; water proceeds from the Soul; birth and death proceed from the Soul; aliment proceeds from the Soul; power proceeds from the Soul; knowledge proceeds from the Soul; reflection proceeds from the Soul; sensitivity proceeds from the Soul; will proceeds from the Soul; the mind proceeds from the Soul; speech proceeds from the Soul; names proceed from the Soul; mantras proceed from the Soul; sacrifices proceed from the Soul—verily all these proceed from the Soul.

2. तदेष श्लोको न पश्यो मृत्युं पश्यति न रोगं नोत दुःखताꣳसर्वꣳ ह पश्यः पश्यति सर्वमाप्नोति सर्वश इति स एकधा भवति त्रिधा भवति पञ्चधा सप्तधा नवधा चैव पुनश्चैकादश स्मृतः शतं च दश चैकश्च सहस्राणि च विꣳशतिराहारशुद्धौ सत्त्वशुद्धिः सत्त्वशुद्धौ ध्रुवा स्मृतिः स्मृतिलम्भे सर्वग्रन्थीनां विप्रमोक्षस्तस्मै मृदितकषायाय तमसस्पारं दर्शयति भगवान् सनत्कुमारस्तꣳ स्कन्द इत्याचक्षते तꣳ स्कन्द इत्याचक्षते॥

"Therefore is the verse 'that man who knoweth this[37] confronts not death nor disease, nor doth he meet with pain and suffering. He observes every thing, and attains every thing in every way'. He is one (before creation), he becomes trified, he becomes pentafid, he becomes septafid, he becomes monafid; he becomes divided

into eleven—into a hundred parts; he becomes ten and one; he becomes a thousand; he becomes twenty.[38] By the purity of his aliment he becomes purified in his nature; by the purification of his nature he verily gets memory; and by the attainment of memory all the attachments of his body are severed." Thus unto him whose passions were overcome did Lord Sanatkumāra, explain what is beyond darkness. Hence is this (portion of the Upaniṣad) called his section—hence is it called his section.

Foot Note

1. The words Itihāsa and Purāṇa occur twice in this Upaniṣad, first in the 3rd chapter (section IV, verse I, ante p. 94) in connection with the Atharvāngirasa hymns, and as the fourth from the Ṛg-Veda, or next in order after the Sāma Veda, and here as the fifth or immediately after the Atharva Veda. But Śaṅkara does not explain them further than by calling them the fifth Veda पञ्चम वेदं। In commenting upon the phrase *Vedānām Veda* he adds "of the Vedas or of the five including the Bhārata, (वेदानां भारतपञ्चमानां) which would imply that the Bhārata, by virtue of its being an Itihāsa, was a Veda. The Bhāgavata Purāṇa has the same idea. In the 4th chapter of the first book of that work there is a passage which says, "Vyāsa, having rescued the four Vedas, Ṛk, Yajur, Sāma and Atharva, relates the Itihāsa and Purāṇa which form the fifth Veda," ऋग्यजुःसामाथर्वाख्यां वेदाश्चत्वार उद्धताः। इतिहासपुराणंच पंचमो वेद उच्यते। This is however opposed to the interpretation given by Śaṅkara in the Bṛhadār-aṇayaka-Upaniṣad (Chap. IV. Verse). There he states that Itihāsa alludes to such passage in the Vedas as advert to anecdotes, such as the anecdotes of Urvasī, Purūravas, etc., and such expressions as 'the gods and the demons fought of yore'; and the Purāṇa relates to ancient historical references, such as, 'the world did not exist before, etc.' Mādhvācārya has this apparent contradiction by observing that the words Itihāsa and Purāṇa are common terms and apply to all works which contain historical narratives. He says that "like the six Aṅgas the Purāṇas, etc., are adapted to give a knowledge of the Vedas and are therefore worthy objects of study. Thus in Yājñavalkya 'the Purāṇa, Nyāya— Mimāṁsā, Dharmasāstra and the Vedāṅgas,' in all fourteen, are Vedas, the receptacles of learning and virtue. Again 'the Veda is made manifest through the agency of the Itihāsa and Purāṇa.; Further, 'the concise Veda dreads the

two' (Itihāsa and Purāṇa lest they should misrepresent it). It has been else where said by him :

The anecdotes of Hariscandra, Naciketā and others related in the Aitareya, Taittirīya, Kāṭhaka and other Sākhās, which are calculated to develope the knoweldege of virtue and Brahman, have been made clear in the Itihāsas. The accounts given in the Upaniṣads of creation, preservation and destruction have been developed in the Purāṇas like the Brahma, Vaiṣnava, etc." and therefore they are eulogistically called Vedas.

This view of the meaning of the words Itihāsa and Purāṇa is supported by the Buddhists, who style all their narrative works Purāṇas, and reckon the Biography of Śākya as the Purāṇa *par excellence.*

षडङ्गवत् पुराणादीनामपि वेदार्थज्ञानोपयोगं दृष्ट्वा विद्यास्थानत्वं याज्ञवल्क्येन स्मर्य्यते।

पुराणन्यायमीमांसा धर्म्मशास्त्राङ्गमिश्रिताः।
वेदाः स्थानानि विद्यानां धर्म्मस्य च चतुर्दशेति।।

इतिहासपुराणाभ्यां वेदं समुपबृंहयेदिति।

बिभेत्यल्पश्रुताद्वेदो मोभयः प्रहरेदिति। अन्यत्रापि स्मर्यते। ऐतरेयतैत्तिरीय काटकादिशाखसूक्तानि हरिश्चन्द्रनाचिकेताद्युपाख्यानानि धर्म्मब्रह्मावबोधयुक्तानि तेषु तेष्वितिहासग्रन्थेषु स्पष्टकृतानि। उपनिषदुक्ताः सृष्टिस्थितिलयादयो ब्राह्मवैष्णवादिपुराणेषु स्पष्टीकृता।

2. In the original this word is expressed by the phrase *Vedānām Veda,* because, says ŚAṆKARA, the Vedas are understood by its aid.

3. *Rāsi,* Arithmetic and Algebra.

4. *Daiva,* the science which treats of accidental physical occurrences.

5. *Nidhi,* the science which regulates the division of time into mahākāla, kāla, etc.

6. *Vākovākyam, Ekāyanam.* It is worthy of note that at the time when this Upaniṣad was composed the words now most in use to indicate logic and polity—*tarkaśāstra* and *nītiśāstra,* were unknown or not current.

7. *Deva Vidyā*—Nirukta, "glossarial explanation of obscure terms especially those occurring in the Vedas."—WILSON.

8. *Brahma Vidyā.* Articulation, ceremonials and prosody.

9. *Bhuta Vidyā.*

10. *Kṣatra Vidyā.*

11. *Sarpa Vidyā.*

12. *Devajana Vidyā,* the sciences of making essences of dancing, singing, music, architecture, painting, etc. (silpa.)—Śaṅkara.

13. It is intended to imply that every object of adoration leads to a special region after death.

14. *Phylanthus emblica.*

15. *Terminalia Chebula.*

16. "Saṅkalpa," says Śaṅkara, "is the power which, after determining what is fit and what is not fit to be done, impels the mind to do that which should be done." It is the same as *determining reason* of Leibnitz and the *activity* of the French philosophers. We have used will as its equivalent with reference to Dr. Read's definiftion to the word as given in his Essays on the Active Powers (Essay II. Chap. 1) He says : "Every man is conscious of a power to determine in things which he conceives to depend upon his determination; to this power we give the name of will. By the intellect we know or understand by the sensitivity we feel as desire, and by the will determine to do or not to do, to do this or do that."

17. Therc is a play upon the word *Saṅkalpa,* from the verb *Sankḷp* "to unite," which cannot be preserved in the translation.

18. The word in the original is *citta,* from *cit* to think or reflect. Śaṅkara defines it as "the nature of thinkingness, that which has the knowledge of the present time, and which has the power of knowing the use of the past and the future." वित्तं चेतयितृत्वं प्राप्तकालानुरूपबोधवत्वंमती- तानागतविषयप्रयोजननिरूपणसामर्थ्यं च. Anandagiri adds that it is that faculty which gives the knowledge relating to objects at its proper times, such as this object is thus obtained and of concluding from a knowledge of the gratification derived by eating at some past time the effect of eating in future. इदं दस्त्वेषं प्राप्तमिति प्राप्तकालवस्तुनो वस्त्वनुरोधी चेतनाख्यो वृत्तिविशेषस्तद्वत्वं चित्तमित्यर्थः। अतीतं भोजनं तृप्तिसाधनं दृष्टं भोजनत्वात्। आगामिनोऽपि तस्य तदेव प्रयोजनमिति निरूपणसामर्थ्यं चित्तमिति. We use sensitivity as its equivalent, that word being "now used as a general term to denote the capacity of feeling as distinguished from intellect and will. It includes sensations both external and internal whether derived from contemplating outward and material objects, or relations and ideas, desires, affections, passions. It also includes the sentiments of the sublime and beautiful,

the moral sentiment and the religious sentiment, and in short every modification of feeling of which we are susceptible."—FLEMING's Vocabulary, *voce,* Sensitivity.

19. The word in the original is ध्यान, *dhyāna* from *dhyai* "to meditate "and consequently to be in a state of repose. The phrase *dhyāyati* (remains) *iva* (like) *pṛthivī* (the earth) therefore means, the earth remains as if in repose; but the original has a play on the word *dhyāya,* which it is desirable should be indicated in the translation.
20. Vijñāna or the cognition of the meaning of the Śāstras.—ŚAṄKARA.
21. *Vide* note to page 220.
22. Regions of jñāna and vijñāna.
23. In the Sanskrit original the phrase "by power" is repeated after every object named.
24. उपसत्ता "companion, intimate and favourite"; समीपगोऽन्तरङ्गः प्रियोभवति says Śaṅkara.
25. द्रष्टा *draṣṭā* आचार्य्यस्यान्यस्य चोपदेष्टुर्गुरोर्द्रष्टा भवति।
26. Ākāśa.—"Space" or "æther."
27. *i.e.,* for Supremacy on Earth and in Heaven.
28. The word prāṇa has been variously translated in the preceding pages as "life" "soul" or the "vital air," according to the context of the passages in which it has occurred with the words preceding and following it. Here reference is, no doubt, made to vitality or life, but as the value of the discussion depends in a great measure upon the meaning we attach to this word, we prefer to insert it bodily rather than run the risk of misinterpreting our author by using an English equivalent of doubtful import. According to the sense we attach to this word the Upaniṣad becomes a supporter of the different doctrines of animism, organicism, dynamicism and the like.
29. Lit., Prāṇa moves by Prāṇa.
30. Adverting to the practice of facilitating the cremation of dead bodies by stirring the fire and altering the position of the limbs with a poker. The argument of the text is, that life is the object of relationship and not the material body.
31. *i.e.,* one who having exceeded the several objects enumerated from "name" (section I) to "hope," say "life is the cause of all things"; "life is everything."
32. Mati मति an ardent desire for any object of thought मन्तव्यविषये आदरः।

33. Śraddhā श्रद्धा belief in the existence of the truth आस्तिक्यबुद्धि।
34. Niṣṭhā निष्ठा respectful attention to the service of tutors गुरुशुश्रूषादिस्तत्परत्वम्।
35. The word bhūmā भूमा "great without limit" निरतिशयबहुः in the original Sanskrit, is in the masculine gender. For obvious reasons we have made it neuter.
36. Lit., unlike can abide in unlike.
37. Lit., observer.
38. The commentator explains the object of these numerals to be to indicate the susceptibility of the Soul to assume innumerable forms.

EIGHTH CHAPTER

SECTION I

हरि: ॐ

1. अथ यदिदमस्मिन्ब्रह्मपुरे दहरं पुण्डरीकं वेश्म दहरोऽस्मि-
न्नन्तराकाशस्तस्मिन्यदन्तस्तदन्वेष्टव्यं तद्वाव विजिज्ञासि-
तव्यमिति ॥

Hari, Om ! Now, within this habitation of Brahman (the human body *Brahmapura) there is* a small lotus like) chamber, and within it a minute vacuity (antarākāśa[1]). That which is within the vacuity is worthy of search; that, verily, should be inquired after.

Although it has been shown in the sixth and seventh chapters that Brahman is independent of all distinctions of quarters, space and time, that it is "truth (sat) alone without a second," and that it is indicated by the phrase, "The soul is all this"; yet for the edification of men of weak minds, whose understandings cannot easily contemplate an object having no distinctions of quarters, space and the like, and yet who cannot obtain their salvation without making that Brahman the object of their adoration (परमार्थविषय), a spot in the lotus-like heart is to be pointed out. Besides, although the Soul is without qualities and can be indicated by the single epithet "truth only," yet for the good of men of weak minds, who cannot comprehend other than human qualities, the Brahman is to be described as possessed of truth, desire, and the like qualities. Further, although the knowers of Brahman generally abstract themselves from women and such other objects, yet as the desire for worldly enjoyments, cherished by the indulgence of many transmigrations, is not to be easily subdued, the particular practices of Brahmacarya, etc., are to be inculcated.

Again, although to the believer in the unity of this Soul, there can be no such distinctions as those of the goer, going and the place to go, for from those distinctions of ignoranace, proceed the ideas of origin, existence, and end; and all such accidents subside in his own self, like the lightning in the sky, the wind *(in space)* and heat in the burnt fuel, yet for those whose intellect is affected by the ideas of goer, going, etc., and who adore the Brahman possessed of qualities and represented by a spot in the heart, a transition through the meridional artery (bazelar artery ?) is to be pointed out in this chapter.

2. तं चेद्ब्रूयुर्यदिदमस्मिन्ब्रह्मपुरे दहरं पुण्डरीकं वेश्म दहरोऽस्मिन्नन्तराकाशः किं तदत्र विद्यते यदन्वेष्टव्यं यद्वाव विजिज्ञासितव्यमिति ।।

Were (his pupils) to ask him (who makes the preceding remark), "Since within this habitation of Brahman, there is a lotus-like chamber, and within it a minute vacuity, what is within it, that is worthy of search ? That verily should be enquired after ?"

3. स ब्रूयाद्यावान्वा अयमाकाशस्तावानेषोऽन्तर्हृदय आकाश उभे अस्मिन् द्यावापृथिवी अन्तरेव समाहिते उभावग्निश्च वायुश्च सूर्याचन्द्रमसावुभौ विद्युन्नक्षत्राणि यच्चास्येहास्ति यच्च नास्ति सर्वं तदस्मिन्समाहितमिति ।।

He would say, "Verily as *extensive* is space, so is the vacuity within the heart. Both the earth and the heaven exist within it. Both Agni, and Vāyu, both the sun and the moon, as also lightning and the stars, and whatever *else* exist in this (universe) as well as what do not—all exist within this vacuity."

4. तं चेद्ब्रूयुरस्मिꣳश्चेदिदं ब्रह्मपुरे सर्वꣳ समाहितꣳ सर्वाणि च भूतानि सर्वे च कामा यदैनज्जरामाप्नोति प्रध्वꣳसते वा किं ततोऽतिशिष्यत इति ।।

Were (his pupils) to ask him (who thus respond), "If within this habitation of Brahman are lodged all these objects, all these created objects and all these human desires, when (the body) wasteth and dies, which for certain it does, what remains behind ?"

5. स ब्रूयान्नास्य जरयैतज्जीर्यति न वधेनास्य हन्यत एतत्सत्यं ब्रह्मपुरमस्मिन्कामाः समाहिता एष आत्मापहतपाप्मा विजरो विमृत्युर्विशोको विजिघत्सोऽपिपासः सत्यकामः सत्यसंकल्पो

यथा ह्येवेह प्रजा अन्वाविशान्ति यथानुशासनं यं यमन्तमभि-
कामा भवन्ति यं जनपदं यं क्षेत्रभागं तं तमेवोपजीवन्ति॥

He says, "The diseases of the body can never reduce it to decrepitude nor the slaughter of the body effect its destruction. This habitation of Brahman is verily and everlasting truth. In it dwell all human desires. It is the Soul, it is far from all vice, it is not subject to death; it is immortal and above affliction. It is neither afflicted by hunger nor thirst. Truthful is its wish; and truth is its resolve. As (evanescently) pass away the rewards of the subjects who become obedient to what is ordained (by kings) and obtain according to their wish—this or this—a province or a field—

6. तद्यथेह कर्मजितो लोकः क्षीयत एवमेवामुत्र पुण्यजितो
लोकः क्षीयते तद्य इहात्मानमननुविद्य व्रजन्त्येताँश्च सत्यान्
कामाँस्तेषाँ सर्वेषु लोकेष्वकामचारो भवत्यथ य
इहात्मानमनुविद्य व्रजन्त्येताँश्च सत्यान् कामाँस्तेषाँ
सर्वेषु लोकेषु कामचारो भवति॥

"As this region, obtained through works, runs to waste (or passes away) and that region, which may be obtained through virture, passes away,—so do they who live without knowing the Soul. For them all these truthful desires become unfruitful in every region. For them who live with a knowledge of the Soul all truthful desires become fruitful in all regions.

SECTION II

1. स यदि पितृलोककामो भवति संकल्पादेवास्य पितरः
समुत्तिष्ठन्ति तेन पितृलोकेन संपन्नो महीयते॥

"Should he desire the region of Pitṛ,[2] he attains it with glory, for verily the moment he wishes it, the Pitṛs receive him with welcome.

2. अथ यदि मातृलोककामो भवति संकल्पादेवास्य मातरः
समुत्तिष्ठन्ति तेन मातृलोकेन संपन्नो महीयते॥

"Next, should he desire the region of Mātṛ,[3] he attains it with glory, for verily the moment he wishes it, the Mātṛs receive him with welcome.

3. अथ यदि भ्रातृलोककामो भवति संकल्पादेवास्य भ्रातरः समुत्तिष्ठन्ति तेन भ्रातृलोकेन संपन्नो महीयते ।।

"Next, should he desire the region of Bhrātṛ,[4] he attains it with glory, for verily the moment he wishes it, the Bhrātṛs receive him with welcome.

4. अथ यदि स्वसृलोककामो भवति संकल्पादेवास्य स्वसारः समुत्तिष्ठन्ति तेन स्वसृलोकेन संपन्नो महीयते ।।

"Next, should he desire the region of Svasṛ,[5] he attains it with glory, for verily the moment he wishes it, the Svasṛs receive him with welcome.

5. अथ यदि सखिलोककामो भवति संकल्पादेवास्य सखायः समुत्तिष्ठन्ति तेन सखिलोकेन संपन्नो महीयते ।।

"Next, should he desire the region of Sakhā,[6] he attains it with glory, for verily the moment he wishes it, the Sakhās receive him with welcome.

6. अथं यदि गन्धमाल्यलोककामो भवति संकल्पादेवास्य गन्धमाल्ये समुत्तिष्ठतस्तेन गन्धमाल्यलोकेन संपन्नो महीयते ।।

"Next, should he desire the region of Gandhamālya,[7] he attains it with glory, for verily the moment he wishes it, the Gandhamālyas receive him with welcome.

7. अथ यद्यन्नपानलोककामो भवति संकल्पादेवास्यान्नपाने सुमत्तिष्ठतस्तेनान्नपानलोकेन संपन्नो महीयते ।।

"Next, should he desire the region of Annapāna,[8] he attains it with glory, for verily the moment he wishes it, the Annapānas receive him with welcome.

8. अथ यदि गीतवादित्रलोककामो भवति संकल्पादेवास्य गीतवादिते समुत्तिष्ठतस्तेन गीतवादित्रलोकेन संपन्नो महीयते॥

"Next, should he desire the region of Gītavāditra,[9] he attains it with glory, for verily the moment he wishes it, the Gītavāditras receive him with welcome.

9. अथ यदि स्त्रीलोककामो भवति संकल्पादेवास्य स्त्रियः समुत्तिष्ठन्ति तेन स्त्रीलोकेन संपन्नो महीयते॥

"Next, should he desire the region of Strī,[10] he attains it with glory, for verily the moment he wishes it, the Strīs receive him with welcome.

10. यं यमन्तमभिकामो भवति यं कामं कामयते सोऽस्य संकल्पादेव समुत्तिष्ठति तेन संपन्नो महीयते॥

"Whatever country he desires, whatever he desires, he attains it with glory, for verily the moment he wishes it it abideth for him.

SECTION III

1. त इमे सत्याः कामा अनृतापिधानास्तेषाꣳ सत्यानाꣳ सतामनृतमपिधानं यो यो ह्यस्येतः प्रैति न तमिह दर्शनाय लभते॥

"They, the truthful desires, are enveloped in untruth. Of those truthful objects there is a false covering. He who is translated from this (world) to that, is never again beheld in this world.

2. अथ ये चास्येह जीवो ये च प्रेता यच्चान्यदिच्छन्न लभते सर्वं तदत्र गत्वा विन्दतेऽत्र ह्यस्यैते सत्याः कामा अनृता–पिधानास्तद्यथा हिरण्यनिधिं निहितमक्षेत्र ज्ञा उपर्युपरि संचरन्तो न विन्देयुरेवमेवेमाः सर्वा प्रजा अहरहर्गच्छन्त्य एतं ब्रह्मलोकं न विन्दन्त्यनृतेन हि प्रत्यूढाः॥

"Whatever man desires and gets not, whether it be, such (of his relatives, and friends,) as are alive, or such as are dead, or whatever else it be (be it food, raiment or drink); all those might be obtained within this (vacuity in the heart); therein dwell those truthful desires, which have untruth for their envelope. As those who are ignorant of the nature of (mineral) beds might pass repeatedly over an undiscovered mine of gold and find it not, so do mankind daily retire to this vacuity (in their sleep) and yet being misled by untruth they find not this Brahmaloka.

3. स वा एष आत्मा हृदि तस्यैतवेद निरुक्तः हृदयमिति
तस्माद्धृदयमहरहर्वा एवंवित्स्वर्गं लोकमेति।।

"Verily that Soul (ātmā) abideth in the heart ! Of a truth its epithet is *hṛdyayam.*[11] Therefore he who knows it daily retires to the region of svarga (heaven) in his heart.

4. अथ य एष संप्रसादोऽस्माच्छरीरात्समुत्थाय परं ज्योतिरु-
पसंपद्य स्वेन रूपेणाभिनिष्पद्यत एष आत्मेति होवाचैतद-
मृतमभयमेतद्ब्रह्मेति तस्य ह वा एतस्य ब्रह्मणो नाम
सत्यमिति।।

"He who has confidence in this, rising from this body and attaining a noble body of light, abides in his own form. This is the (description of the) Soul." He (the narrator in reply to his pupils) continued : "That Soul is deathless : it is devoid of fear; it is Brahman. Of this Brahman the (proper) name is *satya* (truth).

5. तानि ह वा एतानि त्रीण्यक्षराणि सतीयमिति तद्यत्सत्तद-
मृतमथ यत्ति तन्मर्त्यमथ यद्यं तेनोभे यच्छति यदनेनोभे
यच्छति तस्माद्यमहरहर्वा एवंवित्स्वर्गं लोकमेति।।

"Verily (that Brahman is indicated by) these three syllables सतीय *Satīya.* Thereof the syllable *s* स implies immortality; the syllable *ti* ती earthliness, and the syllable *y* य is a particle which joins the other two, and since it joins the two it means restraint of passions. He who knows this attains the region of Svarga."

Section IV

1. अथ य आत्मा स सेतुर्विधृतिरेषां लोकानामसंभेदाय नैतꣳ सेतुमहोरात्रे तरतो न जरा न मृत्युर्न शोको न सुकृतं न दुष्कृतꣳ सर्वे पाप्मानोऽतो निवर्तन्तेऽपहतपाप्मा ह्येष ब्रह्मलोकः॥

Now, that which is the Soul (ātmā) is a bride; it is a support for the preservation of all these worlds from destruction. This bridge cannot be crossed by day nor by night, nor by disease, nor by death, nor grief, nor virtue, nor vice. All defects depart herefrom. This region of Brahma is devoid of vice.

2. तस्माद्वा एतꣳ सेतुं तीर्त्वाऽन्धः सन्ननन्धो भवति विद्धः सन्नविद्धो भवत्युपतापी सन्ननुपतापी भवति तस्माद्वा एतꣳ सेतुं तीर्त्वापि नक्तमहरेवाभिनिष्पद्यते सकृद्विभातो ह्येवैष ब्रह्मलोकः॥

Crossing this bridge the blind cease to be blind, the wounded ceases to be wounded, the afflicted cease to be afflicted. Hence verily on crossing this bridge nights become days. For certainly ever-refulgent is the region of Brahman.

3. तद्य एवैतं ब्रह्मलोकं ब्रह्मचर्येणानुविन्दन्ति तेषामेवैष ब्रह्मलोकस्तेषाꣳ सर्वेषु लोकेषु कामचारो भवति॥

For him verily exists this Brahma-loka who can attain it through Brahmacarya. His desires are satisfied in every region.

Section V

1. अथ यद्यज्ञ इत्याचक्षते ब्रह्मचर्यमेव तद्ब्रह्मचर्येण ह्येव यो ज्ञाता तं विन्दतेऽथ यदिष्टमित्याचक्षते ब्रह्मचर्यमेव तद्ब्रह्मचर्येण ह्येवेष्ट्वात्मानमनुविन्दते॥

Now, that which is called *Yajña*[12] is Brahmacarya. The man who acquires a knowledge of the Brahma-loka through Brahmacarya, attains the region of Brahma. That which is called *Iṣṭa*[13] is Brahmacarya. Through Brahmacarya is that Soul attained which is *Iṣṭa*.

2. अथ यत्सत्रायणमित्याचक्षते ब्रह्मचर्यमेव तद्ब्रह्मचर्येण ह्येव सत आत्मनस्त्राणं विन्दतेऽथ यन्मौनमित्याचक्षते ब्रह्मचर्यमेव तद्ब्रह्मचर्येण ह्येवात्मानमनुविद्य मनुते ।।

Now that which is called *Satrāyaṇa*[14] is Brahmacarya. By Barhmacarya doth one serve his own self (Ātmā). That which is called *Mauna* is Brahmacarya. Through Brahmacarya is that Soul known and meditated upon.

3. अथ यदनाशकायनमित्याचक्षते ब्रह्मचर्यमेव तदेष ह्यात्मा न नश्यति यं ब्रह्मचर्येणानुविन्दतेऽथ यदरण्यायनमित्याचक्षते ब्रह्मचर्यमेव तत्तदरश्च ह वै ण्यश्चार्णवौ ब्रह्मलोके तृतीयस्यामितो दिवि तदैरंमदीयꣳसरस्तदश्वत्थः सोमसवनस्तदपराजिता पूर्ब्रह्मणः प्रभुविमितꣳहिरण्मयम् ।।

Now that which is called *Anāśakāyanam* (fasting) is Brahmacarya. That soul is not destroyed which is known through Brahmacarya. That which is called *Araṇyāyana*[15] is Brahmacarya. *Ara* means an "ocean" and *ṇya* means an ocean; and these two oceans abide in the region of Brahman. In that third heaven from this there are a delightful tank full of gruel, are an *aśvattha* tree from which exudes nectar, and a place of gold built by Brahman and named *Aparājita.*[16] They belong to Brahman.

4. तद्य एवैतावरं च ण्यं चार्णवौ ब्रह्मलोके ब्रह्मचर्येणानुविन्दन्ति तेषामेवैष ब्रह्मलोकस्तेषाꣳ सर्वेषु लोकेषु कामचारो भवति ।।

For them is reserved this region of Brahman who know through Brahmacarya the two oceans *ara* and *ṇya.* Their desires are accomplished in all regions.

SECTION VI

1. अथ या एता हृदयस्य नाड्यस्ताः पिङ्गलस्याणिम्नस्तिष्ठन्ति शुक्लस्य नीलस्य पीतस्य लोहितस्येत्यसौ वा आदित्यः पिङ्गल एष शुक्ल एष नील एष पीत एष लोहितः॥

Now, the arteries of the heart exist steeped in a brown ethereral fluid,—yea in a white, a blue, a yellow, a red ethereal fluid. Verily the Sun exists as brown, as white, as blue, as yellow, as red.

2. तद्यथा महापथ आतत उभौ ग्रामौ गच्छतीमं चामुं चैवमेवैता आदित्यस्य रश्मय उभौ लोकौ गच्छन्तीमं चामुं चामुष्मादादित्यात्प्रतायन्ते ता आसु नाडीषु सृप्ता आभ्यो नाडीभ्यः प्रतायन्ते तेऽमुष्मिन्नादित्ये सृप्ताः॥

As a main road with a village at each end, meets both this and that,[17] so do the rays of the sun meet both this region and that. From that sun they spread. They enter these arteries. Thence they spread. They enter the sun.

3. तद्यत्रैतत्सुप्तः समस्तः संप्रसन्नः स्वप्नं न विजानात्यासु तदा नाडीषु सृप्तो भवति तन्न कश्चन पाप्मा स्पृशति तेजसा हि तदा संपन्नो भवति॥

When man is so asleep that all his faculties are devoid of action and his feelings are at rest, he dreams not. Then is he abiding in these arteries. Then can no sin fasten on him. Then is he refulgent in light.

4. अथ यत्रैतदबलिमानं नीतो भवति तमभित आसीना आहुर्जानासि मां जानासि मामिति स यावदस्माच्छरीरा-दनुत्क्रान्तो भवति तावज्जानाति॥

Now, when he is diseased and about to die, those around him enquire, "Do you recognise me ? Do you recognise me ?" He recognises them as long as he does not depart from his body.

5. अथ यत्रैतदस्माच्छरीरादुत्क्रामत्यथैतैरेव रश्मिभिरूर्ध्वमाक्रमते स ओमिति वा होद्वा मीयते स यावत्क्षिप्येन्मनस्तावदादित्यं गच्छत्येतद्वै खलु लोकद्वारं विदुषां प्रपदनं निरोधोऽविदुषाम्॥

When he quits his body he rises upwards with the aid of the rays aforesaid, resounding *Om.* When his mind ceases to act he attains the sun. That is the way to the region *above.* It is open to the learned, but closed to the ignorant.

6. तदेष श्लोकः। शतं चैका च हृदयस्य नाड्यस्तासां मूर्धानमभिनिःसृतैका। तयोर्ध्वमायन्नमृतत्वमेति विष्वङ्ङन्या उत्क्रमणे भवन्त्युत्क्रमणे भवन्ति॥

Thereof is the verse : "There are a hundred and one[18] arteries issuing from the heart; one of them penetrates the crown of the head. The man, who departs this life through that artery, secures immortality.[19] The rest of the *arteries* lead to *various* transitions, — they lead to *various* transitions."

SECTION VII

1. य आत्मापहतपाप्मा विजरो विमृत्युर्विशोको विजिघत्सोऽपिपासः सत्यकामः सत्यसंकल्पः सोऽन्वेष्टव्यः स विजिज्ञासितव्यः स सर्वांश्च लोकानाप्नोति सर्वांश्च कामान्यस्तमात्मानमनुविद्य विजानातीति ह प्रजापतिरुवाच।

"He who is the Soul, who is bereft of sin,—He, who is not subject to decay, death or repining,—He, who eats not, nor feels the sensation of thirst,—He who is all truthful in his wishes and his resolves,—even He should be sought for and enquired after. He attains all his wishes, he attains all the regions, who, having enquired, knoweth the Soul." Of a truth, thus said Prajāpati.

2. तद्धोभये देवासुरा अनुबुबुधिरे ते होचुर्हन्त तमात्मानमन्विच्छामो यमात्मानमन्विष्य सर्वांश्च लोकानाप्नोति

सर्वाँश्च कामानितीन्द्रो हैव देवानामभिप्रवव्राज विरोचनोऽसुराणां तौ हासंविदानावेव समित्पाणी प्रजापतिसकाशमाजग्मतुः।।

Verily, thus knew the Devas and Asuras. They sad, "We shall enquire after that Soul by knowing which all regions as well as all desires may be attained." Then did Indra, among the Devas, and Virocana among the Asuras, proceed forth, without communicating with each other.[20] Sacrificial fuel in hand[21] both repaired to Prajāpati.

3. तौ ह द्वात्रिँशतं वर्षाणि ब्रह्मचर्यमूषतुस्तौ ह प्रजापतिरुवाच किमिच्छन्ताववास्तमिति तौ होचतुर्य आत्मापहतपाप्मा विजरो विमृत्युर्विशोको विजिघत्सोऽपिपासः सत्यकामः सत्यसंकल्पः सोऽन्वेष्टव्यः स विजिज्ञासितव्यः स सर्वाँश्च लोकानाप्नोति सर्वाँश्च कामान्यस्तमात्मानमनुविद्य विजानातीति भगवतो वचो वेदयनते तमिच्छन्ताववास्तमिति।।

They lived as Brahmacāris for the period of 32 years. Unto them said Prajāpati, "With what intent do you abide here ?" They replied, "The learned believe it to be your lordhship's saying, 'that the Soul which is without sin, which is not subject to decay, death or repining; which eats not, nor feels the sensation of thirst; and whose wishes and resolves are all-truthful—even such a Soul should be sought for and enquired after; and that he attains all the regions and all his wishes who, having enquired, knoweth that Soul.' Wishing to know that we abide here."

4. तौ ह प्रजापतिरुवाच य एषोऽक्षिणि पुरुषो दृश्यत एष आत्मेति होवाचैतदमृतमभयमेतद्ब्रह्मेत्यथ योऽयं भगवोऽप्सु परिख्यायते यश्चायमादर्शे कतम एष इत्येष उ एवैषु सर्वेष्वंतेषु परिख्यायत इति होवाच।।

Unto them said Prajāpati, "The being that you perceive within the eye[22] is that Soul"; and added "it is Brahman, the deathless and fearless." [The pupils taking him literally and believing the Brahman to be a mere shadow, enquired] : "Which is it, revered Sir, that you allude to, the shadow that is seen in water, or that which is perceived in a mirror ?" Prajāpati returned, "Of a certain it is perceived in both"

Section VIII

1. उदशराव आत्मानमवेक्ष्य यदात्मनो न विजानीथस्तन्मे प्रब्रूतमिति तौ होदशरावेऽवेक्षांचक्राते तौ ह प्रजापतिरुवाच किं पश्यथेति तौ होचतुः सर्वमेवेदमावां भगव आत्मानं पश्याव आलोमभ्य आनखेभ्यः प्रतिरूपमिति ।।

(Prajāpati said), "Go and view yourselves in that panful of water, and should you fail to know the Soul, enquire of me." They beheld themselves in a panful of water. Unto them said Prajāpati, "What do ye behold ?" They replied, "We behold *ourselves* in this, Sir, pictures of ourselves to the very hair and nails.

2. तौ ह प्रजापतिरुवाच साध्वलंकृतौ सुवसनौ परिष्कृतौ भूत्वोदशारावेऽवेक्षेयामिति तौ ह साध्वलंकृतौ सुवसनौ परिष्कृतौ भूत्वोदशरावेऽवेक्षांचक्राते तौ ह प्रजापतिरुवाच किं पश्यथेति ।।

Unto them said Prajāpati "Go, and having cleaned your persons and adorned yourselves with costly ornaments and rich clothing, behold yourselves in that panful of water. They, having cleansed their persons and put on costly ornaments and rich clothing, beheld themselves in a panful of water. Of them enquired Prajāpati. "What do you perceive ?"

3. तौ होचतुर्यथैवेदमावां भगवः साध्वलंकृतौ सुवसनो परिष्कृतौ च एवमेवेमौ भगवः साध्वलंकृतौ सुवसनौ परिष्कृतावित्येष आत्मेति होवाचैतदमृतमभयमेतद्ब्रह्मेति तौ ह शान्तहृदयौ प्रवव्रजतुः ।।

They two replied : "Sir, as we are well adorned, well-dressed and cleanly, so do we behold ourselves in this, well-adorned, well-dressed and cleanly." He said, "That is Brahman, the deathless, and fearless." They two went away satisfied.

4. तौ हान्वीक्ष्य प्रजापतिरुवाचानुपलभ्यात्मानमननुविद्य व्रजतो यतर एतदुपनिषदो भविष्यन्ति देवा वासुरा वा ते पराभविष्यन्तीति स ह शान्तहृदय एव विरोचनोऽसुराञ्जगाम तेभ्यो हैतामुपनिषदं प्रोवाचात्मैवेह महय्य आत्मा परिचर्य आत्मानमेवेह महयन्नात्मानं परिचरन्नुभौ लोकाववाप्नोतीमं चामुं चेति।।

Prajāpati, observing them, said, "Since these two are going away without attaining or knowing the Truth, this instruction will be for the defeat of the Devas and Asuras." He, Virocana, with a feeling of satisfaction, reparied to the Asuras, and unto them imparted this instruction : "Self alone is adorable; in this (world) self alone should be served; by adoring and serving one's self both this and the other world may be attained."

5. तस्मादप्यद्येहाददानमश्रद्दधानमयजमानमाहुरासुरो बतेत्यसुराणाꣳ ह्येषोपनिषत्प्रेतस्य शरीरं भिक्षया वसनेनालंकारेणेति सꣳ स्कुर्वन्त्येतेन ह्यमुं लोकं जेष्यन्तो मन्यन्ते।।

Therefore thenceforward the Asuras give no alms, have no faith in good works, and officiate at no sacrifice; hence are they called Asuras. This is their Upaniṣad (canon). Their dead are besmeared with aromatics and adorned with ornaments and costly raiments, and they think that thereby they will overcome this region and that.

SECTION IX

1. अथ हेन्द्रोऽप्राप्यैव देवानेतद्भयं ददर्श यथैव खल्वयमस्मिञ्छरीरे साध्वलंकृते साध्वलंकृतो भवति सुवसने सुवसनः परिष्कृते परिष्कृत एवमेवायमस्मिन्नन्धेऽन्धो भवति स्रामे स्रामः परिवृक्णे परिवृक्णोऽस्यैव शरीरस्य नाशमन्वेष नश्यति नाहमत्र भोग्यं पश्यामीति।।

Now Indra, without going to the Devas, felt frightened,

(saying.) "Verily, this (shadow) becomes well adorned when the body is well-adorned, and well-dressed when (the body) is well-dressed, and clean when the body is clean. Again it becomes blind when the body is blind, defective when the body is defective,[23] and mutilated when the body is mutilated. Further, on the destruction of the body it is destroyed. I can see no good in this."

2. स समित्पाणिः पुनरेयाय तꣳह प्रजापतिरुवाच मघवन्यच्छान्त- हृदयः प्राव्राजीः सार्धं विरोचनेन किमिच्छन् पुनरागम इति स होवाच यंथैव खल्वयं भगवोऽस्मिञ्छरीरे सध्वलंकृते साध्वलंकृतो भवति सुवसने सुवसनः परिष्कृते परिष्कृत एवमेवायमस्मिन्नन्धेऽन्धो भवति स्रामे स्रामः परिवृक्णे परिवृक्णोऽस्यैव शरीरस्य नाशमन्वेष नश्यति नाहमत्र भोग्यं पश्यामीति।।

Therefore, with sacrificial fuel in hand he returned. Unto him said Prajāpati, "You went away with Virocana, perfectly satisfied. O Maghavan : what do you wish by returning back ?" He replied, "Since of a truth, O Lord, this (shadow) becomes well adorned when the body is well-adorned, and well-dressed when the body is well-dressed, and clean when the body is clean; again it becomes blind when the body is blind, and defective when the body is defective and mutilated when the body is mutilated; further, on the destruction of this body it is destroyed. I can see no good in this."

3. एवमेवैष मघवन्निति होवाचैतं त्वेव ते भूयोऽनुव्याख्यास्यामि वसापराणि द्वात्रिꣳशतं वर्षाणीति स हापराणि द्वात्रिꣳशतं वर्षाण्युवास तस्मै होवाच।।

"Even so it is, Maghavan," said (Prajāpati) and continued, "I shall again explain it unto you. Do you abide here for another thirty-two years." He there dwelt for another thirty-two years. Unto him said (Prajāpati).

SECTION X

1. य एष स्वप्ने महीयमानश्चरत्येष आत्मेति होवाचैतदमृतमभयमे-
तद्ब्रह्मेति स ह शान्तहृदयः प्रवव्राज सहाप्राप्यैव देवानेतद्भयं
ददर्श तद्यद्यपीदः शरीरमन्धं भवत्यनन्धः स भवति यदि
स्राममस्रामो नैवैषोऽस्य दोषेण दुष्यति।।

"That which enjoys in a dream the feeling of being gratified by the attainment of a coveted object,[24] is the Soul" : and continued, "it is deathless and fearless; it is Brahman." Verily he (Indra) went away satisfied, but before he reached the Devas he felt frightened (saying), "Verily, this feeler of dreams becomes not blind when the body is deprived of its eyes, and remains unmutilated when the body is mutilated, it is not affected by the defects of the body;

2. न वधेनास्य हन्यते नास्य स्राम्येण स्रामो घ्नन्ति त्वेवैनं
विच्छादयन्तीवाप्रियवेत्तेव भवत्यपि रोदितीव नाहमत्र भोग्यं
पश्यामीति।।

"Nor destroyed by the destruction of the body, nor mutilated by its mutilation : it feels as if it is being destroyed, driven away, put to grief and to weeping. Verily, I can see no good in this."

3. समित्पाणिः पुनरेयाय तꣳह प्रजापतिरुवाच मघवन्यच्छान्त-
हृदयः प्राव्राजीः किमिच्छन् पुनरागम इति स होवाच
तद्यद्यपीदं भगवः शरीरमन्धं भवत्यनन्धः स भवति यदि
स्राममस्रामो नैवैषोऽस्य दोषोण दुष्यति।।

Therefore with sacrificial fuel in hand he returned. Unto him said Prajāpati, "You went away satisfied, O Maghavan, What do you wish in returning back ?" He replied, "Since it (the soul you have pointed out) becomes not blind when the body is deprived of its eyes, and remains unmutilated when the body is mutilated, it is not affected by the defects of the body;

4. न वधेनास्य हन्यते नास्य स्राम्येन स्रामो घ्नन्ति त्वेवैनं
विच्छादयन्तीवाप्रियवेत्तेव भवत्यपि रोदितीव नाहमत्र भोग्यं
पश्यामीत्येवमेवैष मघवन्निति होवाचैतं त्वेव ते भूयोऽनुव्या-

ख्यास्यामि वसापराणि द्वात्रिंः शतं वर्षाणीति स हापराणि द्वात्रिंः शतं वर्षाण्युवास तस्मै होवाच ॥

"Nor destroyed by the destruction of the body, nor mutilated by mutilation;—since it feels as if it is being beaten, driven away, put to grief and to weeping, I see no good in it." "Even so it is, Maghavan," said (Prajāpati) and continued, "I shall again explain it unto you. Do you abide here for another thirty-two years." He dwelt there for another thirty-two years. Unto him said (Prajāpati) :

Section XI

1. तद्यत्रैतत् सुप्तः समस्तः संप्रसन्नः स्वप्नं न विजानात्येष आत्मेति होवाचैतदमृतमभयमेतद्ब्रह्मेति स ह शान्तहृदयः प्रवव्राज स हाप्राप्यैव देवानेतद्भयं ददर्श नाहं खल्वयमेवंः संप्रत्यात्मानं जानात्ययमहमस्मीति नो एवेमानि भूतानि विनाशमेवापीतो भवति नाहमत्र भोग्यं पश्यामीति ॥

"That in which retiring, the sleeper is completely at rest and knows no dreaming, is the Soul," and continued, "It is deathless, and fearless : It is Brahman. "Verily, he (Indra) went away satisfied, but before he reached the Devas he felt frightened (saying), "Verily, it then knows not itself that I am this; nor does it know these elements thus (*i.e.*, as they are); it seems to be altogether destroyed for the time. I can see no good in this."

2. स समित्पाणिः पुनरेयाय तंः ह प्रजापतिरुवाच मघवन्यच्छान्त- हृदयः प्राव्राजीः किमिच्छन्पुनरागम इति स होवाच नाहं खल्वयं भगव एवंः संप्रत्यात्मानं जानात्ययमहमस्मीति नो एवेमानि भूतानि विनाशमेवा- पीतो भवति नाहमत्र भोग्यं पश्यामीति ॥

Therefore with sacrificial fire in hand he returned. Unto him said Prajāpati, "You went away satisfied , O Maghavan, what do you wish in returning back ?" He replied, "It (the soul you have pointed out,) knows not its own self that I am this nor does it know these elements thus (*i.e.,* as they are); it seems altogether destroyed for the time. I can see no good in this."

3. एवमेवैष मघवन्निति होवाचैतं त्वेव ते भूयोऽनुव्याख्यास्यामि नो एवान्यत्रैतस्माद्वसापराणि पञ्च वर्षाणीति स हापराणि पञ्च वर्षाण्युवास तान्येकशतꣳ संपेदुरेतत्तद्यदाहुरेकशतꣳ ह वै वर्षाणि मघवान्प्रजापतौ ब्रह्मचर्यमुवास तस्मै होवाच॥

"Even so it is," replied Prajāpati (and continued) : "I shall again explain unto you this Soul, but nothing beside it. Do you abide here for five years more." He dwelt there for five years more; he completed a hundred and one years. Therefore do good people say, Maghavan dwelt with Prajāpati for a hundred and one years as a Brahmacārin. Prajāpati said unto him;

SECTION XII

1 मघवन्मर्त्यं वा इदꣳ शरीरमात्तं मृत्युना तदस्यामृतस्याशरीरस्यात्मनोऽधिष्ठानमात्तो वै सशरीरः प्रियाप्रियाभ्यां न वै सशरीरस्य सतः प्रियाप्रिययोरपहतिरस्त्यशरीरं वाव सन्तं न प्रियाप्रिये स्पृशतः॥

"Of a truth this body is mortal, O Maghavan ! It is subject to death. Yet is it a resting-place of the immortal and unembodied Soul. When thus embodied, it is verily subject to desirable and repulsive objects. To the embodied there is no release from susceptibility to desirable and repulsive objects. Verily the unembodied never comes in contact with desirable and repulsive objects.

2. अशरीरो वायुरभ्रं विद्युत्स्तनयित्नुरशरीराण्येतानि तद्यथैतान्यमुष्मादाकाशात्समुत्थाय परं ज्योतिरुपसंपद्य स्वेन स्वेन रूपेणाभिनिष्पद्यन्ते॥

"Unembodied are the wind and the clouds, the lightning and the thunder. They are all without body. Issuing forth from yonder sky by the attainment ... (solar) heat, they assume their respective forms.

3. एवमेवैष संप्रसादोऽस्माच्छरीरात्समुत्थाय परं ज्योतिरुपसंपद्य स्वेन रूपेणाभिनिष्पद्यते स उत्तमः पुरुषः स तत्र पर्येति जक्षन्क्रीडन्रममाणः स्त्रीभिर्वा यानैर्वा ज्ञातिभिर्वा नोपजनꣳ स्मरन्निदꣳ शरीरꣳ स यथा प्रयोग्य आचरणे युक्त एवमेवायमस्मिञ्छरीरे प्राणो युक्तः।।

"Even like unto them, man, issuing[25] forth from his body by the attainment of the Great Light, assumes his own genuine form. He is (then) the best of men. He then lords it with eating and playing, and enjoying with woman, or equipages, or relatives, without thinking of the body. Even as cattle are attached to an equipage, so is the Soul (Prāṇa) attached to the body.

4. अथ यत्रैतदाकाशमनुविषण्णं चक्षुः स चाक्षुषः पुरुषो दर्शनाय चक्षुरथ यो वेदेदं जिघ्राणीति स आत्मा गन्धाय घ्राणमथ यो वेदेदमभिव्याहराणीति स आत्माभिव्याहाराय वागथ यो वेदेदꣳशृणवानीति स आत्मा श्रवणाय श्रोत्रम्।।

"Now, within those spaces (Ākāśa orbits) are the eyes, and the eyes are intended for the obervation of the Being who dwells within the eyes. He who willeth 'I shall smell' is the Soul (Ātmā,) wishing to inhale odours. Now, he who willeth 'I shall speak' is the Soul, wishing to articulate speech. Now, he who willeth 'I shall hear' is the Soul, wishing to hear sounds.

5. अथ यो वेदेदं मन्वानीति स आत्मा मनोऽस्य दैवं चक्षुः स वा एष एतेन दैवेन चक्षुषा मनसैतान् कामान् पश्यन् रमते।।

"Now, he who willeth 'I shall think' is the Soul thereof. The mind is the celestial eye, observing all objects of desire. By the aid of the mental celestial eye the Soul enjoys them all.

6. य एते ब्रह्मलोके तं वा एतं देवा आत्मानमुपासते तस्मात्तेषाꣳसर्वे च लोका आत्ताः सर्वे च कामाः स सर्वाꣳश्च लोकानाप्नोति सर्वाꣳश्च कामान्यस्तमात्मानमनु–विद्य विजानातीति ह प्रजापतिरुवाच प्रजापतिरुवाच।।

"Now, because the Devas adored that Soul in the region of Brahman, therefore they obtained all regions, and all their desires were fulfilled. He attains all regions and obtains all his desires, who, having duly enquired, knows the Soul.' Thus said Prajāpati, verily thus said Prajāpati.

SECTION XIII

श्यामाच्छबलं प्रपद्ये शबलाच्छ्यामं प्रपद्येऽश्व इव रोमाणि विधूय पापं चन्द्र इव राहोर्मुखात्प्रमुच्य धूत्वा शरीरमकृतं कृतात्मा ब्रह्मलोकमभिसंभवामीत्यभिसंभवामीति।।

"From blackness I attain multicolour, from multicolour I attain blackness. Like unto the horse which shakes off all dust from its coat, or the moon which escapes from the mouth of Rāhu, I shall purify my body, and becoming free (by the aid of dhyāna), attain, verily attain—the uncreate Brahma-loka."[26]

SECTION XIV

आकाशो वै नाम नामरूपयोर्निर्वहिता वे यदन्तरा तद्ब्रह्म तदमृतः स आत्मा प्रजापतेः सभां वेश्म प्रपद्ये यशोऽहं भवामि ब्राह्मणानां यशो राज्ञां यशो विशां यशोऽहमनुप्रापत्सि स हाहं यशसां यशः श्वेतमदत्कमदत्कः श्वेतं लिन्दुमाभिगां लिन्दुमाभिगाम्।।

"Verily that which is known as Ākāśa[27] is made of name and form. That which is beyond the two (name and form) is Brahman; It is immortal : It is the universal Soul. I shall attain the audience chamber of Prajāpati. I shall attain the glory of Brāhmaṇa. I shall attain the glory of kings (Kṣatriyas), I shall attain the glory of Vaiśyas; I desire all glory; I desire the glory of the glorious; I shall not enter again; no, I shall not enter the white toothless all-devouring slippery abode."[28]

Section XV

1. तद्धैतद्ब्रह्मा प्रजापतय उवाच प्रजापतिर्मनवे मनुः प्रजाभ्य आचार्यकुलाद्वेदमधीत्य यथाविधानं गुरोः कर्मातिशेषेणा-भिसमावृत्य कुटुम्बे शुचौ देशे स्वाध्यायमधीयानो धार्मिका-न्विदधदात्मनि सर्वेन्द्रियाणि संप्रतिष्ठाप्याहिꣳ सन्सर्वभू-तान्यन्यत्र तीर्थेभ्यः स खल्वेवं वर्तयन्यावदायुषं ब्रह्मलोकम- भिसंपद्यते न च पुनरावर्तते न च पुनरावर्तते।।

Verily this was related by Brahmā to Prajāpati, by Prajāpati to Manu, and by Manu to mankind. Having studied the Veda in the house of a tutor, and having paid to the Guru what is his due, one should dwell with his family in a healthy country, reading the Vedas, bringing up virtuous sons and pupils, devoting himself with all his senses to the Universal Soul, and injuring no created being. Having lived thus as long as life lasts, he attains the Brahma-loka. Thence he never returns, verily thence he never returns.

ॐ आप्यायन्तु ममाङ्गानि वाक्प्राणश्चक्षुः श्रोत्रमथो बलमिन्द्रियाणि च सर्वाणि सर्वं ब्रह्मौपनिषदं माहं ब्रह्म निराकुर्यां मामा ब्रह्म निराकरोदनिराकरणमस्त्वनिराकरणं मेऽस्तु तदात्मनि निरते य उपनिषत्सु धर्मास्ते मयि सन्तु ते मयि सन्तु।। ॐ शान्तिः शान्तिः शान्तिः।।

Foot Notes

1. *i.e.,* Brahman called ākāśa or space. It is said elsewhere "his nme is ākāśa, etc." The word is intended to imply that he is, like space, incorporeal and all-pervading.
2. Father.
3. Mother.
4. Brother.
5. Sister.
6. Friends.
7. Essence and garland.
8. Food and drink.
9. Song and music.

10. Women.
11. Lit., "this is the heart."
12. Yajña, the offering of burnt sacrifice.
13. Iṣṭa, adoration.
14. Satrāyaṇa, feeding hermits and the poor.
15. *Araṇyāyana,* dwelling in forests for religious purposes.
16. That which cannot be attained except through Brahmacarya.
17. *i.e.,* both the near and the off village.
18. In order to imply others, the commentator qualifies the number by adding that they are the principal arteries.
19. अमृतत्त्व The state of deathlessness.
20. From a feeling of envy.
21. Alluding to the custom of Brahmacarya which requires that men should, when going to their tutors, carry some such fuel as are meet for fire sacrifice.
22. *Lit.,* the male *puruṣa.* That which the Yogis perceive with their closed eyes and undisturbed and contented mind; adds the commentator.
23. Lit., having a flow of humours from the eyes or nose.
24. Lit., lives subserved. महीयमानः चरति; Lives feeling the enjoyment of the dream that he is being subserved by his wife, servants, etc. महीयमानः पूज्यमानः चरति स्वप्नभोगान् अनुभवति।
25. The issue here is metaphorical. It implies that the intelligent comes to a consciousness of his soul being distinct from his body, and in no way dependent upon it, and thus knowing it not to be his self he enjoys the pleasures of his world without thinking of the body, *i.e.,* without feeling attached to it. Nor are such pleasures prejudicial to his intelligence inasmuch as he is conscious of their true nature.
26. The commentator explains that *śyāma* blackness means the all-pervading Brahman, by acquiring a knowledge of which through dhyāna, we attain the region of Brahman (śabala) and there we attain the nature of Brahman ब्रह्मभावं.
27. Lit, space, but intended here to mean the Universal Soul which, like space, is illimitable and undefinable.
28. The womb.

BIBLIOGRAPHY

Original Sources :

Aitareya Āraṇyaka with the com. of Sāyaṇa ed. by R. Mitra, Bibliotheca Indica, Calcutta, 1876.

Atareyabrāhmaṇa with the com. of Sāyaṇācārya, Anandashrama Press, Poona, 1896.

Āpastamba Paribhāṣā com. by Dhūrtaswāmi & Tr. by Bhattacharya, S.S., Calcutta, 1932

Aṣṭāṅgahṛdaya of Vāgbhatta ed. by H.M. Patel, Sastu Sahitya Vardhaka Karyalaya, Bombay, 1966.

Atharvaveda com by Sāyaṇa ed. by Viśvabandhu, Vishveshvarananda Vedic Research Institute, Hoshiarpur, 1960.

Atharvaveda Pariśiṣṭa pub. by Chaukhamba Orientalia, Varanasi, 1976.

Baudhāyana Dharmasūtra, com. by Govindaswāmī, ed. by Shri Nivāsācārya Government Branch Press, Mysore, 1907.

Bhāgavadgītā, Sastu Sahitya Vardhaka Karyalaya, Bombay, 1939.

Bhāgavat Purāṇa ed by Shastri G.M. Sastu Sahitya Vardhaka Karyalaya, Princess Street, Bombay, 1937.

Brahmāṇḍa Purāṇa ed. by Phanasikar Vasudeva, Nirnaya Sagara Press, Bombay, 1914.

Brahmasiddhānta by Oza Madhusudan, Benaras Hindu University, 1961

Brahmasūtra bhāṣya of Madhva Tr. by Rangacarya B.R., Poona, 1848.

Brahmasūtra bhāṣya of Nimbārka ed. by Pandit Shri Dhundhiraj Shastri, Chawkhamba Sanskrit Series Office, Benaras, 1932.

Brahmasūtra bhāṣya of Rāmānuja Tr. by R.D. Karmarkar, University of Poons, 1934.

Brahmasūtra Sāṅkarabhāṣya, Nirnaya Sagar Press, Bombay, 1948.

Brahmasūtrāṇubhāṣya by Śrī Vallabhācārya, Nirnaya Sagar Press, Bombay, 1924.

Bṛhadāraṇyaka Upaniṣad com. by Śaṅkara, Gita Press, Gorakhpur, 1942.

Bṛhad-Devatā ed. by Mitra Rājā Rajendralala, The Asiatic Society of Bengal, 1892.

Caraṅavyūhapariśiṣṭasūtram by Saunakamuni, Chaukhamba Sanskrit Series, Varanasi, Samvat 1959.

Chāndogya Upaniṣad, Gita Press, Gorakhpur, IInd edn. 1945.

Gautamasūtras with the com. of Vātsyāyana ed. by V.G. Apte Anandashrama Sanskrit Series, Poona, 1922.

Gopatha Brāhmaṇa, ed. by Dieuke Gasstra, Leiden, 1919.

Halāyudhakośa ed. by Joshi Jayashankar, pub. by Prakashana Bureau, Suchana Bibhaga, Lucknow, U.P., 1826.

Jaiminīya Upaniṣad com. by Upaniṣad Brahmayogin, Adhyar Library Madras, 1969.

Jaimini Gṛhyasūta, Tr. by Caland W., Motilal Benarasidass, Delhi, 1922.

Kaṭhopaniṣad with the com. of Śaṅkara ed. by Apte V.G., Anandashrama Printing Press, Poona, 1849.

Kauśikāsūtra com. by Dharila Tilaka Vidyapitha, Poona, 1972.

Kenopaniṣad, pub. by Gita Press, Gorakhpura, 1946.

Kūrmapurāṅa ed. by Bhattacharya R.S., Indological Book House, Varanasi, 1969.

Kuvalayānanda of Appaya Dīkṣita, ed. by Phanashikar, V.S., Bombay, 1937.

Mahābhārat Tr. by Shastri, S.P., Sastu Sahitya Vardhaka Karyalaya, Princess Street, Bombay, 1956.

Manusmṛti Tr. by Shastri G.M., Sastu Sahitya Vardhaka Karyalaya, Princess street, Bombay, 1952.

Muktikā Upaniṣad ed. by Pandit Jibananda Vidyasagara, Sanskrit College of Calcutta, 1872.

Muṇḍaka Upaniṣad, Gita Press, Gorakhpur, 1947.

Māṇḍukya Upaniṣad, Gita Press, Gorakhpur, 1949.

Nirukta of Yāska, Anandashrma Press, Poona, 1926.

Patañjali Vyākaraṇa Mahābhāṣya, ed. by Shastri Guruprasad Rajasthan Sanskrit College Granthamala no. 30, Benaras, 1938.

Praśna Upanıṣad, Gita Press, Gorakhapur, 1945.
Ṛgveda with the com. of Sāyaṇa, Vedic Research Institute, Poona, 1946.
Ṛgvedādibhāṣyabhūmikā by Swami Dayananda S., Pub. by Vaidika Yantralaya, Ajamera, V.S. 1960.
Ṛktantram, A Prātiśakhya of the SV ed. by Shastri Suryakanta, Meharchanda Lachhamandas Sanskrit Book Depot., Lahore, 1933.
Sāhityadarpaṇa of Visvanatha, Chaukhamba Sanskrit Series, 1947.
Śatapathabhāhmaṇa Tr. by Pandita Gangaprasad Upadhyaya, pub. by The Research Institute of Ancient Scientific Studies, New Delhi, 1967.
Śvetāśvatara Upaniṣad, Gita Press, Gorakhpur, 1950.
Taittirīya Āraṇyaka Commented by Bhatta Bhashkar Mishra, Pub. by Govt. Press, Mysore, 1902.
Taittirīya Āraṇyaka com. by Sāyaṇa, Ananda Ashram Press, Poona, 1897.
Taittirīya Brāhmaṇa com. by Bhaṭṭa Bhāskara ed. by Shastri R.S., The Govt. Branch Press, Mysore, 1921.
Taittirīyasaṁhitā with the coms. of Bhaṭṭa Bhāskara Miśra and Sāyanācārya, ed. by N.S. Sontakke & T.N. Dharmadhikarī, Pub. by Vaidika Samsodhana Mandala, Poona, 1970.
Taittirīya Upaniṣad with the con. of Śaṅkara, Ananda Ashrama Press, Poona, 1889.
Taittirīyopaniṣadbhāṣyavārtikam by Sureśvarācārya, Anandasram Printing Press, 1883.
Tarkasaṁgraha of Annambhaṭṭa ed. by Athalye, Y.S., Bhandarkar Oriental Research Institute, Poona, 1974.
Vācaspatyam Bṛhat Sanskṛtābhidhānam, Chaukhamba Sanskrit Series, Varanasi.
Vaikhānasa Gṛhyasūtras, ed. by S. Shastri, Baroda, 1921.
Vaiyākaraṇa Siddhāntakaumudī ed. by Pandit Gopalashastri Nene, Chowkhamba Sanskrit Series Office, Varanasi, 1966.
Vāyupurāṇa ed. by Mitra Rajendralal, The Asiatic Society of Bengal, Calcutta, 1888.
Viṣṇupurāṇa, Gita Press, Gorakhapur, 1934.

General References :

Abhedananda : The Upaniṣadic Doctrine of the Self. Oriental Publishers and Distributors, 1488, Pataudi House, Darya Ganj, New Delhi, 110 002.

Allen, W.S. : 'Phonetics in Ancient India', Oxford University Press, Oxford, England, 1958.

Allen, W.S. : 'Sandhi', Oxford University Press, Oxford, England, 1967.

Altekar, A.S. : 'The Āśrama System' Ghurye Felicitation Volume, ed. by K.M. Kapadia, Popular Books Deport, Bombay-400 007, 1954.

Altekar, A.S. : 'Education in Ancient India', Nanda Kishore and Bros., Benaras, 1944 (2nd edn.).

Apte, V.M. : 'The Practical Sanskrit English Dictionary', Prasad Prakashana, Poona, 1958.

Aufretch, Theodor : 'Gatalogus Catalogorum', Wiesbaden, Vol. I-II, 1962, Leipzing, Vol. III, 1903.

Bal Gangadhar, Tilak : 'The orien or Research into the Antiquity of the Vedas' Pub. by Tilak Bros., Lokamanyan Tilak Road, 568, Narayana Peth, Poona-100 002, 1955.

Balasubramanian, R. : 'Taittiriyopaniṣad Bhāṣyavārtika of Sureśvara, Centre for Advanced Study in Philosophy, University of Madras, 1974.

Belvalkar, S.K. and : 'History of Indian Philosophy', Vol. II, Creative Period, Bilvakunja Publishing House, Poona, 1927.

Bhatta, Vishnuprasad : On the meaning of the title 'Bṛhadāraṇyaka Upaniṣad, Journal of the Oriental Institute, Vol. 23, Nos. 1-2, Baroda, 1973.

Bhattacarya, Debika : 'Comparative study of the Atharvavedic and Indo-European Occult Practices', Pubd. in Journal of the Oriental Institute, Baroda, Vol. 26 No. 4

Blair, C.J. : 'Heat in the Ṛgveda and Atharvaveda', American Oriental Society, 1961.

Bokil, V.P. : 'The History of Education in India', Oriental Book Agency, Poona, 1925.

Burrow, T. : 'The Sanskrit Language', Feber and Feber, 24 Russel Square, London.

Cassells, Ger : 'German English Dictionary', Cassell and Co. Ltd., London, 1957.

Chattterjee, Chinmoy : 'Vedantic Education' Gauranga Cultural Research Institute, Lucknow, 1957.

Chattopadhyaya, Sudhakar: 'Traditional Values in Indian Life', India International Centre, Delhi, 1961.

Cooley, C.H. : 'Social Oranisation A Study of the Larger Mind', Scribner's New York, 1929.

Das, Bhagavana : 'Praṇavavāda of Gārgāyana', Benaras Hindu University, 1910.

Dasgupta, S.N. : 'A History of Indian Philosophy', Vols. I, (1922), II (1940), Cambridge University Press, London.

Dave, T.N. : 'Taittirīya Upaniṣad', A Mine of Cultural and philosophical inoformations, Sharadapitha Pradeep, Vol. 5, No. 2, Dwarka, 1965.

David M. Knipe : 'In the Image of Fire', Motilal Benarasidass, Delhi, 1975.

Deussen Paul : 'Āśrama', ERE, Vol. II, 1951.

Deussen Paul : 'Philosophy of Upaniṣads', Dover Publications Inc., New York, 1966.

Dwivedi, R.C. : 'Selections from Brahmanas and Upanisadas' Motilal Banarasidass, Delhi-7, 1965.

Dhavan, K.K. : 'Poetic Elements in the Upaniṣads' Vishveshvara- nanda Research Institute, Hoshiarpur, 1976.

Fatahsingh : 'The Vedic Etymology' National Publishing House, Delhi-6.

Firth, Raymond : 'Elements of Social Organi-sation', Watts and Co., London, 1951.

Gaden, A.S. : 'Ascentism (Hindu) Encyclo-paedia of Religion and Ethics, Vol. II', T & T Clark, New York, 1953 (3rd edn.).

Gairola, Vacaspati : 'Sanskrit Sāhitya Kā Itihāsa', Chowkhamba Vidyabhavana, Varanasi, 1960.

Ghurye, G.S. : 'Caste and Class in India', Philosophical Library, New York, 1952.

Ginsberg, M. : 'Sociology', Oxford Univer-sity Press, London, 1950.

Gispert Sanch, S.J. : 'Bliss in the Upaniṣads', Oriental Publishers and Distri-butors, New Delhi-110 002.

Hobhouse, L.T. : ERE, Vol. I, end. III, 1955.

Hume, R.E. : 'The Thirteen Principal Upanisads' Oxford University Press, London, 1951 (Reprinted).

Jacobo, H.J. : 'Cosmology, Cosmogony, Encyclopaedia of Religion and Ethics, 'Vol. III, T & T Clark, New York, 1953 (3rd edn.)

Kane, P.V. : 'History of Dharmaśāstra,' Vol. II, Part I, Government Oriental Series, Class B, No.6, BORI, 1941.

Kantawala, S.G. : 'Cultural History from the Matsyapurāṇa', M.S. University of Baroda, Baroda, 1964.

Kapadia, K.M. : 'Hindu Kinship', The Popular Book Depot, Bombay- 400 007, 1947.

Karve, Irawati : 'Hindu Society - An Interpretation', Deccan College, Poona, 1961.

Keay, F.E. : 'Indian Education in Ancient of Latter times', Oxford University Press, Oxford , 1938.

Kaith, A.B. : The Veda of the Black Yajus School, entitled 'Taittirīya Samhitā, Part I, HOS, Vol. 18, Cambridge, Massachusetts, 1914.

Keith, A.B. : HOS Vol. No. 31, 'Religion and Philiosophy of the Veda and Upaniṣads', The Harward University Press, Combridge.

Kunhanaraja, C. : 'Education in Ancient India', The Ádyar Library, 1950.

Kunjunni Raja, K. : 'New Catalogus Catalogorum', University of Madras, Vol. I revised edn. 1959; Vol. II, 1966, Vol. III 1967; Vol. IV 1968; Vol. V 1969; Vol. VI 1971; Vol. VII 1973; Vol. VIII 1974.

Kuppuswami, A. : 'Śrī Bhagavadpāda Śaṅkarācārya', Chowkhamba Sanskrit Series Office, Varanasi, 1972.

Macdonell, A.A. : 'A Vedic Reader', Geoffrey Camberlege Oup, 1954.

Macdonell, A.A. : 'Sanskrit English Dictionary', Longmans Green and Co. Ltd., London, 1893.

MAcdonell, A.A. : 'Vaidic Decatasastra', Benaras Hindu University, 1961.

Macdonell, A.A. : 'Vedic Index Names and Subjects', Vols. I, II, Motilal Banarasidass, Varanasi, 1958.

Maciver, R.M. : 'The Elements of Social Science', 7th edn., Methuen and Complany Ltd., London, 1949.

Maclver, R.M. and Page C.M. : 'Society : An Introductory Analysis', Macmillan & Co. Ltd., London, 1950

Mahadevan, T.M.P. : 'Upaniṣads', Arnold Heinemann Publishers, New Delhi-110 016, 1975.

Mayrhofer, M., : 'A Conscise Etymological Sanskrit Dictionary' Carl Winter, Heidelberg, 1953.

Max Muller : 'The Upaniṣads' SBE, Vol. I, 1926 (2nd end.), Clarendon Press, Oxford, 1883.

Max Muller : SBE, Vol. 23, 'The Zend Avesta' Part I; SBE, Vol. 31, 'The Zend Avesta' Part II, Glarendon Press, Oxford, 1883, 1887.

Modi, P.M. : 'Development of the System of Āśramas', Proc. and Trac. of the 7th AIOC, Baroda, Dec., 1933.

Mookerji, R.K. : 'Ancient Indian Education', Macmillan & Co., Ltd., London, 1947.

Muri, J. : 'Original Sanskrit Texts', tra. by Ram Kumar Rai, Chowkhamba Vidyabhavan Varanasi, 1965.

Narahari, H.G. : Ātma in Pre-Upaniṣadic Vedic Literature', Adyar Library, Madras, 1944.

Nath, R. : 'On the authenticity of the Allopaniṣad' Journal of the Oriental Institute, Baroda, Vol. 26 No. 3, Baroda, 1977.

Palsule, G.B. and Bedekara, V.M. : 'Sixty Upaniṣads of the Vedas', Motilal Banarasidass, Delhi, 1980.

Pandita, Bhagavad Datta : 'Vaidika Vaṅamaya kā Itihāsa', Vol. I, Shree Ramalal Kapoor Trust, Amrtasara.

Prabhu, P.M. : 'Hindu Social Organization', Popular Prakashan, Bombay, 1963, 4th edn.

Radhakrishnan, S. : 'Indian Philosophy' The Macmilan Co., New York, 1956, 7th edn.

Radhakriahnan, S. : 'Philosophy of the Upaniṣads', Georg Allen and Unwin Ltd., London, 1924.

Radhakrishnan, S. : 'The Principal Upanisad', George Allen and Unwin Ltd., London, 1953.

Raghavan, V. : 'Sāmavaeda and Music', Journal of Music Academy, Vol. 33, pp. 127-133, Madras, 1951.

Rai, Ganga Sagar :
1. Śākhās of the Ṛgveda, 'Purāṇa', Vol. VI,
2. Śākhās of the Yajurveda, 'Purāṇa', Vol. VII,
3. Śākhās of the Sāmaveda 'Purāṇa., Vol. VIII,
4. Śākhās of the Atharvaveda 'Purāṇa', Vol. IV, 1964, 1965 1966, 1972 respy.

Ranade, R.D. : 'A Constructive Survey of Upanișadic Philosophy', Oriental Book Agency, Poona, 1926.

Sharma, Jogeswar : 'The Philosophy of Education in the Upanișads', Oriental Publishers and Distributors, New Delhi-110 002, 1978.

Shah, J.G. : 'Śrī Vallabhācārya — His Philosophy and Religion, Pușṭimārga Pustakālaya, Nadiad, 1969.

Sharma, B.N.K. : 'Philosophy of Śrī Madhva', Bharatiya Vidya Bhavan, Bombay, 1962.

Sharma, Baldeva Raj : 'The Concept of Ātman in the Principal Upanișads', Dinesh Publications, New Delhi-110 015, 1972.

Shastry, Alladi M. : 'The Taittiriya Upanișad', Samata Books, Madra, 1980.

Swami, Atmananda : 'Śaṅkara's teachings in his own words', Bharatiya Vidya Bhavan, Bombay, 1958.

Swami, Chinmayananda : 'Discourses on the Taittirīya Upanișad, Madras.

Swami, Madhavananda : 'A Bird's Eye view of the Upanișads' Cultural Heritage of India, Vol. I, The Ramakrishna Mission, Calcutta, 1958.

Swami, Nikhilananda : 'The Upanișads, Phoenix House, London, or Munshiram Manoharlal, Oriental and Foreign Bookseelers, Delhi-110 006.

Swami, Nikhilānanda : 'Vedānta-sāra or essence of Vedānta of Sadānanda Yogindra' Advaita Āśrama, Mayavati, Almora, Himalayas, 1949, 3rd edn.

Swami, Sharvananda : 'Taittiriyopanișad', Sri Ramkrishna Math, Mylapore, Madras, 1949.

Swami, Vivekananda : 'Complete Works of Vivekananda', Vol. II, 1921; Vol. IV, 1923; Vol. V, 1924, Advaita Ashrama, Almora.

Thite, G.U. : 'Sacrifices in the Brāhmaṇa Texts', University of Poona, 1957.

Upandhyaya, Baldeva : 'Śrī Ācārya Sāyana aur Mādhava', Hindi Sahitya Press, Prayag, 1947.

Upadhyaya, Baldeva : 'Śrī Śaṅkarācārya', Hindustani Academy, Allahabad, 1963, IInd edn.

Van, J.M. Boetzelaer : 'Sureśvara's Taittirīyopaniṣad Bhāsyavārtikam' Leiden, Brill, 1971.

Varma, Siddheshwar : 'The Etymologies of Yaska', Vishveshvaranand Institute Publications, Hosherpur, 1953.

Velankar, H.D. : 'Ṛgveda Maṇḍala VII', Bharatiya Vidya Bhavan, Bombay-400 007, 1963.

Venkatachalam : 'A Convencing case of Interpolation in the TU', SP a AIOC (26), Ujjain, 1975.

Venkataraman Iyer : 'Sṛṣṭi Vākṣyās in the Upaniṣads', Vedānta Kesarī, Vol. 53 (11), 1967.

Weber, Albrecht : 'The History of Indian Literature', Kegan Paul, Trench, Trubner & Co. Ltd., Broadway House, 68-74, Carter Lane, E.C. London, Fourth edn. 1904.

Webster : 'New World Dictionary' 2nd edn. American Publishing Co. Pvt. Ltd., New Delhi.

Winternitz, M. : 'A History of Indian Literature' Vol. I, University of Calcutta, Calcutta, 1927.

Index